Caribbean
with Kids

Open Road—More *and* Better Choices!

"Paris Permenter and John Bigley know kids, know parents, and know the Caribbean. They make it as clear as the Caribbean Sea that a family holiday doesn't have to be an oxymoron." – *Amazon.com*

"Definitely get hold of this book if you're considering a family vacation in the Caribbean." – *TravelwithKids.About.com*

Open Road Travel Guides

Open Road Publishing has guide books to exciting, fun destinations on four continents. As veteran travelers, our goal is to bring you the best travel guides available anywhere!

No small task, but here's what we offer:

•All Open Road travel guides are written by authors with a distinct, opinionated point of view – not some sterile committee or team of writers. Our authors are experts in the areas covered and are polished writers.

•Our guides are geared to people who want to make their own travel choices. We'll show you how to discover the real destination – not just see some place from a tour bus window.

•We're strong on the basics, but we also provide terrific choices for those looking to get off the beaten path and experience the country or city – not just see it or pass through it.

•We give you the best, but we also tell you about the worst and what to avoid. Nobody should waste their time and money on their hard-earned vacation because of bad or inadequate travel advice.

•Our guides assume nothing. We tell you everything you need to know to have the trip of a lifetime – presented in a fun, literate, no-nonsense style.

•And, above all, we welcome your input, ideas, and suggestions to help us put out the best travel guides possible.

Caribbean
with Kids

Open Road—More *and* Better Choices!

Paris Permenter & John Bigley

Open Road Publishing

Open Road Publishing

We offer travel guides to American and foreign locales. Our books tell it like it is, often with an opinionated edge, and our experienced authors always give you all the information you need to have the trip of a lifetime. Write for your free catalog of all our titles.

Open Road Publishing
P.O. Box 284, Cold Spring Harbor, NY 11724
E-mail: Jopenroad@aol.com

4th Edition

ISBN 1-59360-032-1
Library of Congress Control No. 2005929017

Contents

Maps

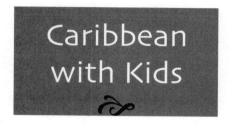

Caribbean
with Kids

1. INTRODUCTION

A new family-friendly attitude is blowing across the Caribbean like a fresh tradewind. Parents who have vacationed here before are discovering the fun of introducing their children to favorite island attractions. Families are playing together and staying together in some of the Caribbean's premier destinations, creating warm holiday memories that will last for generations.

Throughout the Caribbean, you'll find resorts with kids' programs to keep youngsters busy and happy as well as beaches where the whole family can play in the waves, snorkel in shallow waters, or just build sand castles until the sun sets over another perfect day. And if you're ready to take a break from constantly watching the budget as well as the kids, you'll also find many all-inclusive resorts that leave the worries of "how much is left in the vacation budget?" at the door.

Regardless of what you're looking for in an island vacation for the family, there's a place for you in the Caribbean. After you've looked throught this book, selecting your next Caribbean family getaway will be "no problem, mon!"

Chapter 2

OVERVIEW

Ready to cast off those jackets, feel the sun on your face and the sand between your toes? Watch your children romp in the sand, be introduced to new cultures, and share a few days with you that you'll all remember the rest of your lives?

Then it's time to head to the Caribbean. While you may be shoveling snow, the islands are still blessed with weather that's just right for a day of snorkeling, scuba diving, or just sunning.

While they may all share the powdery sand, the aquamarine waters, and the near-perfect weather, Caribbean destinations can be as different as the seashells found along their beaches. Some islands are large and span hundreds of miles; others can be covered in an afternoon bicycle excursion. Culturally, these islands vary from French to Dutch to English; language and currency differ as well. Political structures range from crown colonies to independent nations.

Before we start examining the individual differences, let's look at the region as a whole. The Caribbean spans an area that stretches over 2,000 miles east to west and 1,000 miles north to south, starting just off the coast of Florida and arching down to the coast of South America.

This part of the world is blessed with year-around sunshine, with water warmed by Caribbean currents and shores cooled by gentle trade winds. Winter and summer temperatures differ by only about five degrees.

If you look at a map of the Caribbean, you'll see that the islands arch out like a cracking whip, with the largest islands to the west and the small

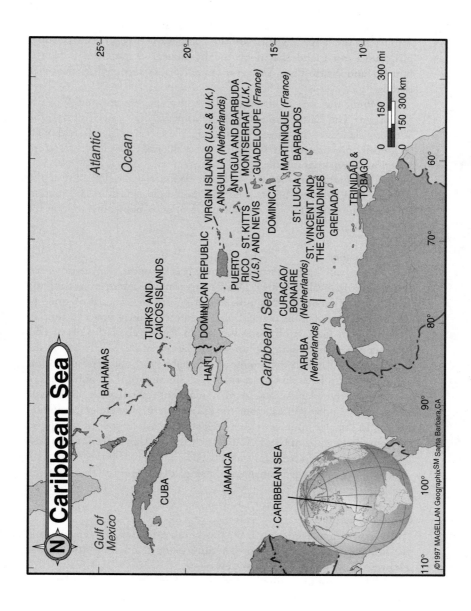

N

Caribbean Sea

Gulf of
Mexico

Atlantic

Ocean

BAHAMAS

TURKS AND
CAICOS ISLANDS

CUBA

JAMAICA

HAITI

DOMINICAN REPUBLIC

PUERTO
RICO
(U.S.)

ST. KITTS
AND NEVIS

VIRGIN ISLANDS (U.S. & U.K.)
ANGUILLA (Netherlands)
ANTIGUA AND BARBUDA
MONTSERRAT (U.K.)
GUADELOUPE (France)

DOMINICA

MARTINIQUE (France)

BARBADOS

ST. LUCIA

ST. VINCENT AND
THE GRENADINES

CURACAO/
BONAIRE
(Netherlands)

ARUBA
(Netherlands)

GRENADA

TRINIDAD &
TOBAGO

Caribbean Sea

CARIBBEAN SEA

©1997 MAGELLAN GeographixSM Santa Barbara,CA

25°

20°

15°

10°

60°

70°

80°

90°

100°

110°

0   150   300 mi

0   150 300 km

islands to the east, curving on down to South America and ending in a "snap" with the ABC islands: Aruba, Bonaire, and Curaçao back to the west.

The whole formation of islands is referred to as the Antilles, usually divided into the Greater Antilles and the Lesser Antilles. The Greater Antilles, as the name suggests, are the Caribbean's largest islands: Cuba, Hispaniola (an island shared by the Dominican Republic and Haiti), Jamaica, and Puerto Rico. The term Lesser Antilles encompasses the other islands.

Often, the area is just divided up into the Eastern and Western Caribbean. The Eastern islands are the same as the Lesser Antilles; the Western islands are the Greater Antilles and the Cayman Islands. Although technically not part of the Caribbean, the Bahamas also shares its azure waters and perpetual summer.

The multiple names given to this region is your first hint at the diversity the Caribbean boasts. The Caribbean holds an endless fascination for us, and hopefully for you, because it *does* offer so many different types of experiences.

Rich in History

The islands have such varied cultures because of the many nations that fought over this valuable area. During this time of unrest, protecting the islands was a major job. Magnificent forts were constructed of stone to defend the islands from marauding buccaneers. Today you can tour El Morro in San Juan, stroll along the lemon sherbet-colored walls of Fort Christiansvaern in St. Croix, photograph the city of Puerto Plata from the Fortaleza San Felipe in the Dominican Republic, or visit imposing Brimstone Hill in St. Kitts, known as the "The Gibraltar of the Caribbean."

Once the islands were settled, many prospered with sugar cane plantations. Today you can tour the islands' heritage of huge plantation houses. In Jamaica, tours provide a peek at the lavish lifestyle once enjoyed by plantation owners at Great Houses such as Rose Hall near Montego Bay, and the newly opened Barnett Estate Plantation also near Montego Bay, with a jitney tour of the sugar, banana, and mango plantation and fine dining in a restored sugar mill.

Winter Getaways

At one time, wintering in the Caribbean meant wealth. Today you'll still find the rich and famous crowd heading to the islands for a little sun, but getaways are affordable for almost everyone.

There's nothing quite like stepping off an airplane, still in layers of clothing, into the Caribbean sunshine. This is the peak season in the islands, a time when travelers from around the globe come to enjoy a respite from the cold.

Different Cultures

Although every island boasts a rollicking Caribbean spirit, their cultures also borrow heavily from their founding fathers. Aromas of fine French food fills the air of Martinique, St. Martin, St. Barthelemy, and Guadeloupe. Dutch architecture creates picturesque waterfront communities in Aruba, Bonaire, Curaçao, Saba, Sint Maarten, and Sint Eustatius. A rich Spanish atmosphere pervades the islands of the Dominican Republic and Puerto Rico. Anguilla, the British Virgin Islands, Montserrat, the Cayman Islands and the Turks and Caicos still operate as British dependencies. In the former British colonies of the Bahamas, Antigua and Barbuda, Barbados, Dominica, Grenada, St. Kitts and Nevis, St. Lucia, Trinidad and Tobago, and Jamaica, the British influence is still strongly felt, with driving on the left side of the road and the Royal family smiling back from postage stamps.

Check Out the Water!

The true island treasure that every Caribbean nation shares are miles of beaches lapped by clear, warm water. The activities in the water are endless: sailing, windsurfing, water-skiing, the list goes on and on. If you'd like to stay above the water, head to the boating capital of the Caribbean, the British Virgin Islands. Several resorts offer combination packages with a week's stay split between a hotel and a yacht.

If you want to venture beneath the waves, you'll find the top dive destinations to be the Cayman Islands, Turks and Caicos, and Bonaire. Divers can hand feed sharks on guided dives in the Bahamas or pet sting rays at Grand Cayman. Or if you're just looking to snorkel, coral reefs are scattered just yards from shore throughout this region.

Why the Caribbean?

The Caribbean is a great destination for parents and children, but don't just take our word on it. We recently interviewed Teresa Plowright, guide at About.com's excellent Travel with Kids website (*travelwithkids.about.com*). Filled with articles, news, reader forums, and tips for traveling families, the site also includes Teresa's site reports on family-friendly resorts. We recently caught up with Teresa and asked her for her Caribbean insight and tips.

•*Why do you think the Caribbean is a good destination for families?*

The answer to this question is like a layer cake: there's so many reasons, each a different flavor, one on top of the other.

Down at the bottom, we have the most basic fact: the Caribbean is a great tropical getaway. For legions of families in the eastern US, certain islands are easily reachable by a short plane ride—a big consideration, when traveling with young kids. Beaches are picture-perfect, and many islands have coral reefs which can offer a thrilling introduction to underwater life. Kids can view the coral and fishlife through glass-bottom boats, or they can try snorkeling, or scuba if over 12 years old.

The next layer is the abundance of family resorts, especially all-inclusive resorts. Families can enjoy beautiful rooms and landscaped grounds, restaurants that specifically cater to kids, and special facilities such as playgrounds, kiddie pools, waterslides, etc. Another nice aspect of a resort stay is that often kids can enjoy a certain amount of independence, and run freely around the grounds, head to the restaurant by themselves to get a drink, etc.

Then there's the activities: glass-bottom boat rides, snorkeling trips, kayaking, waterslides, scuba instruction and outings, wind-surfing, bike-riding, tennis lessons, water-toys in the pools, even mini-golf, trapeze, rock-climbing walls at some resorts. Not to mention the daily scheduled family-type activities such as scavenger hunts, bingo, beach BBQ's, etc.

Next layer is the kids' programs offered by virtually all resorts these days. Even if parents only use the kids' programs for one activity, or one hour, a day, that break can be wonderfully refreshing for parents of little kids—and meanwhile the kids are having fun and making new friends.

Club Med Punta Cana has amazing kids programs, with different activities for 2-year-olds, 3-year-olds, and many age groups; plus a special new concept for teens, The Ramp, a creative structure with a skateboarding slope on one side, an open-air lounge on another side, and on top a neat hang-out area with a canopy where movies can be screened. The final feature is all-inclusive pricing, which reduces hassle for parents: there's no need to worry, "how much will that meal/drink/activity/4th-ice-cream-of-the-day cost?" Meanwhile, kids love being able to help themselves to drinks, ice-cream cones, whatever, without having to ask Mom or Dad. The whole piece of cake means plenty of fun, minimal hassle.

The final feature is all-inclusive pricing, which reduces hassle for parents: there's no need to worry, "how much will that meal/drink/activity/4th-ice-cream-of-the-day cost?" Meanwhile, kids love being able to help themselves to drinks, ice-cream cones, whatever, without having to ask Mom or Dad.

The whole piece of cake means plenty of fun, minimal hassle.

• *What advice would you have for families who are taking their family vaction in the islands for the first time?*

We'd offer two related pieces of advice: try to take some outings outside your resort; and don't overlook the great opportunities for kids to absorb some learning on your trip.

The Caribbean islands are thick with history: Columbus himself landed on several islands. Of course, much of this history is not a happy story:

the destruction of the native inhabitants; the slave trade, and the slave struggles during the plantation era. Still, visiting the Caribbean can provide a huge opportunity to bring history to life. And despite all the past hardships in this part of the world, most visitors today are struck by the exuberance, in manner, music, mood, of the Caribbean spirit: kids can see this too.

To learn about culture and history, take some outings outside your resort. Some islands—such as Curaçao—have towns with beautifully restored colonial streets, where you can wander and find photo ops; some islands, such as the US Virgin Islands, have old forts complete with cannons. St. John, USVI has a self-guided Historic Trail. Many islands have "Great Houses" from the plantation days, which offer tours. Just head to the lobby of your resort, look for the Tour Desk, and check what outings are available. Another excellent option, if you're in Jamaica, is Countrystyle, which will customize tours for your family. Nature tours are another way to enrich your trips, on islands such as St. John USVI with extensive park land.

•*Do the islands make a good destination for families with infants and toddlers?*
Many resorts make a special effort to welcome families with wee kids, and offer nurseries for babies and kids' programs for toddlers. (Beaches Resorts, for example.) For most families, a vacation is meant to be Together Time, but even a short break from parenting can be refreshing for parents of tiny tots. Often, parents of infants and toddlers scarcely have five minutes to themselves during daily life at home: simply lying in a hammock and reading a book for half an hour can be heavenly!

We particularly like the approach at Franklyn D. Resort, and sister resort FDR Pebbles, which both provide every family with a vacation nanny who helps during the family's entire stay. Sometimes the nanny stays right with the family just lending a hand, at the pool or beach; sometimes she takes the kids with her for fun activities. Many families return and ask for the same nannies trip after trip.

As for activities: babies and toddlers don't need a lot to make them ecstatic— a swimming pool, a baby slide, a gentle beach plus a sand-bucket will all pretty much be Heaven for a teeny child.

Final point: at a family resort, parents can feel totally comfortable feeding a tiny child in a restaurant, with all the chaos this can entail. Some resorts have separate kids' meals for dinner time.

•*Do you think all-inclusive resorts are a good value for families both in terms of money and activities?*
Prices vary greatly among different resorts, and even at the same resort depending on time of year. If a person is budget-conscious, there are definitely bargains to be found. The Starfish brand, in the Sandals group, in

particular is aiming to be a value-for-money resort. Other resorts, such as Beaches and FDR, discount 25% or more during off-season.

Yet, even at full-prices, these resorts are delivering a lot for the money spent, when you consider the range of activities offered— for example, scuba diving, which is available to ages 12 and up. Snorkeling trips are also very popular: on many islands, visitors need to take a boat to snorkel on a coral reef, which can easily cost $100 for a family. Your all-inclusive price at a resort also includes all the snacks and drinks your children want: in the hot tropics, at $6 a drink (for, say, a virgin fruit-drink) your kids could run up quite a tab! I think parents really appreciate simply not having to bother about the costs of drinks and activities once they've paid their all-inclusive price. Remember, too, that the Caribbean isn't an inexpensive destination; even relatively modest properties can cost $150 a night for lodging alone; a sandwich can be $12 US, and a lunch for family of four could easily ring up $70.

Chapter 3

BEST PLACES TO STAY

ATLANTIS RESORT, Paradise Island, New Providence Island, Bahamas. Tel. 242/363-3000, Fax 242/363-6309. Toll-free reservations Tel. 800/ATLANTIS; www.atlantis.com. Winter, rooms from $380-720, suites starting at $855; summer, rooms from $340-565, suites starting at $685, cards accepted.

The vacationers looked up through the sea water, the sun filtering down in liquid shafts and illuminating the hundreds of fish around them. Suddenly, the light was blocked by an sinister silhouette —a shark. Directly overhead, the six-foot predator swam with deliberate slowness, making schools of yellow grunts scurry closer to sheltering rocks.

But, unlike the school of fish and the large spiny lobster on the sandy floor below, the tourists were not worried. The visitors in the 100-foot long clear tunnel — the parents with the little boy in a stroller, the teenagers wearing a three-day sunburn, and the couple on their first trip to the Caribbean — just delighted in the view. Surrounded by thousands of tropical fish, sharks, manta rays, and sea turtles in the world's largest open-air aquarium, they had the experience of scuba diving without ever getting wet.

The tunnel and the 14-acre water gardens surrounding it are found at the Atlantis on Nassau's Paradise Island. The hotel is one of the most lavish properties in the entire Caribbean. For all its niceties, the hotel is just a backdrop to the 3.2 million-gallon saltwater habitat, the largest outdoor, open-air aquarium in the world. A 14-acre waterscape, where over 40 waterfalls splash and churn sea water into fish-filled lagoons that weave among walkways and bridges. Over three million gallons of sea water fill the observation tanks, each carefully constructed of man-made stone and coral formations to simulate a marine environment.

Guests flock to the Predator Lagoon for a close-up look at the half dozen reef sharks that swim a constant pattern alongside barracudas and rays. Above the water's surface, guests watch for the shark's tell-tale fin to break the lagoon's surface; underwater, encased in the clear tunnel, they stand within inches of the sharks. The Predator Lagoon is popular with all ages of visitors, from small children who delight at the diving turtles and crawling spiny lobsters to the older visitors and non-swimmers looking for the sensation of scuba diving without getting wet.

Water activities continue above the surface as well. Near Predator Lagoon, a rope suspension bridge swings and sways over the water. Nearby water tricycles churn across Paradise Lagoon, a salt water lagoon that opens to the sea. Here in the calm, protected waters the resort hopes to introduce tropical fish to be enjoyed by beginning snorkelers and children who are not ready to tackle the mild waves on the beach. The most popular spot with children is the Lazy River Ride, which meanders through the Waterscape for a quarter mile. Kids hop on an inner tube and set off on a journey pushed by a gentle current. Nearby, Goombay Baths and Slides are a series of saltwater pools where kids can tumble from one to another. Kids also enjoy a children's pool with a sand play area, an Adventure Water Walk with computer-controlled geysers and fountains, and the calm waters of Paradise Lagoon, a good place to receive an introduction to snorkeling or swimming.

Thrill seekers plunge down the Leap of Faith slide on a replica of a Mayan temple. The slide takes an almost vertical 60-foot drop, plunging riders into an acrylic tunnel in a shark-filled lagoon. The temple is also home to the Serpent slide, which spins through the interior of the dark temple before emerging into Predator Lagoon.

Guests at Atlantis can also take part in one of the most exciting children's programs in the Caribbean: the Discovery Channel Camp at Atlantis. This program is a joint effort by the Discovery Channel and Sun International to use computer and television technology to give children an interactive opportunity to explore. Children ages 5-12 can participate in morning, afternoon or evening sessions. The camp includes several components. The Base Camp is easy to find—just look for the replica of a 17th century Spanish galleon, Atocha. This play and orientation center uses the sails of Atocha as a giant television monitor to display Discovery Channel footage.

The Technology Lab uses state-of-the-art computers, camcorders, scanners, and plenty of imagination. The Science Outpost offers live animal touch tanks and aquariums as well as working microscopes and collections of fossils and bones. The Arts and Crafts area utilizes the crafts of the Bahamas and gives children the chance to direct the creativity in many ways.

BEACHES NEGRIL RESORT AND SPA, P.O. Box 12, Negril, Jamaica. Tel. 876/957-9270, Fax 876/957-9269. Toll-free US phone number 888/BEACHES; www.beaches.com. Winter rates from $670 per person for two nights in a deluxe room, Summer rates from $650 per person for two nights in a deluxe room, all-inclusive. Credit cards accepted.

This impressive property is the answer to all those couples who enjoyed a vacation at Sandals but then wanted to take the kids back the next time. Part of the Sandals family, Beaches brings the all-inclusive fun those couples-only resorts are known for to families, singles, and couples. Here, kids under 2 stay free, and there are child rates for kids from 2-15.

Beaches is perched on Negril's famous Seven Mile Beach and offers something for everyone. Four swimming pools, a sports complex with tennis, volleyball and basketball courts, watersports, you name it, it's here. Kids have a full Kids Camp with age appropriate activities. Young travelers especially enjoy the Xbox Game Oasis Center; play's unlimited and free!

Dining is arranged so families can enjoy time together and apart. Two gourmet restaurants are for adults only while children especially enjoy a pasta bar with brick oven pizza and a Beach Grill, exclusively for kids between 5pm and 9pm.

The latest addition to this resort is the Pirates Island Water Park, an 18,000-square-foot park smack dab in the middle of the resort and definitely one of the most popular aspects of the property with the younger set. (Actually, it's pretty popular with the older set as well.) The park has water slides, water cannons, a misting pool and a lazy river.

Beaches and Sesame Street also have an exclusive arrangement; be on the lookout for Sesame Street characters during your stay. Elmo, Cookie Monster, Grover and Zoe appear in costume throughout the resort. There's even a story hour with Elmo featuring Caribbean stories, nature walks with Grover, dancing with Zoe, and more. For an extra fee, you can even set up a birthday party for your child with special appearances by the characters. Here are Beaches Negril's weekly activities for kids ages 4-7:

Monday: Mask 'a-Raids
8:30am Meet & Greet
9:30am Nature Walk
10am Sand Sculpting
11am Pool
12noon Lunch
1:30pm Fashion Show Rehearsal
2pmMask Making
3pm Cheetah Hunt
4pm Musical Games
4:30pm Playground

5pm Free time
6:30pm Dinner-Mill
7pm Crazy Mask-a-Raids (Nicole's Disco)
8:15pm Clown Show
9:15pm Relax with Disney
10:30pm Kamp Closes

Tuesday: World of Fashion
8:30am Meet & Greet
9:30am Beach Walk
10am Pool Games
11am Hat Making Lessons
12noon Lunch
1:30pm Sega
2pm Tennis Clinic (please sign up. Ages 5-7 yrs.)
3pm Art & Craft
4pm Soccer
4:30pm Mini Golf
5pm Free Time
6:30pm Dinner - Mill
7pm Board Games
8pm Fashion Show - Big Top
8:40pm Relax with Disney
10:30pm Kamp Closes

Wednesday: Island Fantasy
8:30am Meet & Greet
9:30am Exercise
10am Sand Castle Building Contest
11am Pool Games
12noon Lunch
1:30pm Sega
2pm Tennis Clinic (ages 5-7 years)
3pm Reggae Dance Class
3:30pm Miniature Golf
4:30 - 5pm Play Ground
6:30pm Beach Party
9-10pm Disco Party - Nicole's Disco
PARENTS PLEASE TAKE KIDS TO PARTIES

Thursday: Shining Star
8:30am Meet & Greet
9:30am Exercise

10am Mini Golf
11am Pool Games
12noon Lunch
1:30pm Puppet Making
2:30pm Rap Time
3pm Talent Show Rehearsal - Big Top
4pm Lawn Games
4:30pm Playground
5pm Free Time
6:30pm Dinner in the Mill
7pm Sega
8pm Talent Show - Big Top
8:40pm Relax with Disney
10:30p.m Center closes

Friday: The Great Outdoors
8:30am Meet & Greet
9:30am Nature Walk
10am Outdoor Games
11am Pool Games
12noon Lunch
1:30pm Let's Bake
2:30pm Tea Time
3:30pm Art & Craft
4:30pm Water Games
5pm Free Time
6:30pm Dinner in the Mill
7pm Movie
10:30pm Kamp Closes

Saturday: Games Night
8:30pm Meet & Greet
9:30am Exercise
10am Pool Games
11am Hat Making Lessons
12noon Lunch
 1:30pm Treasure Hunt
2pm Sega
2:30pm Art & Craft
3:30pm Miniature Golf
4pm Playground
5pm Free Time
6:30pm Dinner in the Mill

7pm Games Room
9pm Movie
10:30pm Kamp Closes

Sunday: Tropical Delight
8:30am Meet & Greet
9:30am Exercise
10am Miniature Golf
11am Pool Games
12noon Lunch
1:30pm Fashion Show Rehearsal
2pm Tie-dye (please bring t-shirt)
3pm Sandcastle Building
4pm Playground
4:30pm Pool Splash
5pm Free Time
6:30pm Dinner - the Mill
7pm Movie
10pm Kamp Closes

FRANKLYN D. RESORT (FDR), P.O. Box 201, Main Street, Runaway Bay, St. Ann, Jamaica. Tel. 876/973-4591, Fax 876/973-4600. Toll-free reservations Tel. 800/654-1FDR or 888/FDR-KIDS; www.fdrholidays.com. Rates from $560 in summer, from $600 in winter. Credit cards accepted.

FDR has one of the most unique programs in the Caribbean for vacationing families. Each guest is assigned a Vacation Nanny on arrival. She works with the family throughout their entire stay, supervising the kids, washing out bathing suits, or even making sandwiches for hungry young travelers.

All guests stay in one-, two-, or three-bedroom suites. Breakfast, lunch, dinner (and a special kiddies dinner) are included along with all beer, soft drinks, bar drinks, and wine. Guests have use of all sports facilities including sailing, windsurfing, snorkeling, glass bottom boat, kayaking, bicycles, tennis court, and gym.

The children's mini-club includes computer training, satellite TV room, disco, Super Nintendo games, donkey rides, picnics, arts and crafts, kiddies slides and paddling pools, and kiddies disco.

FDR offers a unique service: the chance for couples to get married and honeymoon with their new family. With an increase in second marriages involving children, FDR now offers a special $400 wedding package that includes everything a couple needs to get married. The new family can have time together—and apart, thanks to the Vacation Nanny.

STARFISH TRELAWNY BEACH AND FUN RESORT, Falmouth, Jamaica. Tel. 876/954-2450, Fax 876/954-2149. Toll-free reservations Tel. 800/659-5436; www.starfishresorts.com. Winter rates from $72.50. Summer rates from $ 109. Credit cards accepted.

Starfish Trelawny, managed by the SuperClubs chain, is a great place for families to enjoy their vacation. This resort, which recently underwent an extensive renovation, operates as an all-inclusive but without the full menu of included activities found at the SuperClubs resorts; you will pay an additional fee for some activities. The high-rise resort is about an hour's drive east of Montego Bay. There is a 2-night minimum stay.

While parents enjoy golf, pampering at the spa, and other activities, the kids will be well taken care of at the Kids Club. Children will have a great time with supervised activities all day long. Kids are divided up into age groups of 0–3 years, 4–7 years, 8–12 years and teens to help kids make friends, and activities are assigned based to age level. The Kids Club is open every day from 9 am to 5 pm, and offers water sports, pool, slides, a circus, tennis, basketball, beach visits, theme parties, and contests.

After 5 pm, parents can pay an additional fee for a baby sitter to watch the kids while mom and dad spend a romantic evening alone.

Here is an example of the activities that can expected for the kids:

6 months to 3 years old
9-10am Welcome
10-12:30pm Activities
12:30pm Lunch
1:30pm Quiet Time/ Nap Time
3pm Activities
5pm Closed – Good Evening

4-7 Years old
9-9:30am Welcome
9:30am Flying Trapeze
11am Mask Making
12:30-1:30pm Lunch
1:30pm Sun Shade Activities – Cartoons
3pm Pool
5pm Closed – Good Evening

8-12 Years old
9-9:30am Welcome
9:30am Mask Making
10:30am Flying Trapeze
12:30pm Lunch

1:30pm Sun Shade Activities – Mime Game
3pm Beach
5pm Closed – Good Evening

WYNDHAM SUGAR BAY BEACH CLUB & RESORT, 6500 Estate Smith Bay, St. Thomas, US Virgin Islands. Tel. 340/777-7100, Fax 340/777-7200. Toll-free US reservations number 800/WYNDHAM; www.wyndham.com. Winter from $259, summer from $279. Credit cards accepted.

This 300-room resort is a real rarity in the US Virgin Islands: an all-inclusive property. Here, families can stay, play, and eat for one easy price. Perched high atop by seaside hill, the resort offers spectacular views of St. John and the British Virgin Islands.

The all-inclusive package includes all meals and drinks, an ice cream bar, day and night tennis, all non-motorized watersports, use of snorkel equipment, use of fitness center and Jacuzzi, daily activity programs, nightly entertainment, and beach volleyball.

The KidsKlub keeps young vacationers age three to 12 busy and happy. From 9:30am to 5pm daily, children stay occupied with activities such as kite flying, sea shell hunting, crab races, arts and crafts, and more.

The whole family finds plenty of fun as well. Much of the activity centers around the spectacular pool area. Here three interconnecting pools are alive with the sounds of children's laughter as well as the roar of a man-made waterfall. Visitors reach the pool area across a suspended bridge (look in the hibiscus for a resident iguana on the way down!) and a casual dining area lies just steps away. Beyond the pool area, the beach offers plenty of watersports and has some good snorkeling just yards from the shore, a site where we spotted about 40 small squid one afternoon.

The Wyndham Sugar Bay also boasts the island's only indoor resort amphitheater. Movies are shown here when guests are ready to take a break from the sun and the KidsKlub also uses the site for a weekly movie showing.

Chapter 4

ANGUILLA

Well known among the well-to-do, Anguilla is a favorite getaway for those really looking to get away. Don't expect mega-resorts on this isle; it is definitely for families looking to discover their own fun.

And that's an easy order to fill. This tiny island is the king of the Caribbean beach world, a mecca for beach buffs in search of that perfect stretch of sand. Although only 16 miles from end to end and little more than 35 square miles in all, the island packs in over 30 beaches and numerous nearby cays to tempt sunlovers, snorkelers, sailors, scuba divers, and those just looking for a good beach walk or hike. A few beaches bustle with activity but most are quiet and interruption-free, just pristine boundaries between land and sea.

Fun is also easy to find thanks to the friendliness of the Anguilla people. Anguillians pride themselves on their hospitality. Local residents greet cars with a wave and exchange "good morning" greetings with those they meet. Crime is as rare as you can find anywhere and, if you get lost, just pull over and ask for help. There's a welcoming spirit here that's shared with visitors and instantly makes your family feel right at home.

Anguilla also boasts a high safety factor. Rent a car, buzz around the island, pull over and dine at side of the road joints; you'll feel safe.

All this safety and seclusion does come at a price, however. The island aims for the upper market traveler, who is not shocked by three figure dinner tabs and per night accommodation rates equal to those found in three or four-night budget packages on some other islands. There are some medium-range properties that we have included in this chapter, but by and large Anguilla is for those who don't have to keep an eye on the pocketbook.

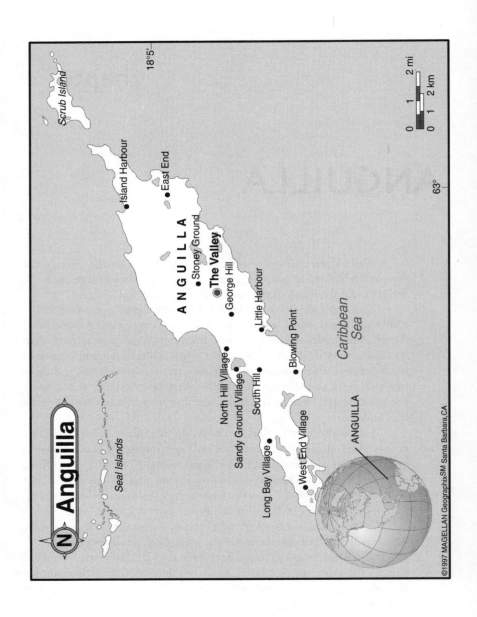

Anguilla

N

Scrub Island

Seal Islands

Island Harbour

East End

ANGUILLA

Stoney Ground

● The Valley

George Hill

Little Harbour

North Hill Village

Sandy Ground Village

South Hill

Blowing Point

Long Bay Village

West End Village

Caribbean Sea

ANGUILLA

18°5'

63°

0   1   2 mi
0   1   2 km

©1997 MAGELLAN GeographixSM Santa Barbara,CA

Are We There Yet?

By Air

Air travelers arrive at Wallblake airport either by American Eagle from American's hub in San Juan, Puerto Rico or by connection from nearby Saint Maarten (either plane or ferry). The flight from Saint Maarten to Anguilla takes approximately 10 minutes and costs about US $58 round-trip (daylight fare); air charter between the two airports runs about $300 per person. Service from Saint Maarten is available on WINAIR, Tel. 599/545-4273, Fax 599/545-3544, Toll-free 800/634-4907, www.fly-winair.com.

Additional service to Anguilla is available from LIAT, Tel. 1-888-844-LIAT (5428) or 268/497-5000, www.liatairline.com, with daily flights from Antigua, St. Kitts, and St. Thomas. Tyden Air, Tel. 800/842-0261, 264/497-0261, or 264/497-2719, Fax 264/497-3079, has charter service anywhere in the Caribbean and day tours to St. Barts, Nevis, and Virgin Gorda as well as daily flights to Saint Maarten. Tyden also offers flights to St. Thomas and St. Kitts. Air Anguilla, Tel. 264/497-2643, offers flights to Saint Maarten. Flying time from San Juan is one hour.

By Ferry

Visitors also arrive by ferry from St. Martin. The 20-30 minute ride from Marigot on the French side of St. Martin to Blowing Point, Anguilla costs US$10 each way (plus a US $3 departure fee each way). The trip takes 20 to 25 minutes.

To take the ferry to Anguilla, stop by the open air ferry station on the north end of the market in Marigot. Go up to the window, pay your $2 departure tax, and sign up on the manifest sheet, listing your name, passport number, and nationality. The ferry fee will be collected on board.

Getting Around the Island

If you'll be traveling around the island very much, by far the most economical transport is a rental car. Taxis are readily available but are not cheap, so a rental car is preferable for most guests. You can ask for a taxi to be dispatched at the airport or the ferry port in Blowing Rock. All taxi fares are fixed.

Public transportation is not available on Anguilla. Taxi service, both in cars and 12-passenger vans, is available throughout the island. All taxis are on a call basis. We used Austin's Taxi Service, Tel. 264-497-6660, beeper 2111-239, and can recommend this service for its thorough knowledge of the island.

Rental car prices vary with operator and model, but a typical mid-size or a jeep runs about $35 per day. A three-month Anguillan permit is required of all drivers. The fee is US $20; this license can be obtained from the rental car companies.

Where Are We Staying?

CAP JULUCA, Maundays Bay. Tel. 264/497-6666, Fax 264/497-6617. Toll-free reservations Tel. 888/8JULUCA; www.capjuluca.com. From $825 in high season; low season rates start at $325. Credit cards accepted.

Cap Juluca, named for the native Arawak Indian Rainbow God, is an exclusive getaway for those looking for privacy and pampering. The 72 guest rooms and junior suites, seven suites, six pool villas all offer complimentary mini bar, marble baths, and hair dryer. Some units include kitchen with refrigerator and dining room. Guest facilities include three tennis courts, croquet, beach, pool, Sunfish, kayaks, windsurfing, fitness center, snorkel trips and sunset cruises.

Cap Juluca offers a children's program called "Cap Juluca Kids" during the peak family season: Easter holidays and the months of July and August. The program is complimentary for guests and includes a full day of activities and theme field trips several times a week as well as lunch and a Cap Juluca kids' T-shirt. The program runs Monday through Friday from 9am to 5pm.

Children have the opportunity to learn through themed activities such as "Anguilla Today," a day of fun that highlights the island's residents, animals, ponds, and the sea; "Amerindians and Arawaks," with a visit to an island cave to hunt for fossils and crystals; "Fishing and Salt Production," to explore a fishing village; "Boat Racing," with a visit to the island's traditional boat builders. The most popular trip explores Gavanah Cave where the island's first archaeological find, a giant rodent fossil, was discovered in 1868. The rodent weighed 345 pounds but, to the relief of everyone, hasn't resided on the island in over 100,000 years!

After the two-hour field trips, children enjoy activities at the resort including puppet shows, journal writing, music, photography, nature hikes, games, and arts and crafts. The program is available for children age four to 12.

COVECASTLES, Shoal Bay West. Tel. 264/497-6801, Fax 264/497-6051. Toll-free reservations Tel. 800/223-1108; www.covecastles.com. $1,095 for one-bedroom villa, $895 for one-bedroom beach house in high season.

This villa resort caters to the guest looking for privacy, peace, and quiet. These stark white two- and three-bedroom getaways have a contemporary exterior and a tropical decor inside. Complimentary amenities include snorkeling, Sunfish sailboats, sea kayaks, bicycles, tennis, video players and library, concierge service, cable TV, and a personal housekeeper. Also available at additional charge are deep sea fishing, sailing excursions, tennis instruction, massage, and more.

CUISINART RESORT AND SPA, Rendezvous Bay. Tel. 264/498-2000, Fax 264/498-2055. Toll-free reservations Tel. 800/937-9356; www.cuisinartresort.com. From $570 in high season; low season rates from $395.

If you cook, you've no doubt heard of CuisinArt. This beachfront resort is owned by the same company. Part of the Leading Small Hotels of the World, this exclusive property is known for its pampering luxury, its fine dining, and its attention to detail.

Along with cooking classes, this resort offers its guests tennis, watersports, a beautiful swimming pool, boat charters, mountain biking, scuba diving, a mile-long beach, a full-service spa, boutique, art gallery, and a variety of cafes and restaurants.

For the kids, CuisinArt has a playground, and will orgainize children's activities upon request. There is also a kids' menu, inlcuding brick over pizzas, a game room with a pool table, babysitting, and cribs upon request. Older kids can take the cooking classes offered twice per week, and learn to play baci on the resort's two courses.

MALLIOUHANA, Meads Bay. Tel. 264/497-6111, Fax 264/497-6011. Toll-free reservations Tel. 800/835-0796; www.malliouhana.com. From $620 in high season; low season rates $275.

This intimate, 56-room hotel is perched on cliffs overlooking a tranquil sea and yet another example of a perfect Anguillian beach. Guest rooms here are private, spread among 25 manicured acres.

Complimentary facilities include use of snorkeling and fishing gear, waterskiing, cruises to nearby cays, windsurfing, Sunfish, Prindle catamarans, four tennis courts (three lit for night play), two pools, Jacuzzis, and fitness facilities.

Malliouhana has plenty of activities for the kids, too. The Children's Place, located on Meads Bay Beach, has a "shipwrecked" pirate ship complete with water cannons, which is fun for young visitors to explore and climb. Kids will have a blast climbing over a ropewalk, then slideing down a 60-foot water slide into the water. An 11-foot-deep pool is equipped with springboards, and there is a staffed playground nearby with a sun shelter with video games and ping pong

What Can We Do Now?

If this is your first visit to the island, invest in an island tour led by one of the tour companies or a taxi driver. **Guided island tours** are available from most taxi drivers for $40 for one or two people, $5 for each additional person and will help give you a good overview of the island. From there, you can rent a car and motor around to the beaches and natural attractions scattered around the island (remember, though, driving is on the LEFT).

Anguilla is home to several small museums. The National Trust is currently at work on a museum in The Valley, but several privately owned collections welcome visitors. The **Heritage Collection**, Pond Ground, Tel. 264/497-4440, is the work of Colville Petty, an authority on Anguilla's rich history. Housed in part of Petty's home, the museum spans the entire range of the island's history, from its Amerindian days to the 1967 Revolution. Kids enjoy the collection of Arawak artifacts, including an Arawak shell necklace, a hollowed conch shell that served as an early drinking vessel, and spindle whorls, used to spin cotton to make hammocks and religious symbols for the Arawaks are also on display. This fascinating museum is open Monday through Saturday, 10 to 5pm and Sunday by appointment. Talking to Colville Petty about the island's history is well worth the price of admission. Admission is US $5, children under 12 are $2.

Anguilla enjoys a rich West Indian culture. Have a look at the traditional song and dance with a visit to the **Mayoumba Folkloric Theatre**, La Sirena Hotel, Tel. 264/497-6827, a group that plays every Thursday night at La Sirena hotel in Meads Bay. Call for reservations.

Kids five to 10 years old also have a unique opportunity to interact with Anguillians. Children are invited to a weekly Saturday morning **storytime** at the Anguilla National Library, The Valley, Tel. 264/497-2441, a Caribbean-style building designed by a local architect. The National Library is seeking assistance with the purchase of books, computers, software, and audiovisual materials. Contact the Anguilla Library Service, The Valley, Anguilla, BWI, Tel. 264/497-2441.

Sports & Recreaton

Young swimmers will find many opportunities for **snorkeling**. A marked snorkel trail is found off Shoal Bay East. Maintained by the National Trust, the site has been mapped and can be easily followed by most snorkelers. Stop by the National Trust office at the National Museum in The Valley or ask your hotel's concierge for a map of this snorkel trail. To check on the snorkel trail or to obtain a map, call the National Trust, Tel. 264/497-5297.

Certified **scuba divers** in your family can enjoy a look at one of seven wrecks that lie in the waters off Anguilla. Four were sunk in 1990 as part of an ecological program and all the wrecks are intact and upright on the ocean floor. Anguilla has two dive operations, located in Sandy Ground and Island Harbour. Rates average about $45 US for a single tank dive, $80 for a two-tank dive, and $55 for a night dive.

Regardless of your children's ages and swimming abilities, you'll discover that one of Anguilla's best assets is its **beaches**. Miles of shining sand pave the perimeter of this island, which is often cited as one of the top beach destinations in the Caribbean (with good reason). The atmosphere at the various beaches varies from playful to placid. Regardless of which beach you select, the mood is friendly and low-pressure.

A few beach vendors are found on the island's busiest stretch of sand, **Shoal Bay**, but even here the sales are very low-key and you'll be able to enjoy undisturbed sunbathing all afternoon. Shoal Bay is a true classic, one of the best in the Caribbean. Nearly chalk white sand stretches for two miles. Shoal Bay has the most typical "beach" atmosphere in Anguilla, with casual eateries sprinkled along the sand. Beach chairs and umbrellas are rented by the day for a few dollars. This beach is a terrific choice for a family day of fun in the sun. Young swimmers generally find the water calm, and snorkeling is excellent on the northeast end of the beach.

Other good beach choices include **Sandy Ground**, stretching alongside the community of Sandy Ground (a favorite with boaters, windsurfers and water-skiers, so not the best choice for those with young swimmers), **Rendezvous Bay** (great for beachwalking), **Maundays Bay**, at Cap Juluca (good for beachwalking). A good adventure is to take a boat out to one of the many cays and islets surrounding Anguilla. Check with boat operators for a day trip to **Prickly Pear Cays** or **Sandy Island**, both known for their snorkeling, or for a unique experience load up everyone for a day trip to one of the uninhabited islands: **Anguillita Island**, **Sombrero Island**, or **Dog Island**. A boat can drop you for a full day's excursion, most departing from Sandy Ground. Bring along a picnic lunch and feel like Swiss Family Robinson.

For a unique experience, families should check out **Dolphin Fantaseas**, Meads Bay, Tel. 264/497-7946. This tour increases the public knowledge of dolphins by offering swims in a dolphin pool. Swims are offered daily at 9:30, 11:30, 2, and 4 for US $105.

Horseback riding is available through El Rancho Del Blues, Blowing Point, Tel. 264/497-6164. One hour rides on the beach and in the countryside are offered at 9, 11, 2, and 4; riding lessons are also available.

If you've got any football (soccer to Americans) fans in the family, drop by the Ronald Webster park, located north of the Post Office in The Valley. You'll find a game most weekend afternoons.

What Can We Buy?

Shopping is not one of Anguilla's strong points, especially for kids looking for small souvenirs. Artist's galleries are sprinkled throughout the island, but these are pricey reminders of an island vacation. Cap Juluca has a nice gift store but take out a loan first.

A good option is an afternoon of shopping in St. Martin. Take a ferry ride to Marigot, St. Martin for a day at the market. Kids of all ages find trinkets, clothes, jewelry, shells, carvings, and other goodies in all price ranges. The market is colorful, fun, and friendly.

What Else Do We Need to Know?

Currency. The Eastern Caribbean (EC) currency is legal tender. Value is set at $1US=2.68EC. US dollars are also accepted.

Driving. Driving is English style, on the LEFT.

Electricity. The island has 110 volt electrical currents.

Information. For more information on Anguilla, contact the Anguilla Tourist Board, Tel. 800/553-4939 , or write Anguilla Tourist Information Office, Coronation Avenue, The Valley, Anguilla, BWI. Staff members are available from 8 to 5 Atlantic Standard Time (one hour ahead of Eastern Standard Time).

Information on Island. While on the island, stop by the Tourist Board office in The Valley at Factory Plaza, Tel. 264/497-2759.

Website. The official Anguilla Tourist Board website is www.anguilla-vacation.com.

Island Report Card	
Transportation to island	B
Transportation around island	B+
Family Resorts	B
Family Restaurants	B-
Friendly atmosphere	A+
Activities for kids	B+
Weather	A
New cultures for kids to experience	A
Safety	A+

Chapter 5

ANTIGUA

What Antigua boasts are beaches: 365 of them, the tourism folks claim. There's a beach for every activity level: stretches of white sand border turquoise waters teeming with marine life, beaches where your family can walk and hardly see another soul, beaches where you can shop for local crafts and buy a burger at beachside grill, and beaches where you can just curl up under a tall coconut palm and sit until the sun sinks into the sea and marks the end of another Caribbean day.

Pre-Colonial Antigua was originally inhabited by the Siboney Indians. In 1493 Christopher Columbus named the island in honor of Santa Maria de La Antigua of Seville, a saint at whose namesake church Columbus had prayed before his journey to the Americas.

Antigua has had close ties to England, ever since an English patrol from St. Kitts landed on the island in 1632 and claimed it for the mother country. Since 1981, however, the twin island nation of Antigua and Barbuda has held the status of an independent country.

This 108-square mile limestone and coral island is somewhat scrubby with rolling hills, especially on the southern reaches. The capital city is St. John's, home of most of the tourist shopping and the cruise port.

The south shore of the island is favored by yachties, who call into Nelson's Dockyard at English Harbour.

Are We There Yet?

By Air

Air travelers will arrive at V.C. Bird International Airport, located near

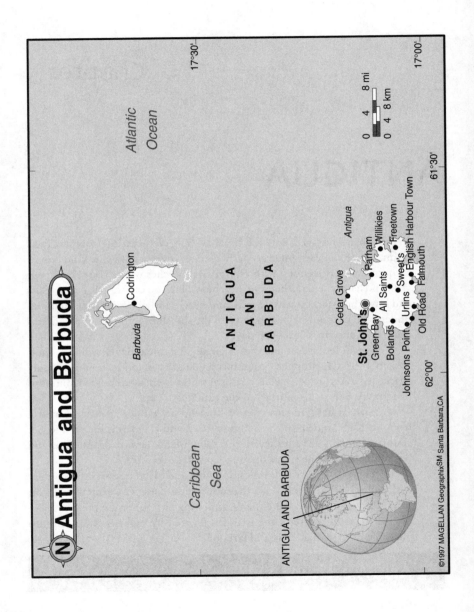

Antigua and Barbuda

N

Caribbean
Sea

Atlantic
Ocean

17°30'

Barbuda

Codrington

ANTIGUA
AND
BARBUDA

17°00'

61°30'

Antigua

Cedar Grove
Parham
Willkies
Freetown
Sweet's
English Harbour Town
Falmouth
St. John's
Green Bay
All Saints
Urlins
Bolands
Old Road
Johnsons Point

62°00'

ANTIGUA AND BARBUDA

0 4 8 mi
0 4 8 km

©1997 MAGELLAN GeographixSM Santa Barbara,CA

the capital city of St. John's. Served by American Airlines, Air Canada, British Airways, BWIA, Caribbean Star, LIAT, Virgin Airlines, USAirways, and others, the airport is also a bustling hub for many interisland flights.

Antigua is also a popular destination for many cruise ships. The terminal is located in downtown St. John's and is within walking distance of the main shopping areas.

Getting Around the Island

Taxi travel is the most common means of transportation, especially for families not comfortable with driving on the left side of the road. Taxi fares from the St. John's area to Nelson's Dockyard on the far side of the island run about $50 US round trip.

Rental cars are available; a temporary Antiguan driver's license is required. The license can be obtained at the V.C. Bird International Airport or at any Antiguan police station. We found that some roads are a little bumpy, and that a full tank of gas (as well as a spare tire) was recommended for visitors who would be traveling out on the island away from the major destinations.

Where Are We Staying?

CURTAIN BLUFF RESORT, Tel. 268/462-8400, Fax 268/462-8409. Toll-free US phone number 888/289-9898; www.curtainbluff.com. Winter rates from $850, summer rates from $495, double occupancy. Credit cards accepted.

This exclusive hotel is located on a private peninsula with two beaches. The all-inclusive property includes all meals, drinks, afternoon tea, watersports, tennis, golf, and even mail service so you can send those postcards home.

Families looking for sports will find a variety of activities to meet their needs at this resort. There are four lighted tennis courts with three full-time tennis pros availible, a pro shop with a racquet stringing facilities. There is also a squash court, putting green, lawn croquet, and fitness center. The 18-hole course at Harbour Club and Cedar Valley is only a short taxi ride from Curtain Bluff.

There is also a variety of watersports inlcuding scuba diving, deep sea fishing, sailboating, windsurfing and kayaking. For those who just want a little relaxation, there are beach chairs, sun chaises, hammocks and floats.

Note: Children are not permitted during the month of February, peak season. At other times, kids under 12 are welcomed with special menus and early seatings, a playground, and an air-conditioned playroom with DVDs and computer games. Twice a year (during the winter holidays and spring break), the resort offers a special Kids Camp for two weeks at a half-day or full-day rate. Kids registered for the camp enjoy beach games, arts and crafts, shell collecting, movies and treasure hunts.

HAWKSBILL BEACH RESORT, St. John's, Tel. 268/462-0301, Fax 268/462-1515. Toll-free reservations Tel. 800/223-6510; www.hawksbill.com. Winter rates from $280, summer from $165. Credit cards accepted.

Located just a few minutes from St. John's, this quiet resort is our favorite kind: quiet, restful, and located on, not one, but four superb beaches. With a primarily British contingency, the resort is somewhat reserved but just a few minutes from the action of St. John's. Kids' supper is served from 6pm to 7pm.

Activities at this resort range from relaxing to adventurous. Family members looking for quiet activities can go out on a paddle boat, play tennis or go shopping at the Hawksbill boutique. More daring members can try sailing, waterskiing or snorkeling. At the end of the day, everyone can meet back up to enjoy music, limbo dancers or cocktail parties.

JOLLY BEACH RESORT, Bolans Village, Tel. 268/462-0061, Fax 268/ 562-2302. Toll-free reservations Tel. 800/223-6510l; www.jollybeachresort.com. Winter rates from $175, summer from $175. Credit cards accepted.

This all-inclusive resort has a family-friendly atmosphere from its Kidz Club to casual activities for the whole family ranging from pinball to table tennis. The supervised children's program is open weekdays only from 9:30am to 12:30pm and 2 pm to 5 pm; the club is available for chilren ages 3 to 12 years old. Along with weekends, the supervised children's program is also not available on public holidays.

Other activities include tennis (four courts lit for night play), water polo, volleyball, pool aerobics, a gym, and more. Non-motorized watersports are part of the all-inclusive package and include Hobie Cats, Sunfish sailboats, windsurfers, kayaks, paddleboats, snorkeling and more. Scuba, waterskiing, and banana boat rides are available for an additional charge, as is golf.

SUNSAIL COLONNA CLUB, Hodges Bay, Tel. 268/462-6263, Fax 268/462-6430. Toll-free Reservations Tel. 800/327-2276. www.sunsail.com. All-inclusive winter rates from $145, summer from $95. Credit cards accepted.

If your family loves the water and sailing, then they'll love Sunsail. This international company, with clubs as far away as Turkey, is a favorite among the sailing world. Here you'll find an array of vessels to take out and enjoy and, if you don't know stern from bow, you can take expert lessons here as well, all part of the all-inclusive plan.

Sunsail isn't fancy but all rooms are air conditioned and include satellite TV, telephone, mini refrigerator, and tea and coffee making facilities. There are numerous twin and double rooms as well as apartments and 2-3 bedroom villas. The resort has a restaurant, pool, tennis, volleyball, and table tennis.

But the real attraction here comes in the form of watersports. The resort hugs a small cove where instruction is available in dinghy, catamaran, and yacht sailing as well as waterskiing and windsurfing. If your skills are up to par, you can take a vessel out or participate in one of the resort programs such as a yacht regatta or dinghy regatta. Waters are their most challenging during the winter months but summer usually brings milder trade winds and conditions better suited to beginners.

The resort also offers excellent child care facilities so parents can take part in watersports. The Kids Clubs run six days per week year around and include lunch. Facilities for children include a nursery, playroom, baby listening, kids' pool, and baby sitting; teenagers have use of tennis courts, sailing, waterskiing, inner tubes, and bananas.

There are several clubs, depending on your child's age:
•Mini Club. This club is for children 4 months to 2 years.
•Penguin Club. This is for children 2 to 4 years.
•Sea Urchin. Children 5 to 7 years can participate in this club.
•Junior Gyber. Preteens 8 to 12 years take part in this club.
•Beach Team. Teens 13-16 years take part in these activities.

What Can We Do Now?

Antigua's most family activity is a trip to its splendid **beaches**. Some of the most popular spots are Dickenson Bay, where you'll find beach bars and watersports action, Hawksbill beaches on Five Island peninsula, home of a clothing-optional beach, and Runaway Beach, also lively with watersports activities.

If it's beach seclusion you're after, then consider a day to Antigua's sister island, **Barbuda**. Day trips to this uncommercialized island, which is also popular with bird watchers because of its population of frigate birds, are available from several operators. Barbuda lies about 30 miles north of Antigua.

Nature lovers will also find plenty of activity on Antigua. **Scuba diving** and **snorkeling** is a popular activity. Certified divers can enjoy a variety of dives, from walls to wrecks.

Antigua is also rich in historic attractions as well. The most visited is **Nelson's Dockyard National Park.** Built in 1784, this dockyard was the headquarters for Admiral Horatio Nelson. Today you can retrace the history of this site at the Dow's Hill Interpretation Centre or at the complex's two museums: Admiral's House and Clarence House, former home of Prince William Henry, later known as King William IV of Britain.

What Can We Buy?

The primary shopping area on the island is in St. John's, near the cruise ship terminal. This area doesn't have the charm of many Caribbean shopping districts, and is somewhat littered, smelly, and dirty. Still, it's worth a two- or three-hour excursion to have a look at the goods offered in the small boutiques.

Redcliffe Quay is a scenic place to shop and have lunch. You will find plenty of cool shade, brick courtyards, and restored buildings where you can shop for Caribbean items in a charming atmosphere.

If you'd like to get away from the tourist center, take a walk up to Market Street for shops aimed at the local residents, including many fabric stores offering beautiful tropical prints.

Outside of St. John's, head to Harmony Hall in Brown's Bay Mill. This art gallery, which originated in Jamaica, features work by many Caribbean artists. Original works as well as prints and posters are for sale, accompanied by crafts, books, and seasonings that capture the spice of the island.

What Else Do We Need to Know?

Currency. The Eastern Caribbean (EC) dollar is the legal tender. It is exchanged at a fixed rate of $1US=2.68EC. American dollars are also accepted.

Driving. Driving is on the LEFT.

Information: Contact the Antigua and Barbuda Department of Tourism, 610 Fifth Avenue, Suite 311, New York, NY 10020, Tel. 888/268-4227, Fax 212/541-4789. In Canada, contact the Antigua and Barbuda Dept. of Tourism and Trade, 60 St. Clair Avenue East, Suite 304, Toronto, Ontario MT4 1N5, Tel. 416/961-3085, Fax 416/961-7218.

On the island, contact the Antigua and Barbuda Department of Tourism, Government Complex, Queen Elizabeth Highway, St. John's, Antigua. West Indies. Email: deptourism@antigua.gov.ag , Tel. 268/462-0480, Fax 268/462-2483

Website. Another good source of information is the Antigua and Barbuda Department of Tourism web page at www.antigua-barbuda.org.

Island Report Card	
Transportation to island	A
Transportation around island	B+
Family Resorts	B
Family Restaurants	B-
Friendly atmosphere	B-
Activities for kids	B+
Weather	A
New cultures for kids to experience	B
Safety	B+

Chapter 6

ARUBA

Aruba is not the tropical paradise found on islands like Jamaica or St. Lucia. Palm trees and tropical flowers cluster only around well-groomed resorts and desert landscapes.

But that's not to say Aruba is without beauty—you just have to know where to look, that's all. You'll have to venture to the rugged Atlantic shore and watch the tumultuous waves carving the natural bridge, continually changing the demarcation line where the land meets the sea. Or you can hike to some of Aruba's highest hills, curious bumps on the landscape, and look out at the cunucu or countryside for traditional Dutch-style houses with their sun-baked orange tile roofs.

But perhaps the best way to see the beauty of Aruba is to look into the faces of the Aruban people, the island's greatest asset. This tiny island, a mere 70 square miles, truly is a melting pot of cultures. Over 43 nationalities are represented here, and with them a melange of languages. Arubans learn from an early age the benefits and necessity of working with other nations and learning different languages is a skill that most young Arubans master. This island is the perfect place to bring your young linguist to inspire the desire to learn.

The language of the Aruban home is Papiamento, a mixture of Spanish, Portuguese, French, Dutch, Indian, English, and even some African dialects. Papiamento is the language of the streets. To the ear, it resembles Spanish. Here are some common Papiamento phrases:

- **Bon Bini.** Welcome.
- **Con ta bai?** How are you?
- **Mi ta bon.** I am fine.

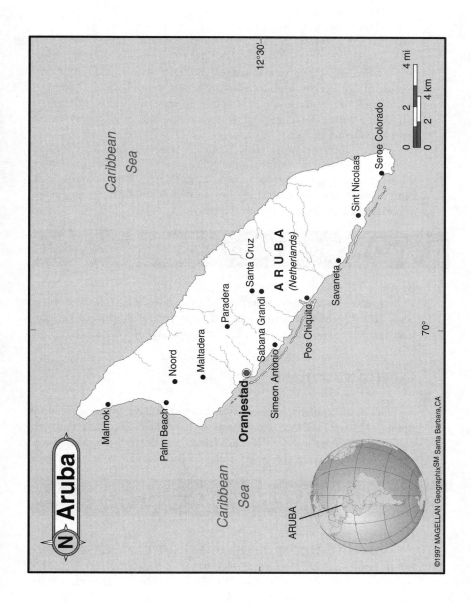

Aruba

Caribbean Sea

Caribbean Sea

Malmok
Palm Beach
Noord
Maltadera
Paradera
Santa Cruz
Sabana Grandi
Oranjestad
Simeon Antonio
Pos Chiquito
Savaneta
Sint Nicolaas
Seroe Colorado

A R U B A
(Netherlands)

12°30'
70°

ARUBA

©1997 MAGELLAN GeographixSM Santa Barbara,CA

0 2 4 mi
0 2 4 km

•**Bon dia.** Good morning.
•**Bon nochi.** Good evening.
•**Pasa bon dia.** Have a good day.
•**Hopi bon.** Very good.
•**Ayo.** Good-bye.

When youngsters head to school, they receive instruction in Dutch, because of Aruba's continuing ties to the Kingdom of Holland. Once they reach third or fourth grade, instruction in English begins. Spanish is introduced during the junior high years, and in high school students select from French or German.

That familiarity with many languages translates into a welcoming atmosphere for visitors of any nationality. There is no hostility to tourists on this island; no language barrier to overcome. There is just a spirit of "Bon Bini" or "Welcome" which greets visitors from the moment they arrive in the airport and continues throughout their visit.

Are We There Yet?

By Air
Aruba is a 2-1/2 hour flight from Miami or four hours from New York. Service into Queen Beatrix International Airport is available from American, Continental, Delta, KLM, United, USAirways, and others.

Getting Around the Island

Taxis are available in resort areas or you can have one dispatched by calling 22116 or 21604 on island. Rates are fixed (no meters), so check with your driver before the ride. Taxi rates from Palm Beach to Oranjestad run about US$16; you may pay in US dollars. Rental cars are widely available.

Where Are We Staying?

Oranjestad
RENAISSANCE ARUBA BEACH RESORT AND CASINO, L.G. Smith Boulevard 82, Oranjestad, Tel. 011/297-583-6000, Fax 011/297-582-5317. Toll-free reservations 800/421-8188;. Low season rates from $160-380, High season rates from $230-$450. Credit cards accepted.

This resort offers two distinct options: the Marina Hotel (on the land side and popular for adults who want to be closer to the nightlife) and or the

The Renaissance Ocean Suites, the best family choice thanks to its oceanside location and all-suites offerings. In the Ocean Suites, the recently renovated guest rooms include a king bed, a living room with a queen sofa bed, minibar, fridge, coffeemaker, high-speed internet access (there is a surcharge for access), and either a balcony or patio.

While Mom and Dad relax at the casinos or spa, the kids can enjoy the children's program, called the Patamingo Club. (What's a Patamingo, you ask? According to Renaissance legend, the patamingo is a half-duck, half-flamingo who lives on Renaissance Island (just offshore) and lays two or three chocolate eggs every morning, ones gathered daily by the employees and handed out to lucky children.

The supervised kids' club is available for children ages 5-12 and includes both daytime and nighttime programs. Day activities include arts and crafts, face painting, Papiamento lessons, dance lessons, and beach Olympic games. In the evenings, your kids can enjoy movies, miniature golf, and more. The day program runs from 9:30 am to 4:30 pm daily; the cost is $20 for a half-day stay or $35 for a full day, both including lunch. The evening program is available Friday and Saturday nights only from 6 pm to 9:30 pm; the price is $25 and includes dinner. For more than one child in the family, each additional child pays only half price. Babysitting services are also available.

Eagle & Palm Beaches

ARUBA MARRIOTT RESORT AND STELLARIS CASINO, L.G. Smith Boulevard, Palm Beach, Tel. 011/297-586-9000, Fax 011/297-586-0649. Toll-free reservations Tel. 800/223-6388; www.marriotthotels.com/auaar. Winter rates $340-$399, Summer rates $175-$290. Credit cards accepted.

This 413-room hotel is one of the tops on Palm Beach, a flashy property with a free-form pool, oversize guest rooms, and just about any activity a family could want.

Every guest room at this resort is equipped with any amenity that could be needed, including a minibar, in-room safe for passports, a balcony or patio to enjoy the Caribbean breeze, and there are cribs available upon request.

While Mom and Dad are having fun in the 10,700 square-foot casino, the kids can play in the game room, or take part in the resort's children program. There are also baby sitters availible for the younger kids.

Just next door, a condominium development managed by Marriott offers family-sized units with kitchen facilities, another top choice for families. Guests at the condos have full use of the hotel facilities.

HOLIDAY INN SUNSPREE RESORT ARUBA, J.E. Irausquin Boulevard #230, Tel. 011/297-58-63600, Fax 011/297-58-65165. Toll-free reservations Tel. 800/HOLIDAY in US, Toll-free reservations Tel. 800/ GET-BOUNTY in Canada and Puerto Rico; www.aruba.sunspreeresorts.com. $188-269 in high season for all-inclusive program in high season, $135 per person off season. Credit cards accepted.

The 600-room Holiday Inn Aruba Beach offers the Bounty all-inclusive Vacation program. The package includes room (with air-conditioning and satellite TV), buffet breakfast daily, full service lunch and dinner daily in a choice of indoor and outdoor restaurants, snacks, unlimited liquor, beer, wine, and soft drinks, theme parties, watersports, tennis, hotel tax, tips, and, especially for families, a supervised kids' program.

Camp Bounty, the program for children age 4-12 (although the program can be adjusted for toddlers 2-4 and teens 12-15), runs daily from 9am to 5pm. The program includes breakfast and lunch with program coordinators, daytime snacks, arts and crafts, and plenty of activities. Children enjoy kite flying contests, drawing and coloring contests, sand sculpting, hoola hoop contests, pool and beach Olympics, shell hunting, talent shows, face painting, dance lessons, scavenger hunts, and more. After program hours, baby-sitting is available.

Check for special promotions during summer and fall months; in the past, this hotel has run a "kids stay free" promotion where children stayed in the same room as parents without charge.

HYATT REGENCY ARUBA RESORT AND CASINO, J.E. Irausquin Boulevard, #85, Palm Beach, Tel. 011/297-586-1234, Fax 011/ 297-586-5478. Toll-free reservations Tel. 800/233-1234; www.hyatt.com and http://aruba.hyatt.com/. Winter rates $440, Summer rates $240. Credit cards accepted.

One of Aruba's most luxurious properties, the 360-room Hyatt is located on the northern end of Palm Beach. Like other Hyatts, this property is for anyone looking for a body holiday: be pampered in the health and fitness facility, slice across the clear Caribbean on a sailboat at the watersports facility, or just luxuriate in the warmth of the sun at the three-level pool complex.

We love this Hyatt property not only for its excellent beach and good location but also for its friendly staff. This hotel boasts one of the friendliest and most helpful staffs we've ever encountered, a factor that helps make a vacation here a sure success.

Camp Hyatt (locally called Camp Watapana), for children age three to 12 years, includes activities such as Papiamento lessons, local arts and crafts, and nature hikes. The camp includes an arts and crafts center, an outdoor playground, a Nintendo playstation, and over 100 types of games and toys. Family Camp, with fun for all members of the family, includes activities such as glass-bottom boat rides, photography classes, and watersports.

The resort is located on a long, wide stretch of beach. Kids also find plenty of water action in the three-level pool which includes a three-story waterslide.

LA CABANA ALL SUITE BEACH RESORT AND CASINO, J.E. Irausquin Boulevard #250, Eagle Beach, Tel. 011/297-58-79000, Fax 011/297-58-70834. Toll-free reservations Tel. 800/835-7193 in US and Canada; www.lacabana.com/resort. Winter rates from $210 double occupancy, Summer rates $132 double occupancy. Credit cards accepted.

Located across the street from Eagle Beach, this orange sherbet-tinted property has plenty of action, including a huge casino. All guest rooms are suites—from studios for families to three bedroom suites for families, and all include a fully equipped kitchenette. You can opt for an all-inclusive plan or a room only.

La Cabana offers kids' programs for every age. The Club Cabana Nana program for children 5 to 12 offers activities from 10:30am until 3:30pm daily, except Wednesdays when the program runs from 5pm to 8:30pm. The program runs year around. Kids receive a Club Cabana Nana T-shirt, lunch daily (pizza on Wednesday nights), and plenty of activities from which to choose: scavenger hunts, mini-golf, sandcastle building, talent show, and more. Papiamento lessons are a fun and educational part of the program, along with a botanical tour of the property and lessons on the island's history and culture.

Teens aren't forgotten either. The Teen Cabana Culture Club entertains ages 13 to 17 with windsurfing, snorkeling, billiards, mini-golf, beach disco parties, and more. There may be some additional costs for this program, depending on the activity planned. The Teen Cabana Culture Club takes place every Thursday and the price includes lunch and a T-shirt.

Concierge Bernadette Davis at La Cabana Resort recommends several Aruba activities for families:

1. Tiri Kochi Park: a playground park where kids can play.

2. Kibaima Park: A mini zoo and recreational park. They have miniature Aruban village houses, a replica coin house, a replica stamp house, redesigned miniature houses of children's classic stories such as Cinderella, the Seven Dwarfs, and the Three Bears. This park is good for children age nine and under.

3. Baby Beach: A perfect beach for children with no current or tide. It's a family beach that's calm and shallow. There are picnic huts and lots of shade; all ages will enjoy.

4. Adventure Golf. Great for kids with arcade machines, a boat ride for children age five and up. Mini golf for all ages with an Italian restaurant on premise.

RADISSON ARUBA CARIBBEAN RESORT AND CASINO, J.E. Irausquin Boulevard, #81, Palm Beach, Tel. 011/297-586-6555, Fax 011/297-586-3260. Toll-free reservations Tel. 800/333-3333; www.radisson.com. Winter rates $245-$365, summer from $189. Credit cards accepted.

This 358-room hotel has plenty to keep families busy on the beach with water-skiing, wave runners, catamarans, scuba instruction, the list goes on and on. The kids' program includes a myriad of activities ranging from volleyball to bocce ball to beach Olympics. Baby-sitting available. The whole family can enjoy the 1500-foot-wide beach and the Olympic-sized pool.

What Can We Do Now?

As home to both the cruise port and the airport, your first look at Aruba will probably be in the city of **Oranjestad**. This beautiful city, where nearly every building sports a fresh coat of paint and a distinct Dutch style, is well worth spending an afternoon wandering the safe, clean streets and enjoying the friendly atmosphere.

Also make sure to have a look at the rest of the island. The biggest tour operator is **DePalm Tours** (Tel. 297/824400, www.depalmonline.com), with desks in every major hotel. This firm offers an excellent half-day tour aboard air-conditioned motor coaches with hotel pick-up. At the conclusion of the tour, you can return to your hotel or get off in downtown Oranjestad for an afternoon of shopping.

DePalm Tours also operates **open air jeep tours** of the island's rugged countryside. The open-air, yellow jeeps bounce along the desert terrain for the best view of this unique island. We've done this with our daughter and the ride is an exhilarating one, especially for teens (reconsider it for young children.) Pack old clothes for this one; you'll be covered in dust. DePalm also rents ATVs, a very popular (and sometimes, honestly, a little scary on busier roads) way to get around town.

Island tours reveal a terrain with a windswept family beauty that families learn to love for its contrast of ochre colors against the turquoise sea and for its rugged beauty. You'll have an excellent view of the cunucu, or countryside, atop **Casibari Rock Formation**. It's a fairly easy climb (although you'll find yourself bent over and squeezing between rocks a few times), but wear good shoes for this trek.

Families also should visit the **natural bridge**, like the divi-divi tree, a symbol of Aruba. This bridge was carved by the tumultuous sea waves that continue to crash on the rocks and spray visitors. You'll always find a crowd at the natural bridge, which is somewhat touristy with a bar and souvenir shop, but it's still worth a visit, especially if you're doing some photography along the way.

A favorite family activity is a ride aboard the **Atlantis Submarine**, Tel. 800/253-0493. This 65-foot vessel is a real submarine and take travelers on a one-hour excursion to see what lies below Aruba's waves. Photo tip: Bring fast film (ASA 400 or higher) for this excursion. You won't be able to use your flash inside the sub but there are many good photo opportunities, especially of your children looking through the portholes at the coral reefs beyond.

Want to feel like part of the sea? There's no better way that with **SeaTrek** (Tel. 297/824400, www.depalmonline.com), available from DePalm Island for ages eight and up. (Kids with asthma cannot take part, though, due to use of pressurized air.) Wearing SeaTrek's special dive helmet, you get the experience of actually walking, in a moon-walk style, right on the floor of the ocean, guided by scuba divers the entire time. The walk takes about 25 minutes and is a fun adventure with swimmers and non-swimmers alike; you don't even need to get your hair wet if you don't want to (and glasses can be worn beneath the helmet.)

Need a break from the sun or a rainy weather option (not likely on this very arid island, but you never know)? At the Renaissance's Crystal Theater, you can watch the 25-minute **Experience Aruba Panorama**, which show-cases the island on a big screen 66 feet high. The movie is show on the hour from 11 am to 5 pm, Monday through Saturday.

Sports & Recreaton

Guided **horseback rides** at Rancho Del Campo are popular with many families. On tours, you can ride through Aruba's only national park: **Arikok National Wildlife Park**, home of Indian rock markings, gold digging ruins, and a restored cunucu home. Don't forget to bring long pants for the horseback ride!

Of course, much of Aruba's allure is the sea, both for its beaches and the action in the water. On the southwest end of the island, **Palm and Eagle beaches** are some of the most popular because of their proximity to the major hotels, but for the calmest waters head to **Baby Beach**. Located on the far southern tip of the island near the town of San Nicolas, it is well-known for its lake-calm waters and a favorite with families. Swimmers should avoid the waters of the island's north shore, which are rough and often plagued by undertow.

For a closeup look at Aruba's undersea life, families with children age 8 and older can opt for **SNUBA** at DePalm Island. You don't need any scuba or snorkeling experience; your instructor will show you how to breath through a regulator connected by an air hose to a tank the floats on the water's surface. After a class, you'll take a private underwater tour down to a depth of 20 feet. You can see both the area's coral formations or see the Antilla, a 430-foot shipwreck. The entire experience takes about an hour.

Both SNUBA and Sea Trek are located on De Palm Island, a private coral island that's just offshore. The island includes plenty of watersports fun as well as restaurants; many cruise ship passengers take advantage of the all-inclusive package at De Palm Island for the day. The package is also available for hotel visitors and includes round trip transportation from your hotel to the island.

Aruba offers some of the Caribbean's top **windsurfing**. Fisherman's Hut is an ideal beginner's site because of its calm, shallow waters, and most resorts offer beginners lessons so your teens and preteens can get a taste of a new sport.

What Can We Buy?

Crafts are few, and most are imported from South America. Kids will find some inexpensive craft items at the mall and also at a small market (filled with picturesque displays of tropical fruit) near the cruise dock in Oranjestad. Here you can also find a true souvenir of the island: an Aruba license plate for US $4.

Aruba definitely ranks as a top Caribbean shopping destination. International goods — perfumes, china, crystal, jewelry, cameras, and clothing—are best buys. Unlike the practice of many islands, bargaining is not customary in Aruba.

Stores are open 8am to 6:30pm, Monday through Saturday, and usually close for two hours during lunch. If a cruise ship is in port, you may find some shops open on Sunday.

The primary shopping district stretches along Oranjestad's waterfront. Malls as colorful as sherbet line this route, tempting shoppers with goods that range from T-shirts and Delft Blue salt and pepper shakers to European tres chic designer outfits and fine jewelry.

Seaport Mall and Seaport Marketplace have the lion's share of the mall business. The Mall is located adjacent to Renaissance Resort and includes high-priced shops on its lowest level. Upstairs, boutiques offer moderately priced resort wear, jewelry, china, and more for a total of over 65 shops.

If you forget someone special on your list, you'll also find shops at the Queen Beatrix International Airport.

What Else Do We Need to Know?

Banks. Hours are 8am to 4pm. ATMs are found at the Caribbean Mercantile Bank and the ABN-AMRO Bank. Either major credit cards or Cirrus network bank cards may be used.

Currency. The Aruban florin is the official currency although US dollars are also widely accepted. At press time the exchange rate was $1US to A.Fl. 1.77 although this fluctuates.

Driving. Driving is on the right side of the road.

Electricity. North American appliances may be used without adapters. Voltage is 110 volts, 60 cycles.

Hospitals. The Dr. Horacio Oduber Hospital near Eagle Beach is a modern facility with 280 beds. The local number is 74300.

Information. The toll-free number for Aruba information is Tel. 800/TO-ARUBA. On Island Information: While on Aruba, contact the local office at L.G. Smith Boulevard 172, Tel. 011/297-582-3777, Fax 011/297-583-4702.

Website. Check out the official website at: www.aruba.com.

Island Report Card	
Transportation to island	A
Transportation around island	A
Family Resorts	A-
Family Restaurants	A
Friendly atmosphere	A+
Activities for kids	A-
Weather	A+
New cultures for kids to experience	A
Safety	A+

Chapter 7

BAHAMAS

For family travelers, the most popular stop in the Bahamas is Grand Providence Island, home of the capital city of Nassau. Located just a half hour flight from Miami, this island may be just a stone's (or a conch shell's) throw from the U.S. mainland, but it gives visitors a wonderful taste of Caribbean life.

One of the most popular islands in the Bahamas is Nassau, the island that's almost synonymous with "Bahamas." The atmosphere in Nassau is a delightful combination of the British and the Caribbean. The Parliament House, a pink building from which the British ruled the Bahamas until 1972, still stands in the middle of the bustling city. The country still retains many British influences, with the Royal family smiling back from the currency and postage stamps. Driving is on the left side of the road.

The heart of Nassau is Rawson Square. Make your first stop at the Visitors Information Center for brochures and maps before starting off on busy Bay Street, the shopping district. Here gold and gem stores make this one of the region's top duty-free stops.

From the cruise port you'll also see a tall, curving bridge. This leads to Paradise Island, the most luxurious area of Grand Providence Island. Once named Hog Island, this area was revitalized by investments by Donald Trump and Merv Griffin and now by South African businessman Sol Kerzner.

Another plush area is Cable Beach, located 10 minutes by cab from downtown Nassau. This stretch of sandy beach is lined with high-rise hotels. Shuttles take guests at these resorts to Nassau several times daily.

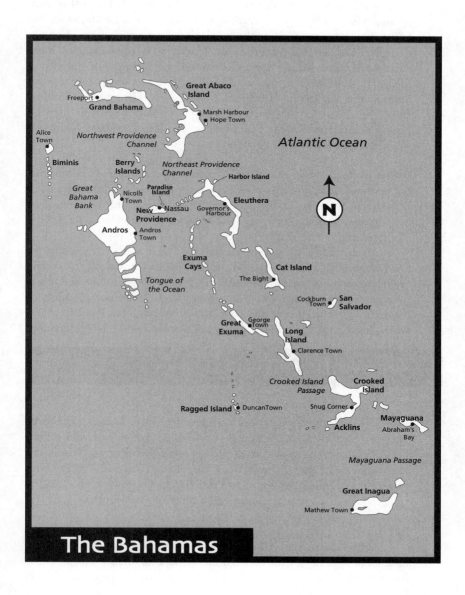

Great Abaco Island

Freeport •
Grand Bahama

Marsh Harbour
Hope Town

Alice Town

Northwest Providence Channel

Atlantic Ocean

Biminis

Berry Islands

Northeast Providence Channel

Harbor Island

Great Bahama Bank

Paradise Island

Nicolls Town

Nassau

Eleuthera

New Providence

Governor's Harbour

Andros

Andros Town

Exuma Cays

Cat Island

The Bight

Tongue of the Ocean

Cockburn Town

San Salvador

Great Exuma

George Town

Long Island

Clarence Town

Crooked Island Passage

Crooked Island

Ragged Island

DuncanTown

Snug Corner

Mayaguana

Acklins

Abraham's Bay

Mayaguana Passage

Great Inagua

Mathew Town

N

The Bahamas

Technically, the Bahama islands lie outside the boundaries of the Caribbean. But, except for a few days when the islands are cooled by winter's chill, you'll have a hard time telling the difference. These 700 islands, sprinkled like seashells across shallow water, share the same sun, sand, and festive atmosphere as their southern neighbors.

But Nassau is far from the only destination in the Bahamas. Grand Bahama Island is indeed a grand destination, starting with the city of Freeport. Stroll the streets of this bustling port and enjoy shopping for international and locally made goods. Market shops sell perfumes, clothing, and crafts, and usually has live music along its outdoor waterfront. Beyond Nassau and Grand Bahama Island fall the Out Islands, smaller landforms where the pace is slow and leisurely.

You may want to book your visit in spring, summer, or fall to be assured of a warm weather vacation. Winter temperatures are usually balmy, but occasionally a cold front reaches its chilly fingers into these waters and drops temperatures to spring-like levels. On an early March visit, we dug into our luggage for sweatshirts and, although temperatures were perfect for island touring, found that it too chilly for comfortable swimming.

While we're warning you, be careful of March and April bookings for another reason: spring breakers. Those low-cost downtown properties (and even some of the Paradise Island and Cable Beach resorts) swell with students during these weeks. Because of the charter packages, Nassau is the Caribbean for the masses and, during this time, that means raucous students. For a quiet, family getaway, consider an alternate month or a different destination.

Are We There Yet?

By Air

Nassau International Airport is served by Delta, American Eagle, Air Jamaica, Air Canada, Continental, USAirways, Bahamasair, and others. Paradise Island also has a small airport with flights from Miami, Ft. Lauderdale, and West Palm Beach aboard Paradise Island Airways from Miami, Fort Lauderdale, and West Palm Beach, Tel. 800/SUN-7202.

Nassau is about a two and a half hours from New York.

By Ship

Cruise ship passengers arrive right in town at the Prince George Dock. Located just off Bay Street between the island and Paradise Island, cruise passengers find they're right in the heart of the action. Cruises also call on Grand Bahama Island.

Getting Around the Island

You'll find plenty of taxis throughout Nassau. Public mini-buses, called jitneys, are widely available and run during business hours. They're slower and more crowded than a taxi ride, but an inexpensive option if you're not in a hurry. Catch jitneys on Bay Street next to the Hilton British Colonial. Be sure to check the destination with the driver before you board, and have correct change (drivers don't give change).

Car rental desks are available at the airport and major hotels. Plan on plenty of traffic within Nassau, however, and don't forget that you'll be driving on the left.

Where Are We Staying?

ATLANTIS RESORT, Paradise Island, Tel. 242/363-3000, Fax 242/363-6309. Toll-free reservations Tel. 800/ATLANTIS; www.atlantis.com. Winter, rooms from $380-720, suites starting at $855; summer, rooms from $340-565, suites starting at $685. Credit cards accepted.

See Chapter 3, "Best Places to Stay," for a detailed write-up.

BRITISH COLONIAL HILTON NASSAU, downtown Nassau, Tel. 242/322-3301, Fax 242/302-9009. Toll-free reservations Tel. 800/HILTONS; www.nassauhilton.com. Winter rates from $210, Summer rates from $200. Credit cards accepted.

This upscale hotel sits at the head of Bay Street, a reminder of Nassau's early hotel days. It's a warm reminder of our early hotel days as well, as the scene of our first visit to the Caribbean. It has a small beach of its own, and it is just steps away from the duty-free shops (and the fast food restaurants if you're watching your pennies).

Today this hotel is largely a business hotel but, if you're in town for a convention or on business, makes a fine place for your family to stay as well. Guests of the British Colonial Hilton Nassau will be pleased to find that within the hotel, there is a barber shop, beauty salon, car rental desk, concierge service, currency exchange, gift shop, recreation desk, news stand, and tour desk. Guests are also able to use the hotel's fitness room and pool.

For kids, there is a babysitting service, and cribs are high chairs are available.

COMFORT SUITES PARADISE ISLAND, Paradise Island Drive, Paradise Island, Tel. 242/363-3680 , Fax 242/363-2588. Toll-free reservations Tel. 877/424-6423 ; www.comfortsuites.com. Winter and summer rates from $190. Credit cards accepted.

This property is located next door to Atlantis Resort, a lower-cost alternative to the mega-resort but with use of the neighbor's facilities. (Kind of like having a neighbor with a great pool—the advantages without the upkeep!) You'll have full signing privileges at Atlantis plus use of its waterpark, restaurants, beach, and more. Also, kids can take part in Atlantis' Discovery Channel camp.

Children age 15 and under stay free if in a room with parents or grandparents, if no additional bedding is needed. Teens 16 and over are charged as adults.

HOLIDAY INN SUNSPREE RESORT, Harbour Drive, Paradise Island, Tel. 242/363-2561, Fax 242/363-3803. Toll-free reservations Tel. 800/HOLIDAY; www.paradiseislandbahama.com. Rates from $260. Credit cards accepted.

This all-inclusive resort makes budget planning simple. Guests have their choice of three on-site restaurants, an expansive pool, a child-safe snorkeling lagoon, tennis, and more.

The KidSpree Kids Club is available for ages four to 12 (teens are welcome to join in as well) with arts and crafts, scavenger hunts, beach games, and more. The camp is part of the all-inclusive program and there's no charge if the parents remain to supervise their children. For parents who drop off kids, there is a fee.

There's a maximum of four persons in a room and an additional charge per child. Children ages 4-12 are charged $35 per night; teens 13-17 are charged $65 per night.

RADISSON CABLE BEACH CASINO AND GOLF RESORT, West Bay St., Tel. 305/932-0222, Fax 954/236-3060. Toll-free reservations Tel. 800/777-7800; www.radisson-cablebeach.com. Winter rates $205-$245, Summer rates $165-$225. Credit cards accepted.

The Radisson Cable Beach offers round-the-clock action both on and off the beach. Every room in the high-rise hotel offers an ocean view. For real luxury, splurge with a junior suite located at the end of each floor. We did and enjoyed sunrise from the bedroom balcony and sunset from the living room balcony. A shopping arcade (with surprisingly good prices, we found) connects the Radisson with the neighboring Wyndham Crystal Palace Casino.

An all-inclusive program is available and, for us, is the top choice for families. Participants wear a wristband that allows them unlimited use of all sports, plus all meals, drinks, snacks, and tips.

As part of the all-inclusive program, kids under 12 stay, eat, and play free when sharing a room with one full paying adult (one child per adult, two children per room maximum).

Camp Junkanoo offers daily supervised fun on a half- or full-day basis. Children are divided into two age groups: four to six and seven to 11. The ratio of children to child coordinators is six to one and children are always monitored and kept in a secure area. Typical activities include a treasure hunt, beach Olympics, arts and crafts, pool and lagoon games, ice cream contests, candy bar bingo, movies, and field trips such as to the Crystal Key Underwater Observatory and Marine Park or Ardastra Gardens and Zoo.

Here's a typical day at Camp Junkanoo:

- •9:30-10am   Register
- •10am   Nature Walk
- •11am   Treasure Hunt/Face Painting
- •12noon   Lunch time
- •1:30   Afternoon registration
- •2:30   Arts and Crafts/Ping Pong
- •3:30   Water Balloon relay
- •4pm   Relaxing hour
- •4:30   Pick up time

Complimentary cribs are offered and baby-sitting is available at nominal charge.

WYNDHAM NASSAU RESORT AND THE CRYSTAL PALACE CASINO, Cable Beach, Tel. 242/327-6200, Fax 242/327-6459. Toll-free US phone number 800/222-7466; www.wyndhamnassauresort.com. Winter rates from $159, summer from $149-189. Credit cards accepted.

With 867 rooms, Cable Beach's largest hotel is tough to miss. The large room property literally glows in the dark, with colored lights over each balcony giving the hotel the look of a seaside candy cane. This is one of the liveliest nightspots in town, thanks to its super-sized casino and glitzy revue.

The resort bustles during daytime hours as well with a private beach, large pool, and miniature golf course on site.

Guest rooms, decorated in tropical colors, can house two adults and two children. Up to two children under 12 can stay in a room with an adult without charge. Cribs are also available without charge. However, be aware that the resort levies a $15 per day, per person fee for all guests age 12 and over which covers the energy surcharge, maid's gratuity, and unlimited use of the miniature golf course.

Kids Klub is for young travelers ages four and up. Each of the counselors is trained in both CPR and first aid according to the resort. Kids' activities include arts and crafts, computer games, scavenger hunts, beach games, and more. The cost of the program is $10 per hour for the first child with a $5 per hour charge for additional children. A four-hour block per child costs $25 per child or $15 for additional kids in the family; for a five to eight-hour day, the price is $40 for the first child and $20 for additional family members. The Kids Klub is open 9 am to 5 pm daily with an evening option of 5 pm to 11 pm Thursday through Saturday. Babysitting is also available for $15 per hour.

Grand Bahama Island
   WESTIN AND SHERATON AT OUR LUCAYA BEACH AND GOLF RESORT, Grand Bahama Island, Tel. 242/373-1333, Fax 242/350-5060. Toll-free US reservations number Tel. 877-OUR-LUCAYA, www.ourlucaya.com. Winter rates $390-$480 for three nights, per person; Summer rates from $660-$690 for three nights per person. Credit cards accepted.

   This massive resort is actually two properties in one: the Westin and the Sheraton. The Westin is located on the far end of the property and is a quiet getaway that's favored by couples and adult travelers without kids.

   The Sheraton is the largest block of the property, a high-rise with plenty of activities for all ages. Our Lucaya is a good choice for parents and kids. Guest rooms are decorated with a Caribbean flair, and there are four outdoor pools to choose from. Parents can relax at the resort's Senses Spa and fitness center, while kids enjoy Camp Lucaya.

   Camp Lucaya is an educational facility for kids 2.5 to 12 years, but that doesn't mean that kids won't have fun! Kids can participate in arts and crafts using native Bahamian materials, hear local fairy tales and myths, attend theme parties, go on excursions with the explorer's club, participate in beach olympics, and take part in other exciting activities. Camp Lucaya is open from 9 am to 5 pm every day, and until 10 pm on Thursday through Saturday during peak periods. For the youngest travelers, there's also a nursery available between 9 am and 5 pm (closed for lunch.) There's a maximum stay of two hours and the charge is $10 per hour, per child.

   Here is a typical weekly schedule of activities at Camp Lucaya:

Monday Land-ho!
10:00 am – noon "Under de sun"
1:00 pm – 3:00 pm Pirates treasure hunt
3:30 pm- 5:00 pm sports

Tuesday Under the Sea
10:00 am - 12:00 noon "Sun n splash"
1:00 pm – 3:00 pm Caribbean crafts
3:30 pm- 5:00 pm Sand and sea games

Wednesday Up, up and away
10:00 am - 12:00 noon Outdoor activities
1:00 pm – 3:00 pm Arts n' crafts
3:30 pm – 5:00 pm The game train

Thursday Music Makes the World Go round
10:00 am - 12:00 noon Rake 'n scrape games
1:00 pm – 3:00 pm Sports
3:30 pm – 5:00 pm Caribbean crafts
7:00 pm –10:00 pm Junkanoo jamboree

Friday Living Happily Ever After
10.00 am - 12:00 noon Imagine that!
1:00 pm – 3:00 pm Bahama mama tales
3:30 pm – 5:00 pm Time machine
7:00 pm-10:00 pm Da movie hut

Saturday Living Creatures
10:00 am - 12:00 noon Jungle mania
1:00 pm – 3:00 pm Caribbean crafts
3:30 pm – 5:00 pm Outdoor safari
7:00 pm-10:00 pm Jungle jam disco

Sunday Under the Sea
10:00 am - 12:00 noon "Sun n splash"
1:00 pm – 3:00 pm Caribbean crafts
3:30 pm – 5:00 pm Sand & sea games

For the kids under 2 and half, Our Lucaya offers a nursery staffed with well-trained baby sitters. The nursery is open from 9 am to 5 pm, but closed from 12:30 to 1:30 pm. There is a maximum stay of two hours.

What Can We Do Now?

The heart of Nassau is Rawson Square. Make your first stop here at the **Visitors Information Center** for brochures and maps before starting off on busy Bay Street, the shopping district. Here gold and gems are sold as well as popular souvenir t-shirts, baskets, and hats. At Rawson Square, horse-drawn **surreys** wait for passengers, who pay $10 (be prepared to negotiate) for a two-person, half-hour ride along picturesque Bay Street.

One of the best views of the area's marine life is at **Atlantis**, Paradise Island. This spectacular resort is home to a one-of-a-kind marine environment filled with sharks, stingrays, lobster, giant grouper and more citizens of the local waters. Even if you're not a guest at this resort, stop by for a look at The Dig, the indoor walk-through aquarium. It's a great attraction for children, filled with replica relics as well marine life.

A longtime attraction is the **Ardastra Gardens and Zoo**, Tel. 242/323-5806, www.ardastra.com. The only zoo in the Bahamas, Ardastra features 300 species of animals and 50 species of birds including monkeys, iguanas, and marching pink flamingos. Stop here if you have time, but we felt that this is one stop that can be cut from busy itineraries. The caged animals are depressing to view, and the personnel here are far from friendly.

History buffs should head over to **Fort Charlotte** for a free guided tour of the largest fort in the Bahamas. Perched high on a hill overlooking Cable Beach, this fort never saw action but today sees plenty of activity as tourists come to enjoy a bird's eye view and a look at the fort's dungeons, cannons, and exhibits.

One of the most popular activities in Nassau is a day at **Blue Lagoon Island**, Tel. 242/363-1000. This "uninhabited" island lies about half an hour's cruise from the dock at Paradise Island and offers beautiful beaches, hammocks beneath towering palms, and plenty of watersports. For additional charges, visitors can parasail, swim with stingrays, or meet dolphins (make reservations early for this choice). The most popular option with kids includes feeding, petting, and swimming with the friendly dolphins; these can be booked as a separate attraction without a day at Blue Lagoon Island by calling 242/363-1003. To save money, bring your own snorkel gear.

One of the region's newest museums is Nassau's **Pirate Museum**, Tel. 242/356-3759, www.pirates-of-nassau.com, an interactive display of the bucaneering history of the Bahamas. Climb aboard the replica pirate ship Revenge while you learn about the real pirates of the Caribbean. Kids under 12 get in free!

Grand Bahama Island

We enjoyed the **Lucayan National Park**, Grand Bahama Highway. This 40-acre park is filled with mangroves, pine, and palm trees. Six miles of charted caves are also found here as well as a secluded beach, hiking trails, and picnicking. This park is home to an enormous network of underwater caves although diving is prohibited without a permit from UNEXSO and even swimming in the caves is a no-no.

For families who want to swim, cross the highway and visit **Gold Rock Beach**. This wide swath of sand is edged with pine trees (perfect for hanging your clothes on) and is a great place to walk hand-in-hand in peace and quiet. The waters here are warm and shallow and perfect for a cool dip. There are no facilities here, so bring along something to drink.

On Grand Bahama, another favorite stop is the **Garden of the Groves** botanical garden. This 12-acre botanical garden is home to over 10,000 varieties of flowers, trees, and shrubs from around the world. Quiet, shaded paths wind through the gardens; you can take time and sit by a waterfall and hear the call of native birds.

Sports & Recreaton

One of the most popular activities in Nassau is a day at **Blue Lagoon Island**, Tel. 242/363-1000. This "uninhabited" island lies about half an hour from the dock at Paradise Island and offers some beautiful beaches, hammocks beneath towering palms, and plenty of watersports activity. For additional charges, visitors can parasail, swim with stingrays, or meet dolphins (make reservations early for this choice). One option includes feeding, petting, and swimming with the friendly mammals. (The dolphin encounters can also be booked as a separate attraction without a day at Blue Lagoon Island, Tel. 242/363-1003.) If you make this trip, bring a towel for everyone in the family and, to save money, your own snorkel gear.

A fun way to view the sea creatures of the Bahamian waters is by participating in **Hartley's Undersea Walk**, Tel. 242/393-8234, www.underseawalk.com. The procedure is simple: put on a watertight diving helmet (yep, the old-fashioned brass kind) and off you go. Be sure to call for reservations for this one because the excursions fill up fast.

Those looking for a unique experience on Grand Bahama can leave from Port Lucaya to join the **Dolphin Experience** Tel. 242/373-1003 www.ourlucaya.com. With this program, there are four ways to get to know the dolphins. The Close Encounter is a two hour excursion where guests stand in water and touch the dolphins (great for the kids!). The second way is the Swim With The Dolphins level, where guests can swim in protected waters with the mammals. The Assistant Trainer Program is an all-day program with a minimum age of 16, and provides a behind the scenes look at the Dolphin Experience. The Open Ocean Programs allows dolphins to follow their trainers, who are in a boat, out to sea where they can choose whether or not to come back to the facility. The Dolphin Dive takes the dolphins and guests one mile off shore and let them learn about each other in 40-50 feet of water.

What Can We Buy?

Bahamian souvenirs mean everything from straw hats to sapphire jewelry, depending on your budget. Children find many inexpensive items including T-shirts (the best bargain is the three for $10 offer in some stands), seed necklaces for $1, small straw purses, and straw hats. Kids can also get their hair, or even just a small section, braided. For just a few braids, expect to pay about $1 per braid including beads.

Perfume prices are regulated by the government, so you will find the same prices at any of the "perfume bars" which are frequent in Nassau. Everything from French to American perfumes, colognes and aftershaves are sold in the perfume bars, as well as in many clothing stores.

What Else Do We Need to Know?

Currency. The currency is the Bahamian dollar, equivalent to the US dollar.

Driving. Driving is on the LEFT side of the road.

Electricity. The current is 120 volts.

Information. For information on the Bahamas, call toll-free Tel. 800/BAHAMAS.

Language. English, with a Bahamian lilt, is spoken throughout the Bahamas islands.

Time. The islands are in the Eastern time zone. From April through October, daylight savings time is observed.

Website. Check out the official website at: www.bahamas.com.

Island Report Card	
Transportation to island	A+
Transportation around island	A
Family Resorts	A
Family Restaurants	A
Friendly atmosphere	B+
Activities for kids	A+
Weather	B+
New cultures for kids to experience	B+
Safety	A-

Chapter 8

BARBADOS

Barbados is a pear-shaped island with gentle rolling hills. Agriculture still rules much of the landscape, and cane is still king. Although sugar prices have dropped severely in recent years, the crop is a Barbadian mainstay. A drive through the island will take you through a jungle of cane, often with nothing but the road before and behind you visible during the peak of the growing season.

The most easterly of the Caribbean islands, Barbados has strongly differentiated east and west sides. On the Atlantic side, currents are strong, and jagged cliffs and sea caves are carved by the water's force. In contrast, western beaches offer placid Caribbean waters with excellent visibility, little current, and a gentle trade breeze.

This island has welcomed tourist for hundreds of years, as far back as George Washington who came here to enjoy the healthful climate (much needed by his tuberculosis-stricken brother, Lawrence).

Today Barbados has the most proper British atmosphere found in the Caribbean. As you drive through the island, look for both men and women in cool white suits on the cricket fields. In the afternoons, take time to enjoy high tea. And listen to the voices of the Barbadians or Bajans (rhymes with Cajun): their accent is almost British.

Are We There Yet?

By Air

The Grantley Adams International Airport is served by American

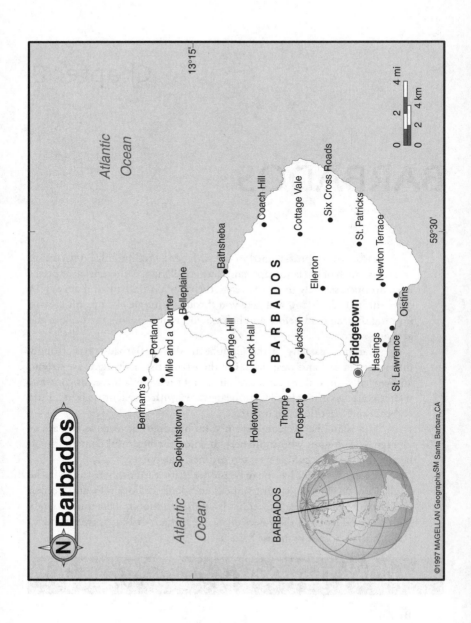

Airlines, BWIA, Air Jamaica, LIAT, Virgin Atlantic, British Airways, and Air Canada. Flying time from New York to Barbados is about four and half hours.

By Ship

Cruise ship passengers arrive at the Bridgetown port facility. The enhanced terminal, designed to resemble an island street, now offers 19 duty-free shops, 13 local retail stores, and many vendors as well as tourist information booths, car rentals, and dive shops.

Getting Around the Island

Taxis are prevalent but not inexpensive. A drive from the airport to the Speightstown-area hotels will run you close to US$30. Rental cars are available; a Barbados drivers license (US $5) is required. Many visitors rent "Mini-Mokes," a cross between a jeep and a dune buggy for about $50 US daily. And, don't forget, driving is on the left side of the road.

Island tours are offered by several operators. Highland Outdoor Tours, Inc. offers adventure excursions, including a horseback trek across the island, safari rides, and plantation tours.

Where Are We Staying?

ALMOND BEACH VILLAGE, St. Peter, Tel. 246/422-4900, Fax 246/422-0617. Toll-free reservations Tel. 800/425-6663; www.almondresorts.com. Winter rates from $570, summer from $460-580. Credit cards accepted.

The Village caters to both couples and families. A children's program keeps the little ones happy while the two of you play a round of nine-hole golf, enjoy watersports right on property, or just lounge around the long expanse of sand.

The Kid's Club is set in the Village's Family Entertainment Center on the southern edge of the property. Here 64 guest rooms are specially reserved for family travelers and swimming pools, a playground, an ice cream shop, a pizza parlor, a restaurant with a special kids' menu and more make even the youngest traveler feel welcomed. Registration in the Kid's Club is complimentary as part of the all-inclusive program, whether families are staying within the Family Entertainment Center or elsewhere on the property.

The Kid's Club Nursery is for children up to the age of four, with a child to caregiver ratio of three to one. The nursery is open from 9am to 5pm daily, closed for the lunch hour. Kids five and up enjoy various activities appropriate to their age. With a child to caregiver ratio of 12 to one, schoolage children are grouped from 5 to 7 and 8 to 12. Child fun includes board games, a mini-pool table, VCR, Jukebox, and Foozeball. Outside the center, supervised fun includes watersports, arts and crafts, beach games, on-site nature walks, storytime, treasure hunts, and more. Parents can enroll children in the program for all or part of a day or just for a single activity. Children can also be escorted to lunch or dinner by Kid's Club staff while parents enjoy a meal out.

Almond Beach takes special care with child safety. Children are supervised by staff at all times. Playrooms are kept locked and children in the Kid's Club are returned only to an adult known by the children or one previously identified as a family member or friend.

The Family Plan for both single and two parent families permits the first child under 16 to stay free when traveling with one or two paying adults (except for standard rooms). All other children are charged US $50 per night (except for standard and deluxe rooms).

BOUGAINVILLEA BEACH RESORT, Maxwell Coast Road, Christ Church, Tel. 246/418-0990, Fax 246/428-2524. Toll-free reservations Tel. 800/988-6904; www.bougainvillearesort.com. Winter rates from $220, summer rates from $165.

Located on the south coast of Barbados, this 100-suite property is ideal for families who are looking a little of everything. From relaxation to sports, this resort has it all.

Bougainvillea's salon offers services from haircuts and styling to Swedish massage to nail services. Also on the property, La Tienda Gift Shop is the perfect place to pick items for friends and family back home. Choose from books, beach items, local art, and jewelry. Everyone is sure to find something to remind them of their trip. Recreation at Bougainvillea ranges from active sports like tennis, sailing, and scuba diving to leisure activities such as cocktail parties and sunset cruises.

While the adults are getting pampered at the salon or taking a pleasure cruise, the kids will be well taken care of. The Kids Club operates every day from 10:30 am to 2:30 pm and is for kids from 3 to 12 years old.

Bougainvillea Beach Resort host a Kids Club for children between the ages of 3 to 12 years old from 10:30am to 2:30pm daily. This service provides professional adult supervision and a wide range of activities for your child, while you are away from the Resort on business or pleasure. For babies and toddlers of all ages, the Resort offers an in room baby sitting service. You'll be confident that your loved ones are in the best of care when you can't be there. Kids can participate in arts and crafts, scavenger hunts, games, miniature golf, and fly kites. There are also plenty of picnics, tours, and pool time. For meal time, there is a special menu just for kids with all of their favorite foods. There is also baby sitting available for the young ones.

FAIRMONT GLITTER BAY, St. James, Tel. 246/422-5555, Fax 246/422-3940. Toll-free reservations Tel. 800/257-7544; www.fairmont.com. Winter from $529, summer from $259. Credit cards accepted.

You'll feel the elegance and refinement of Barbados and Britain at Glitter Bay, constructed as the home of shipping magnate Sir Edward Cunard. The Mediterranean-style structure, with white stucco walls and Spanish clay roofs, is located on a half mile long beach. Glitter Bay's sister resort is the Royal Pavilion (see below), so guests enjoy reciprocal privileges and services of both resorts. You can also golf at the island's golf course, the Royal Westmoreland.

For all its elegance, Glitter Bay welcomes families with a special program. Kids under 18 stay free in their parents' room, and kids also have use of the Cub's Club, aimed at children 4-12. Kids are divided up into smaller groups by age, where they can get to know other travellers of their own age. The daily program includes a variety of activities. There is also a baby sitting service offered at Glitter Bay, as well as cribs.

FAIRMONT ROYAL PAVILION, Tel. 246/422-5555, Fax 246/422-3940. Toll-free US phone number 800/257-7544; www.fairmont.com. Winter rates from $679, summer from $289. Credit cards accepted.

This elegant property is designed for guests looking for the finest money can buy: from a grand entrance lined with the finest boutiques such as Cartier, to the 72 junior suites that overlook the sea. In your room, you'll be pampered as well with twice daily maid service, a private terrace or patio, and a decor that combines elegance and tropical splendor. Children aren't permitted at Royal Pavilion during high season.

The sister property of this resort is Glitter Bay, and guests share facilities and services with that property. Guests also enjoy golf privileges at the Robert Trent Jones, Jr.-designed course, the Royal Westmoreland.

HILTON BARBADOS, Needham's Point, St. Michael, Tel. 246/ 426-0200, Fax 246/ 228-7730, Toll-free 877/GO-HILTON; www.hiltoncaribbean.com. Winter from $360, summer from $150. Credit cards accepted.

This new 350-room hotel is just 15 minutes from the airport, a real bonus for families after a long flight. The hotel has many family-friendly policies: kids under 18 stay from in a room with adults, kids under five receive all meals for free, and kids 5-12 receive breakfast free and 50% off all other meals with accompanying adults. Families who stay a minimum of three nights also get one free babysitting service, up to four hours in length. All kids also receive a children's gift.

SAM LORD'S CASTLE, Long Bay, St. Philip, Tel. 246/423-7350, Fax 246/ 423-6361, Toll-free 888/765-6737; www.samlordscastle.com. Winter from $360, summer from $275. Credit cards accepted.

This resort is more than a hotel, it's a regular tourist attraction. Built in the 19th century, this castle was the property of the pirate Sam Hall Lord who, according to legend, lured passing ships onto the east coast rocks. Of course, no real castle would be complete without its resident ghost, and at Sam Lord's they say his truly still rests on his four-poster bed.

The hotel has a supervised kids' club for ages 5-12 which runs daily from 10 am to 4 pm. Babysitting is also available upon request.

What Can We Do Now?

Barbados is home to many **beaches** where families can snorkel in calm Caribbean waters or enjoy windswept vistas on the Atlantic shoreline. Swimmers should head to the Caribbean coast; precautions should be taken not to get over waist deep in the often-dangerous Atlantic currents, which are preferred by windsurfers and sailors. Swimmers are better off with the calm waters found on Mullins Beach, Crane Beach, and Dover Beach. The natural beauty of Barbados can also be enjoyed in many of its other attractions. Hold hands and enjoy a ride into **Harrison's Cave**, where damp rooms reveal their hidden formations, waterfalls, and pools. A sea cave rather than a cavern, the **Animal Flower Cave** is named for the sea anemones found in its pools.

If you're wondering what lies beneath the ocean's depths, take a cruise aboard the **Atlantis Submarine**, Tel. 246/436-8929 or 800/253-0493, which cruises to a depth of 150 feet below sea level. It's an excellent way for non-divers to see the rich marine life and the wrecks that surround this island.

If the two of you will be enjoying many excursions, check out the **Heritage Passport Program**, sponsored by the Barbados National Trust. Sixteen sites are included on the pass, which offers about a 50% savings on admission (a mini passport is available for fewer stops). The passport includes admission to Harrison's Cave, St. Nicholas Abbey, Mount Gay, and many other sites.

What Can We Buy?

The primary shopping area on the island is found in Bridgetown along Broad Street. Here the two of you will find fine goods of every variety: luggage, designer clothing, china, crystal, silver, cameras, the list goes on.

Barbados is a tax free haven, so you'll enjoy savings. Only liquor must be delivered to the airport or the cruise port; other purchases can be carried out from the store.

In Bridgetown, Cave Shepherd shop offers china, crystal, fine clothing, electronics, and perfumes. Located on Broad Street, this shop has been serving Barbados visitors and residents since 1906. Today it includes a Columbian Emeralds International outlet with fine jewelry as well as two restaurants, an activities desk for island tours, photo lab, and American Airlines office. Other Bridgetown shopping malls include Sunset Mall and DaCostas Mall, with over 35 shops offering everything from perfumes to china to cameras.

For island crafts, drop by the Medford Craft Village in St. Michael. Hand-carved items such as birds, boats, clocks, and fish are made here from local mahogany.

What Else Do We Need to Know?

Currency. The Barbados dollar (BDS) is the official currency. Bd converts at 1.98BDS=$1US. The rate does not fluctuate but is fixed to the US dollar. Both US and Canadian dollars are widely accepted.

Electricity. The current on the island is 110 volts/50 cycles.

Information. Contact the Barbados Tourism Authority, Tel. 800/221-9831. In Canada, the Barbados Tourism Authority can be reached at Tel. 416/214-9880 in Ontario.

Time. Barbados is on Atlantic Standard Time, one hour ahead of Eastern. Daylight savings time is not observed.

Website. Check out the official Website for more information: www.barbados.org.

Island Report Card	
Transportation to island	B+
Transportation around island	A
Family Resorts	B+
Family Restaurants	B+
Friendly atmosphere	A-
Activities for kids	B+
Weather	A
New cultures for kids to experience	B+
Safety	A

Chapter 9

BERMUDA

Since the days of Mark Twain, Bermuda has attracted travelers seeking a luxurious retreat with warm summers and temperate winters, perfect for a round of golf or a game of tennis. Located off the North Carolina coast, the island has long been a favorite getaway with honeymooners, golf buffs (boasting more golf courses per square mile that any other country in the world), and travelers looking for a safe, upscale island destination free from beach vendors.

Today, the island is fast becoming a favorite with families as well. Parents and kids alike will find a full range of activities both on and off the beach.

Although technically not part of the Caribbean, Bermuda has all the sun, sand, and surf of its southern neighbors. Located 650 miles off the coast of Cape Hatteras, North Carolina, Bermuda ranks as one of the most elegant of the island destinations. It combines a slightly formal British atmosphere and its country's position as one of the world's richest countries with the island's semi-tropical climate to create a setting where palm-lined roads connect Easter egg-colored houses.

With weather that's often described as only two seasons — spring (69 degree average in January) and summer (85 degree average in July)— Bermuda is a family's delight.

Although many consider Bermuda to be one island, the country is actually formed by about 180 small islands. Seven of these islands are connected by causeways and bridges, and this forms the landmass referred to as "Bermuda."

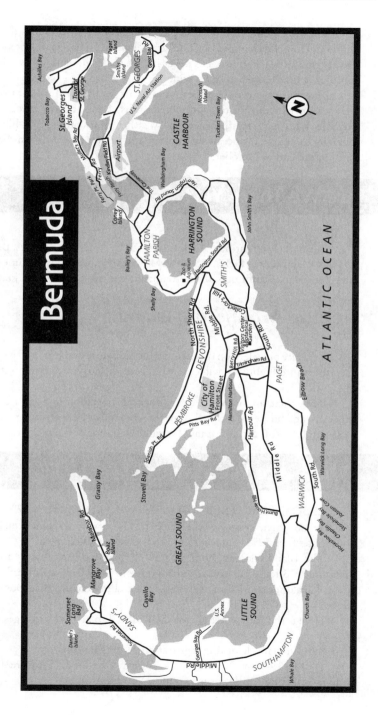

The broken shoreline means a plenitude of beaches, most found on the south side from Southampton to Tucker's Town. Most hotels are not located directly on the beach, but one is never far away: Bermuda is, at its thickest point, only one and a half miles wide.

One point to note about Bermuda is that, unlike the Caribbean, here high season falls during the summer months. Look for low prices from November through April (when the weather is usually spring-like but generally too chilly for ocean swimming) and higher rates from mid-April through the end of October.

Are We There Yet?

By Air

Bermuda International Airport is served by American Airlines, British Airways, Continental, Delta, US Airways, and Air Canada. Flying time from New York is just 90 minutes; from Atlanta budget two hours for the journey.

Getting Around the Island

Taxis are prevalent on this island which has no rental cars. A drive from the airport into Hamilton will cost $22; from the airport to Somerset runs $44.

Since there are no rental cars, your transportation options are taxis, minivans, and bus service as well as motor scooters, not a practical option for most families. You can hire a taxi for sightseeing for $30 per hour.

Where Are We Staying?

ELBOW BEACH BERMUDA, Tel. 441/236-3535, Fax 441/236-8043. Toll free US phone number Tel. 800/233-7434; www.mandarinoriental.com. Winter rates from $275, summer from $465. Credit cards accepted.

The island's largest hotel has a full menu of activity options: 5 championship tennis courts, a putting green, volleyball, a half mile sand beach, kayaking, snorkeling, Olympic sized climate controlled pool, and more.

Here is the daily schedule for the **Kid's Club** activities for ages 4-14:

9:00-9:45am, Morning registration & preparation
10:00-11:45am, Nature Walk, Beach Olympics, Treasure Hunt, Hide-n-Seak, Sandcastle, Beach Games, Youth Aerobics

12:00-1:00pm, Lunch, Afternoon registration
1:30-3:15pm, Lego Tower, Sun Visor, Glas Candy, T-shirt Painting, Tissue Kite, Pencil Toppers,Crazy Cookies
3:30-5:30pm, Video & board games
6:00 pm, Dinner & a movie
7:30-9:15 pm, Mask Making, Karate Demo, Picture Frame, Clay/Playdo, Gombay Demo, Animal Magnet, Shell Jewelry
10:00 pm, Closing Time

FAIRMONT HAMILTON PRINCESS HOTEL, Tel. 441/295-3000, Fax 441/295-1914. Toll free US phone number Tel. 800/441-1414; www.princessbermuda.com. Winter rates $160-245, summer rates $179-$229. Credit cards accepted.

Located on the edge of Hamilton Harbour, this downtown hotel has a cooperative agreement with its sister hotel, the Fairmont Southampton Princess so guests can enjoy both facilities. This property is geared more to business travelers but does offer several family-friendly features, including babysitting services, free cribs, and a family program.

This is an ideal hotel for getting to know the island. There is a variety of tours offered from the Hamilton Princess. Kids should especially enjoy the Glass Bottom Boat Safari, which gives guests a look at the underwater world around Bermuda. Coral reefs, fish, and other marine life will amaze all passengers. There are several other tours that will aquaint guests with the history of the island, as well as the sites of Hamilton.

FAIRMONT SOUTHAMPTON PRINCESS HOTEL, Tel. 441/238-8000, Fax 441/238-8968. Toll free US phone number Tel. 800/441-1414; www.fairmont.com. Winter rates $259-$309, summer rates $399-$459. Credit cards accepted.

This luxury resort stands on a high above the sea with views of the island. The large resort includes golf, a spa,

The resort also includes many family-friendly features. Explorer's Camp Bermuda, located in the Lower Lobby, offers activities and educational tours for kids. The program is complimentary with just a transportation fee for activities located off the property. "We designed the program so families can have a vacation to treasure," explained Jerome Swainson, Guest Services Manager. "At Explorer Camp, parents can join in or if they want 'adult time out,' they can leave the kids with us and know they are going to be well looked after and have a great time!"

The program is year around and offers three age groups: Tree Frogs (4 - 6 years), Longtails (7 - 9 years), Sharks (10 - 12) and Navigators (13 and up). Activities range from beach volleyball, cricket, and soccer to scavenger hunts, rock climbing, beach bonfires, and theme parties. The Explorer

Camp also has a computer lab and science center with microscopes and a reading lab with headsets. pool sports, badminton, basketball and croquet.

The Camp also takes young visitors on excursions around the island with visits to sites such as the Bermuda Aquarium, zoo, Royal Naval Dockyard, Maritime Museum, Crystal and Grotto Caves, and more. Kids can also enjoy the Dolphin Quest for an interactive session with dolphins. The Dolphin Quest is usually located right at the hotel but, at press time, had been temporarily relocated to the Naval Dockyard while the habitat at the Fairmont Southampton Princess was expanded. In the evenings, kids age 7 and over can take part in the 7-Up Club, another complimentary program from 6:30 pm until 10:30 pm The program includes movies, arts and crafts, and games.

Babysitting is available 24 hours daily. High chairs and strollers are also available for guests.

WYNDHAM BERMUDA RESORT & SPA – SOUTHAMPTON BEACH, Tel. 441/238-8122, Fax 441/238-8463. Toll free US phone number Tel. 800/441-1414; www.wyndham.com. Rates from $319. Credit cards accepted.

This expansive resort (formerly the Sonesta) is home of Bermuda's only water park, making it a real favorite with families. Wahoo! Utilizes 230,000 gallons of water, in a whole medley of water options: a main pool, three activity pools, a 110-foot-long translucent body slide, "a lazy river" with a 140-foot-long open-air river for tubing, rafting and swimming, a hot tub, and more. Mindful of Bermuda's cooler weather (remember, it's technically not part of the Caribbean), the waterpark is heated.

Along with the waterpark, another draw for families is the Island Explorers Children's Program, aimed at kids ages 5 to 12. The program is available from June 1 through Labor Day only as well as major holidays. The program, which includes activities ranging from storytelling to arts and crafts, is free for guests but there is a small charge when activities include off-property visits. (There is a charge for lunches). Babysitting is also available.

The resort itself is located on the south shore of the island, surrounded by 33 acres plus three excellent beaches.

What Can We Do Now?

One of the island's most popular family attractions is the **Bermuda Aquarium and Zoo**, Tel. 441/293-2727. The Bermuda Aquarium and Zoo is an excellent stop for families looking for a break from the beach.

From the moment you step from the sunny outdoors to the dark, cool interior of the aquarium, you'll be transported into the undersea environment that lies just off Bermuda's pink beaches. The well-kept tanks each feature local marine life ranging from green morays to grey triggerfish. Free audio handsets allow visitors to hear more about the tank's residents.

The aquarium is just the introduction to the large complex, however. Outside, harbor seals play in their tanks or laze in the sunshine. Nearby, the **Natural History Museum** houses exhibits on everything from whaling to undersea exploration.

The **Local Tails** building contains some of the best exhibits for children. Young travelers can pick up a conch in the touch tank, listen to the call of a local bird or use a remote operated camera to explore an aquarium.

Outside stands the zoo. Along with free-ranging peacocks and exhibits of lemurs and sloths, the zoo is especially noted for its Australasia exhibit. Animals are separated from visitors by flowering water to provide an unobstructed view. Matschies Tree Kangaroo, tree shrews, Murray river turtles, and binturong or bear cat are found in the display.

Another excellent family stop is the **Royal Naval Dockyard**. Recently restored, these extensive dockyards offer a half day of activity including shopping mall housed in an history structure, a crafts market, and, best of all, the **Bermuda Maritime Museum**, Tel. 441/234-1418. Save at least two hours for a visit to this extensive collection which is located in the island's largest fort. Kids will find special signage at many displays where they can learn more about Bermuda's maritime history and facts on everything from how to make a compass to why early sailors thought the island was haunted.

If it rains during your visit, there's always one place that's got perfect weather: the **Crystal Caves**, Tel. 441/293-0640. This limestone cavern was accidently found in 1907 by two boys playing cricket and since that time has been open to the public. You'll enjoy a look at cave formations and small pools in this underground wonderland.

What Can We Buy?

Definitely not the place for shoppers on a budget (although, if budget is a prime concern, you probably wouldn't be vacationing here anyway), Bermuda's shops may give you a slight case of sticker shock. Remember, however, that there's no sales tax on the island so that souvenir is just a little more affordable.

You'll find the best selection of shops along **Front Street** in the city of **Hamilton**. Jewelry, china, crystal, and other high-dollar items rule but look carefully and you'll find the usual tourist offerings as well, from t-shirts to teddy bears.

The best buy is on Bermuda-made items, which range from nautical-themed items to a unique item we once purchased: a miniature "onion" crate that held tiny soaps. The onion crate harks back to the island's well-known Bermuda onions. And there's always another distinctive souvenir that's easy to pack: the world-famous Bermuda shorts.

What Else Do We Need to Know?

Currency. The legal currency is the Bermuda dollar, pegged equally to the US dollar. US currency is widely accepted throughout the country.

Driving. Driving is on the LEFT.

Information. For more on Bermuda, call the Bermuda Department of Tourism office, Tel. 800/223-6106 or 800/BERMUDA or write the Bermuda Department of Tourism, 205 East 42nd Street, 16th Floor, New York, NY 10017.

Website. Check out the official Bermuda website at: www.bermudatourism.com.

Island Report Card	
Transportation to island	A
Transportation around island	B+
Family Resorts	B+
Family Restaurants	B+
Friendly atmosphere	A
Activities for kids	A
Weather	A-
New cultures to experience	B+
Safety	A+

Chapter 10

BRITISH VIRGIN ISLANDS

Hoist the sails and gather way. Grip the wheel in your hands and cut a feather through aquamarine waters to a quiet Caribbean cove. Drop anchor and motor a small launch to an empty beach for a gourmet picnic lunch on white sand.

Sound like a boating fantasy? It is, but in the British Virgin Islands, it is also reality. Year around, skippers and would-be boaters come from around the world to sail these calm waters and take advantage of a group of 50 islands that call themselves "Nature's Little Secrets." Unlike their nearby American cousins, these Virgin Islands are not a shopper's paradise, but one for nature lovers looking for quiet getaways, empty beaches, and a maritime atmosphere. Families will find that kids can romp and enjoy local life on some of the safest islands in the Caribbean.

Boats of every description come to this capital of the Caribbean boating world. But long before today's sleek vessels made the BVI a popular port of call, Christopher Columbus plied these waters. The explorer landed on the island of Tortola in 1694. The multitude of surrounding tiny islands reminded Columbus of the tale of Saint Ursula and her 11,000 virgins so he named these the Virgin Islands.

Although there are over 50 islands in the chain, only a handful have facilities for travelers. **Tortola**, named for the turtle doves found here, is the largest island with only 21 square miles. Don't let distance fool you, however. Because of steep hills, a car trip around or across the island is a slow undertaking.

One of the best ways to see Tortola, and all the British Virgin Islands, is by boat. Even if you don't know a rigging from a rudder, you can enjoy

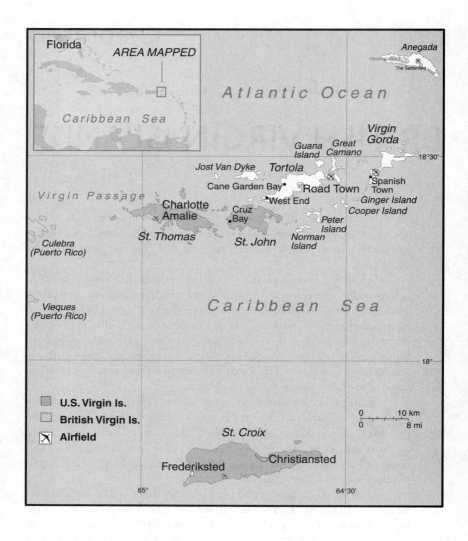

a vacation at sea thanks to skippered boat programs. For about the same cost as a stay at a luxury resort, you can enjoy a week aboard a vessel with a skipper to man the wheel and a cook to prepare local dishes like fried conch or rice and peas.

Tortola's largest community, **Road Town**, is the home office of the largest charter yacht company in the world. Visit The Moorings to view the huge fleet of yachts managed by the company and owned by sailors around the globe.

Set your course for **Jost Van Dyke**, an island named for a Dutch pirate. Jost (pronounced Yost) Van Dyke is a real getaway, a Robinson Crusoe kind of place without luxury hotels, gourmet restaurants or pricey shops. What Jost Van Dyke does have are nearly deserted beaches, coral reefs teeming with colorful fish, and a place called Foxy's.

Foxy's Tamarind Bar is a landmark in the world of Caribbean boaters. It is located beneath palm thatched roofs plastered with boat flags, skippers hats, and business cards left here by visitors. The restaurant serves West Indian specialties like curried chicken *rotis*, but the real treat is Foxy himself. Foxy, a.k.a. Philicianno Callwood, is a one-man show greeting incoming guests with impromptu songs sung to a calypso beat.

Jost Van Dyke may be named for a pirate, but the best known pirate connections in the BVI are **Norman Island** and **Dead Chest**. Norman Island is thought to have been the inspiration for Robert Lewis Stevenson's *Treasure Island*. Dead Chest is the island where the pirate Blackbeard allegedly marooned 15 men and one bottle of rum, starting a fight that left no survivors. The incident inspired the mariners' ditty: "Fifteen men on a dead man's chest. Yo ho ho and a bottle of rum."

A popular port of call is **Virgin Gorda** (the fat virgin), the second largest island in the BVI. The Baths, Virgin Gorda's most photographed attraction, can be reached by land or sea. Left by volcanic upheaval, The Baths are formed by giant boulders that provide a picturesque contrast to the white beach. Duck between boulders to enter the sea cave where you can wade in the cool, shady baths.

Although some hotels feature local musicians, don't look for casinos or nightclubs in these Caribbean islands. The BVI makes no claim to being a swinging destination, and even in the large resorts most activity stops by 11pm.

The reason is simple. Only hours away, the sun will again rise on another Caribbean day. And across the British Virgin Islands, boaters want to be ready.

Are We There Yet? & Getting Around

By Air

Service to Tortola's Beef Island International Airport is available from San Juan on American Eagle and local carriers such as Fly BVI, Winair, and Caribbean Star. Other vacationers prefer to fly directly into St. Thomas and ferry over to Tortola.

By Ferry

Island hopping is a way of life in the BVI and the most common way is aboard ferries. One-hour service from St. Thomas is available daily to Road Town and West End in Tortola aboard Smith's Ferry Service, Tel. 284/494-2355. Service from West End to Cruz Bay, St. John is available from Inter-Island Boat Service, Tel. 284/495-4166.

Where Are We Staying?

BIRAS CREEK, Virgin Gorda, Tel. 284/494-3555, Fax 284/494-3557. Toll-free reservations Tel. 800/872-2392; www.biras.com. Winter: from $810, Summer: from $525. Credit cards accepted.

Tucked on the north end of Virgin Gorda on a 140-acre peninsula, this recently renovated resort is a favorite with families looking for a relaxing getaway. The 32-suite property recently was purchased by Bert Houwer, who had vacationed at the hotel for 14 years. You can't get a much better guest recommendation than that.

Biras Creek makes a good getaway for family vacationers looking to spend time at the private beach, walking on nearby nature trails, and exploring Virgin Gorda. Each suite includes bicycles (and children's bikes for the youngest travelers) so your family can explore. Families also enjoy use of two tennis courts, and complimentary use of snorkel fins, windsurfers, sailboats, and motor dinghies, including free instruction. Complimentary snorkel trips to the surrounding islands are also offered.

When you're ready to take a break, guest assistants (GA's) can entertain the children with an afternoon filled with treasure hunts or crab races.

Consideration for young visitors encompasses the restaurants as well. The restaurant offers early dinners with a special children's menu.

BITTER END YACHT CLUB & RESORT, Virgin Gorda, Tel. 312/944-5855, Fax 284/944-2860. Local Tel. 284/494-2746. Toll-free reservations Tel. 800/872-2392; www.beyc.com. From $490 in winter, from $465 in summer. Credit cards accepted.

This 100-room resort is located at the "bitter end" of the BVI on the North Sound. Reached only by boat, this resort gives you the feeling of staying at a yacht club, where days are spent in close connection with the sea. The resort boasts 150 vessels, the largest fleet of recreational boats in the Caribbean. Many guests arrive via their own craft and simply dock for their stay. Those without a boat can stay in a resort room or aboard one of the club yachts. Spend the day in your "room" boating among the islands, then return to port at night and enjoy a quiet meal in the resort's elegant restaurant.

Children are an important part of the clientele at the Bitter End. Families have complimentary use of over 100 watercrafts, from sailboats to windsurfers to Boston Whaler tenders. Children can also participate in the Bitter End's Nick Trotter Sailing and Windsurfing Class. The Junior Sailing Program offers half-day lessons for young mariners age seven to 12 on a year around basis. (Lessons are complimentary during the summer months as well as during school holidays.)

Other family oriented activities at the resort include snorkel lessons with the watersports staff, guided nature hikes or striking out on your own on the hiking trails, and cruises to the Baths and Anegada in the BVI. Families can also take out a Boston Whaler skiff to a nearby private island for a quiet picnic.

LITTLE DIX BAY, Virgin Gorda, Tel. 284/495-5555, Fax 284/495-5661. Toll-free reservations Tel. 800/928-3000 or 800/525-4800; www.littledixbay.com. From $495 in winter, from $325 in summer. Credit cards accepted.

We have fond memories of our stay at Little Dix: lazing beneath a palm palapa, snorkeling just offshore, enjoying our rondoval guest room with a wonderful view in every direction, dining outdoors to the music of whistling tree frogs.

Apparently plenty of other families also have good memories of Little Dix; it boasts a wonderful repeat business. Many customers have been coming since the days Laurance Rockefeller first developed this property in 1964. Today the hotel still has the same attention to service as it did in its Rockresort days; you'll find that the ratio of employees to guests is one to one.

The resort, for all its comforts and old Caribbean style, is also family friendly, allowing one children under the age of 16 to stay free when rooming with a parent. The resort also offers the Children's Cove supervised program, aimed at children ages 3 to 12. The program activities include treasure hunts, kitemaking, iguana searches, and local crafts. The program has two levels, ages 3 to 6 and 7 to 12.

Programs for younger children include sand candle making and seashell painting while older kids learn tennis and kayaking. The resort also offers special activities for teenagers.

LONG BAY BEACH RESORT, Tortola, Tel. 284/495-4252, Fax 284/495-4677. Toll-free reservations Tel. 888/833-1233; www.longbay.com. Winter from $260. Credit cards accepted.

They call this resort Long Bay but we found that they might as well change the name to Long Beach. A mile-long white sand beach is the central focal point of this 105-room resort located near West End. All rooms, both hilltop and beachside, have views of the beach and the quiet waters of Long Bay.

MOORINGS MARINER INN & YACHT CHARTERS, Road Town, Tortola, Tel. 284/494-2331, Fax 284/495-2226. Toll-free reservations Tel. 800/535-7289; Price varies with size of yacht and number of passengers. Credit cards accepted.

Ahoy mates, here's your chance to take to the seas on your own yacht. Well, maybe the yacht's not technically yours, but for a few days it will be home to yourselves and usually two or three other families. You can rent a stateroom aboard a yacht and enjoy a luxurious trip around the islands (or for true luxury you can rent the entire boat, complete with the services of a captain and a cook.) The Moorings is the world's largest charter yacht company, an operation that started right in tiny Road Town.

PETER ISLAND, Peter Island, Tel. 770/476-9988, Fax 770/476-4979. Toll-free reservations Tel. 800/346-4451 in US; www.peterisland.com. From $835 in winter, from $605 in summer. Credit cards accepted.

This is true luxury: a resort that occupies an entire island. Owned by the Amway Corporation (a fact that most visitors are unaware of except for the can of Amway spot remover in the closet), Peter Island is truly a place where relaxation can flourish like the bougainvillea, hibiscus, and sea grapes that dot its hills. This 1,800-acre island is paradise for families. It starts with your arrival by private launch from Tortola, and continues as you check in and see your guest room: a combination of Scandinavian and Caribbean styles.

What Can We Do Now?

One top destination in the BVI (or, for that matter, in the Caribbean) is **The Baths**. This 682-acre park is located on Virgin Gorda, and it's so unique that once you visit it you'll be able to spot this park in any Caribbean video or magazine. Unlike most Caribbean beaches which are mostly flat, this site is scattered with massive granite boulders. As smooth as riverbed stones, these gargantuan rocks litter the sea and the beach. They also form shadowy caves where you can swim in water that's lit by sunlight filtering through the cracks. This unique site is unspoiled (just one or two concession-aires and no hagglers) and a fun snorkeling spot as well.

Hikers should save time for a visit to **Sage Mountain National Park** on Tortola. The BVI's highest point has an altitude of 1,780 feet and is lush with greenery that can be viewed from its many gravel walkways.

Sports & Recreation

Divers will find plenty of activity in the waters off any of the British Virgin Islands. The best known **dive spot** is the wreck of the RMS Rhone, a mail steam packet that broke up in a storm. You may be familiar with this wreck—it was used in filming The Deep. The bow lies just 80 feet below the surface, making it an easy wreck dive (and usually even visible for snorkelers). Other top dive sites include Alice in Wonderland, a deep dive with mushroom-shaped corals, the Chikuzen wreck, a 246-foot fish-filled wreck just 75 feet below the surface, and Santa Monica Rock, located near the open ocean and a good place to spot large fish.

What Can We Buy?

Unlike the "other" Virgin islands, shopping is not a major attraction of the BVI. However, you will find a good variety of shops in Road Town and West End at Soper's Hole. Spices are also popular buys, from hot sauces to West Indian mustards to chutney. One of the best selections is found at Sunny Caribbee, Main Street, Road Town, Tel. 284/494-2178, has a good collection of things Caribbean, including local crafts, cookbooks, and art prints.

For inexpensive buys, visit the open-air market on Main Street. Here you can haggle for jewelry, T-shirts, calabash bags, and straw hats. The mood is friendly, and you'll be entertained most days by steel band musicians.

What Else Do We Need to Know?

Currency. The US dollar is legal tender in the British Virgin Islands.
Driving. Driving is on the LEFT side of the road.
Electricity. The BVI uses 110 volts, 60 cycles throughout the islands.

Information. Contact the British Virgin Islands Tourist Board, Tel. 800/835-8530 in the US. Information on Island: Call the B.V.I. Tourist Board in Road Town, Tel. 284/494-3134.

Website. Check out www.bvitouristboard.com for a variety of island information.

Island Report Card	
Transportation to island	B
Transportation around island	A
Family Resorts	B-
Family Restaurants	B-
Friendly atmosphere	A
Activities for kids	B
Weather	A
New cultures for kids to experience	B+
Safety	A+

Chapter 11

CAYMAN ISLANDS

Ready, set, dive.

Whether you're a certified diver or a non-swimmer, the Cayman Islands are the place for you to act out your Jacques Cousteau fantasies. Grab some sunscreen and make your way to the luxurious Grand Cayman, one of the easiest Caribbean destinations for vacationers to reach. Less than two hours from Houston and just over an hour from Miami, visitors will find it a place where crime is low, public peddling is prohibited, and the living is definitely easy. The islands have one of the highest standards of living in the world. Boasting an average household income is $56,000CI (US $68,292), a status as one of the top financial centers in the world, and a low unemployment rate, this destination is one that is a natural magnet for vacationers looking for a luxurious getaway.

Just 80 miles northeast of Grand Cayman but worlds apart in terms of atmosphere, **Little Cayman** is tailor made for families looking for secluded scuba diving, fly or tackle fishing, and nature appreciation. Appropriate to its name, Little Cayman spans only 11 miles in length and two miles at its widest point. Boasting none of the glitz of Grand Cayman, Little Cayman does greet guests with all the basic comforts, including several small lodges and condominiums with air-conditioning, satellite television, and telephone service.

With just over 100 permanent residents, the island's largest population is that of birds and iguanas. Over 2,000 Little Cayman Rock Iguanas inhabit the island, so many that "Iguana Crossing" and "Iguana Right of Way" signs are posted throughout the island to protect the five-foot long lizards.

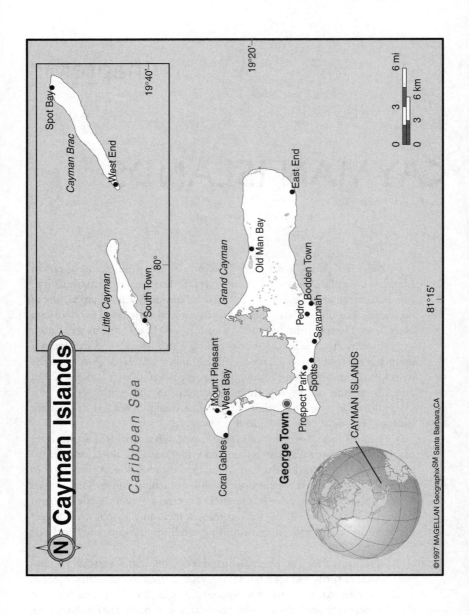

If Grand Cayman is the flashy big brother of the Cayman Islands, swelled with pride about its lavish condominiums, full-service resorts, international dining, and top-notch diving, and Little Cayman is the family's youngest sibling, favored for its petite size and almost shy demeanor, then **Cayman Brac** is the middle child.

This middle sibling, however, is far from overlooked. Cayman Brac has its own special qualities, assets that include world-class diving along undersea walls, hiking in the most rugged terrain found in the Cayman Islands, caves that tempt exploration, birdying, and much more.

The island is named for the "brac," Gaelic for bluff, which soars up from the sea 140 feet on the island's east end. It's the most distinct feature of this 12-mile long, one mile wide island located 89 miles east-northeast of Grand Cayman and just five miles from Little Cayman.

With a population of only 1,300 residents, Cayman Brac is closer in pace to Little Cayman than its big brother, Grand Cayman. Residents, or Brackers, are known for their personable nature and welcome vacationers to their sunny isle.

By far, though, the most popular family destination among these three is **Grand Cayman**. Although it has been a popular destination for many years, Grand Cayman drew the attention of moviegoers across the country because of its prominent role in the movie The Firm, an adaptation of the John Grisham book starring Tom Cruise and Gene Hackman. Much of the movie was filmed at the Hyatt Regency and at popular dive sites just offshore. (And, yes, the stars actually did dive the coral reefs for many scenes.)

Hackman and Cruise may have starred in their dive scenes, but at Stingray City the stingrays definitely receive the leading role. Enjoyed by both divers and snorkelers, Stingray City is a shallow sandbar located offshore where numerous operators take vacationers to enjoy what is one of the most unique experiences in the Caribbean. Accustomed to being fed, the stingrays (which range is size from about one to six feet across) are docile and friendly, brushing against swimmers and even allowing themselves to be held and petted. About 30 stingrays frequent this area.

Little Cayman

Little Cayman's chief draw is its **ecotourism**: diving, fishing, and bird watching. The late Phillipe Cousteau called the island's Bloody Bay Wall one of the best dives of his life; today its still a favorite with divers.

Anglers come to this tiny isle for its excellent **bonefishing**. Bonefish and permit, both caught in the flats, and tarpon, reeled in from brackish Tarpon Lake, draw fishermen. The Southern Cross Club fishing lodge first attracted anglers to these waters; today McCoy's Diving and Fishing Lodge also caters to fishermen. Guests at other island resorts can arrange fishing guides from these lodges.

Birders enjoy the **Booby Pond Visitors Centre**, open Monday through Saturday 2-5pm. Operated by the National Trust, this pond is the home of the Caribbean's largest breeding colony of Red-Footed Boobies and a breeding colony of Magnificent Frigate Birds. Visitors can view the birds from two telescopes (available for use any time) and see exhibits on the birds of Little Cayman in the visitors center. Admission is free although donations are welcomed.

Small resorts, condominiums, and an efficiency apartment complex make up the accommodations offerings.

Cayman Brac

The most recognized site on the island is the Brac, the sheer bluff that is visited by hikers and non-hikers alike. This area is a favorite for birdwatching, one of the most popular activities on Cayman Brac. Here the 180-acre **Parrot Reserve** is home to the endangered Cayman Brac Parrot. Only 400 of the birds remain in the wild on this island.

Among Cayman Brac's most unique features are its many **caves**. The Bluff is pocked with caves that frame beautiful seaside views. Several of the 18 caves on Cayman Brac have been explored and five are frequently visited by vacationers. Rebecca's Cave, east of Divi Tiara Hotel, is marked with signs. The best known of the island's caves, sadly this one is named for a young child who died here during the Great Hurricane of 1932.

Without a doubt, **diving** is one of the island's prime attractions. Over 50 excellent dive sites tempt all levels of divers. The latest attraction is a Russian frigate deliberately sunk in September 1996. Renamed the **M/V Captain Keith Tibbbets**, this 330-foot freighter was built for use by the Cuban navy. It lies approximately 200 yards offshore northwest of Cayman Brac. The bow rests in about 90 feet of water; the stern is just 40 feet below the surface. The sinking of the vessel was recorded by Jean-Michel Cousteau Productions in a documentary film "Destroyer at Peace."

Bonefishing is another top draw for many Cayman Brac vacationers. Guides lead anglers on half- and full-day excursions to seek bonefish in the shallows; deep sea fishing is another popular option and groups of up to four can book a charter for a chance at a trophy catch.

Small resorts, condominiums, and an efficiency apartment complex make up the accommodations offerings. Cayman Brac's largest resort is the 59-room **DIVI TIARA BEACH RESORT**, Tel. 800/367-3484, or 345/948-1553, Fax 345/948-1316 or see www.diviresorts.com. A favorite with scuba divers, the resort includes a dive shop, underwater photo center, and more.

Another popular property with divers is the 40-room **BRAC REEF BEACH RESORT**, Tel. 800/327-3835 or 345/948-1323. Located off Channel Bay on the island's southeast shore, this resort includes a pool,

Jacuzzi, restaurant, bar, dive shop, snorkeling, fishing, tennis, underwater photo center and gift shop. The 16-room Brac Caribbean Beach Village at Stake Bay offers a dive shop, snorkeling, and tennis.

Getting There: Direct flights to Cayman Brac Gerrard Smith Airport are available from Miami, Tampa, Atlanta and Houston or from Grand Cayman aboard Cayman Airways , Tel. 800/422-9626 from US, Tel. 800/441-3003 from Canada. Twice daily service from Grand Cayman is provided on small prop planes with Island Air, Tel. 345/949-5252, Monday through Friday 9am to 5pm; Fax 345/949-7044. Flights depart several times daily. The flight takes one hour and ten minutes, making a brief stop in Little Cayman. Round trip tickets are US $110.

Flights are also available on Island Air from Cayman Brac to Little Cayman and cost US$40 round trip.

While on the island, rentals are available from B & S Motor Ventures, Ltd., Tel, 345/948-1646, Brac Rent-A-Car, Ltd., Tel. 345/948-1515, and Four D's Car Rental, Tel. 345/948-1599.

Are We There Yet?

By Air

You'll arrive in the Cayman Islands at Owen Roberts International Airport, a stylish facility that resembles a Polynesian structure. The principle carrier into this port of entry is Cayman Airways, Tel. 800/G-CAYMAN, the national carrier with flights from Miami, Tampa, Atlanta, and Houston. Service is also available from American Airlines, Northwest Airlines, Continental, USAirways, Air Jamaica, and America Trans Air.

Direct flights to Cayman Brac are available from Miami, Tampa, Atlanta and Houston or from Grand Cayman.

By Ship

Cruise ship passengers arrive in George Town, a wonderfully charming community brimming with shops and restaurants along its clean waterfront.

Getting Around the Island

Transportation around Grand Cayman is easy. Take your pick from taxis and group tours as well as rental cars, vans, jeeps, and sedans. Car rentals begin at about $30 per day; expect to pay about $43 per day for a 4x4 vehicle. On Grand Cayman, 4x4 vehicles are commonplace and many travelers enjoy driving around the island in the open air vehicles. Air conditioned sedans and are also commonplace and often a better choice for families and those who want to secure their valuables while at the beach or in town. Most agencies feature American and Japanese models. Some offer unlimited mileage, free pick up and drop off, and free airport transfers.

Where Are We Staying?

Most visitors to Grand Cayman stay along Seven Mile Beach just outside of George Town. Along this busy stretch you'll find luxurious hotels, fine restaurants, nightclubs, and most of the activity on the island.

BRITANNIA VILLAS, Seven Mile Beach, West Bay Road at the Hyatt Regency, Tel. 345/949-1234, Fax 345/949-8032; www.britanniavillas.com. Toll free reservations Tel. 800/233-1234. Low season rates from $295.

Note: At press time, Britannia Villas remained closed following damage from Hurricane Ivan, although reopening was planned for late in 2005.

If your family would like to stay in a condominium but would like the services of a hotel, the Britannia Villas might just be for you. These elegant villas lie beyond the Hyatt Regency guest rooms adjacent to the Britannia golf course (across the road from the beach but connected with a covered walkway above the traffic). The Britannia Villas are especially popular with families and include all the hotel amenities including pools, restaurants, beach bar, spa, fitness center, children's club, and more.

Along with standard rooms, the property includes 70 one-, two-, three-, and four-bedroom villas and 10 bi-level suites. The Britannia Villas are especially popular with families and include a full range of hotel amenities, from six pools to diving and tennis. "They're an economical choice for families mostly because they are spacious and combine the cost of two rooms into one accommodation," explains William M. Conolly, vice president of sales and marketing. "Families do not have to eat out all the time but have the option of preparing meals or snacks at their desire."

GRAND CAYMAN MARRIOTT BEACH RESORT, Seven Mile Beach, Tel. 345/949-0088, Fax 345/949-0288. Toll-free reservations Tel. 800/228-9290; www.marriott.com. Winter rates $195-$290, summer rates $190-$290. Credit cards accepted.

Located two miles from George Town and about four miles from the airport, this convenient property (formerly the Radisson) is located on a beautiful stretch of Seven Mile Beach. Swimmers and snorkelers can enjoy calm waters and a small coral reef just offshore or learn scuba diving. Booking dive trips is through the on-site shop. Oceanfront rooms include private balconies with good beach views and are worth a somewhat long walk to the elevators in this 315-room hotel. Facilities include casual and fine dining, pool and hot tub, dive shop, wave runners, windsurfing, shopping arcade, and full service spa.

GRAND CAYMANIAN BEACH CLUB AND RESORT, Crystal Harbour Drive at SafeHaven, Tel. 345/949-3100, Fax 345/949-3161; www.grandcaymanian.ky. Low season rates from $175-$330, high season rates from $215-$410.

This condominium property is especially ideal for families members who love golf. Located just steps from the SafeHaven golf course, the property is a drive from Seven Mile Beach. It is located on the North Sound, although there is a shuttle service to Seven Mile Beach. This timeshare is a joint venture between Royal Resorts and the local Thompson Group.

The resort, popular with families, offers 44 flexivillas in a variety of sizes as well as four grand villas and six townhouses. Each includes a full kitchen, living room, and dining room, and full maid service and room service are available. The resort activities include a swimming pool, waterfront restaurant, on-site scuba diving, snorkeling, deep-sea fishing, wave runners, windsurfing, a private dock for boating and fishing, and concierge services.

The resort offers a special children's pool, and organized children's events.

HYATT REGENCY GRAND CAYMAN, Seven Mile Beach, Tel. 345/949-1234, Fax 345/949-8528. Toll-free reservations Tel. 800/55-HYATT; www.hyatt.com. Winter rates from $455, Summer rates $220-$390. Credit cards accepted.

Note: At press time, only the beachside rooms of the Hyatt Regency were open due to damage from Hurricane Ivan. Renovations are underway on the original side of the property, scheduled for completion in early 2006.

One of Grand Cayman's most beautiful resorts, the Hyatt is not located directly on the beach but does offer its guests use of a private beach club across the street with full watersports. You may recognize parts of this resort from the movie The Firm (it's the place where Gene Hackman and Tom Cruise stayed). The 289-room hotel includes many levels of rooms and suites plus luxury villas. Landscaping as beautiful as a botanical garden, the hotel flows from a great main house to grounds dotted with royal palms and ponds filled with colorful koi, and a freeform swimming pool, complete with bridges and pool bar.

All rooms include air-conditioning, mini-bar, satellite TV, coffee makers, telephones, and more. Resort facilities include four restaurants and five bars, private beach club, pool and hot tub, dive shop, 24-hour room service, watersports, dive shop, golf, health club, beauty spa, and more.

The Hyatt Regency Grand Cayman offers guests a unique cultural program to introduce guests to the island's history, culture, and flora and fauna. Horticultural tours led by the resort's landscaping experts point out sea grape, travelers' palm, silver thatch palm, and more. For a peek at the island's past, visitors can talk with a local historian. For more hands-on experiences, a coconut husker can teach the secrets of obtaining the edible portions of this thick fruit, while local artists show the skills needed to make rope, baskets and hats from silver thatch palms.

This hotel is also home to Camp Hyatt, the supervised children's program for toddlers (potty trained) to 12-year-olds. Camp activities include day activities with everything from arts and crafts to visits to local sites such as the Cayman Turtle Farm and Rum Point. Night activities (from 6-10pm) include miniature golf, Caribbean limbo, table tennis, and movies.

WESTIN CASUARINA RESORT, Seven Mile Beach, Tel. 345/ 945-3800, Fax 345/945-3804. Toll-free reservations Tel. 800/WESTIN-1; www.westin.com. Winter rates start at $390, Summer rates begin at $225-375. Credit cards accepted.

This upscale beach resort is built on a strip of Seven Mile Beach bordered by willowy casuarina trees. The hotel has 343 guest rooms, most with breathtaking views of the sea from step-out balconies. The hotel has the feel of a conference property, with a slightly dress-up atmosphere in the main lobby.

Facilities include beachfront, casual and fine dining restaurants, pools, whirlpools, tennis, fitness facilities, beauty salons, masseuse and masseur.

Guest rooms come equipped with everything that families could need. There are rooms with extra sitting rooms for extra space, cribs and rollaway beds are available upon request. There are plenty of water sports like sailing, snorkeling, and diving available. Guests who want to learn to dive can take advantages of the hotel's scuba lessons.

The Westin Casuarina Resort is also home to the Westin Kids Club. Upon check-in, families receive a Westin Kids Club sports bottle that can be filled with complimentary beverages at mealtimes. Young visitors also receive coloring books and bath toys; special amenities are also available for infants. Parents receive safety kits with adhesive bandages, electrical outlet covers, identification bracelets, and a list of local emergency phone numbers. Jogging strollers are available upon request at no additional cost. Whenever possible, guest rooms are set up in advance with high chairs, cribs and other items as appropriate.

WYNDHAM SUNSHINE SUITES, 1112 West Bay Road, Seven Mile Beach. Tel. 345/949-3000, Fax 345/949-1200. Toll-free reservations Tel. 877/786-1110; www.sunshinesuites.com. Low season rates from $160-$205, winter rates from $240-$285.

For families with an eye on the budget, Grand Cayman's Sunshine Suites Resort by Wyndham provides hotel accommodations in the heart of Seven Mile Beach without the high price of beachfront hotels and condos. Located across the street from the beach and adjacent to The Links at Safehaven golf course, this all-suites hotel has a lot to offer cost-conscious travelers. This resort combines the atmosphere of a resort with the pricing of a motel. The hotel has few recreational features of its own but is surrounded by attractions within walking distance including golf and Seven Mile Beach.

Sporting a Caribbean look with lemon-colored guest room blocks built around a central pool, the hotel has a casual and relaxed atmosphere. Sunshine Suites Resort is often quiet during the day as guests explore the island, enjoy the beach, or play a round of golf.

The hotel is composed of 130 suites in three categories. Families of more than two people should reserve a deluxe suite or a one-bedroom suite, which is ideal for most families. Twenty-nine deluxe suites, for up to four guests, have two queen beds. The hotel also has 60 one-bedroom suites, each with a separate bedroom with a king sized bed; the living room contains a queen sized sofa sleeper. Rooms are decorated in bright Caribbean colors, and white tile floors lend a sunny look to the large suites. All include fully equipped kitchens with a coffee maker, complimentary coffee and tea, stovetop, all cooking and eating utensils, and a microwave. All rooms also include 34 channel cable TV, individually-controlled air conditioning, ceiling fans, and baths with aromatherapy products.

Other guests facilities include a guest laundry with coin operated washers and dryers, safety deposit boxes, irons/ironing boards, and hair dryers.

On-site recreation includes a freshwater swimming pool with locked storage area for scuba gear; rinse tanks are available for washing wetsuits and equipment.

Three meal plans are available: the full American plan (American breakfast, lunch and dinner with coffee, tea, juice, sodas and iced tea included with meals but no alcoholic beverages), the All Inclusive Plan (all the above as well as domestic beer and house wine by the glass with meals), and Modified American Plan (breakfast, lunch or dinner with coffee, tea, juice, sodas and iced tea.) There's no charge for meal plans for infants under 2 years and special rates for kids 2-12 years old.

What Can We Do Now?

To experience the entire island, consider an **island tour**. We signed up for a tour with Burton Ebanks, Tel. 345/949-7222, a local with an extensive knowledge of the entire region. We headed off for the day to view the 76 square-mile island.

Outside the city of George Town, the population is sparse and the atmosphere is rural. Located about 25 minutes from George Town, the **Queen Elizabeth Botanic Park**, Tel. 345/947-9462; www.botanic-park.ky, is a 65-acre park filled with native trees, wild orchids, as well as birds, reptiles, and butterflies. Here our family enjoyed a self-guided tour and a quiet look at the flora and fauna that make the Cayman Islands special.

From the North Side most tours travel to the East End, home of the **Blow Holes**. Park and walk down to the rugged coral rocks that have been carved by the rough waves into caverns. As waves hit the rocks, water spews into the air, creating one of the best photo sites on the island.

Just under 30,000 people populate the island, and almost half live in the capital city of **George Town**. Save a few minutes for a tour of the **Cayman Islands National Museum**, Harbour Drive, Tel. 345/949-8368. This excellent two-story museum traces the history of the Cayman Islands, including the islands' natural history. George Town bustles with life any time of day as a center for shoppers and diners. Among historic government buildings, you'll find plenty of shops selling Cayman souvenirs and restaurants featuring both Caribbean cuisine and international dishes.

Continuing past George Town lies the world's only **Turtle Farm**, West Bay, Tel. 345/949-3894; www.turtle.ky. Here you'll have a chance to get up close and personal with green sea turtles, viewing them as eggs, hatchlings, and in various sizes as they work their way up towards adulthood. Some reach 600 pounds, and can be viewed slowly swimming in an open-air tank in the center of the farm.

The Turtle Farm is one of the Caribbean's most popular attractions for children. They can learn a great deal about these marine creatures as well as other wildlife found on Grand Cayman at this farm. The favorite part for children is the holding tank, where they can pick up a turtle. (A tip: Have your child hold the turtle vertically. As long as he's held horizontally, he'll flap around and try to "swim" away.) This is a great place for some terrific vacation photos.

There's no visiting Grand Cayman without seeing what lies beneath the water's surface. But you don't even have to get wet to enjoy the underwater sights of the Caribbean. The **Atlantis submarine**, George Town, Tel. 800/253-0493, offers hourly dives six days a week. For 50 minutes, you'll feel like an underwater explorer as you dive to a depth of 100 feet below the surface. It's a unique opportunity to view colorful coral formations and sponge gardens, and identify hundreds of varieties of tropical fish. The submarine has individual porthole windows for each passenger, plus cards to help you identify fish species. A pilot and co-pilot point out attractions during the journey.

Although Grand Cayman has long been the home of the Atlantis submarine, it is also home base for the **Nautilus**, Tel. 345/945-1355. This 80-foot semi-submersible submarine, docked in George Town, has provided a one-hour tour to view the rich marine life of the bay. The sub goes out about three-fourths of a mile offshore offering visitors a chance to view two shipwrecks and to watch a diver feed a variety of tropical fish. Good for families with children and for anyone claustrophobic, travelers sit in a glass hull six feet beneath the surface but can go up on deck anytime during the trip. Tours are usually offered at 11am and 3 Monday through Saturday, but times vary at times. Guests can choose to go out for one hour, or to stay for an extra half-hour for snorkeling and swimming. The one-hour tours are priced at $35 per person and $15 for children, and the hour-and-a-half tours are $39 for adults and $19 for children.

Another option is a ride on an **Atlantis Research Submersible,** also operating from the Atlantis office. Plunging down to a depth of up to 1,000 feet below the surface, this vessel offers a one of a kind experience that might appeal to older teens with a keen interest in marine biology. The 22 foot sub carries two passengers and a pilot and is the only vessel of its type open to the public. Several times a day, it plunges down the Cayman Wall to depths far beyond the range of sports scuba divers. A large, three foot diameter convex window allows the two passengers to sit side by side in front of this viewport.

The view varies with the depth: from 200 to 400 feet below the surface are colorful sponges and corals in what's termed the "sponge belt." Hundreds of sponges blanket the vertical wall in forms ranging from 20 foot long orange rope sponges to gigantic barrel sponges. From 650 to 1000 feet, living formations give way to limestone pinnacles that house deep sea creatures such as stalked crinoids, porcelain corals and glass sponges. Termed the "haystack" zone, the haystacks or limestone blocks stand over 150 feet tall. Here light no longer penetrates the sea and the research sub illuminates the inky blackness with powerful lights. The highlight of many trips is a visit to the Kirk Pride, a shipwreck that sits on a ledge at 800 feet. This 180 foot freighter sank in a storm in 1976 and its fate was unknown until the wreck was discovered by an Atlantis Research Submarine in 1985.

A far less expensive option is the **Seaworld Explorer**, located next to Atlantis Submarine on South Church Street. Like the Nautilus, it is a good option for those who might feel a little claustrophobic about a submarine adventure (it does not go below the water's surface). Visitors descend into a glass observatory and view marine life as well as two shipwrecks. The

Explorer travels to the Cali, a schooner that hit the reef in 1944, and the Balboa, a freighter from Cuba destroyed by a hurricane. Today the wrecks are encased in corals and filled with fish life. Seaworld Explorer tours last one hour.

To feel like one of the pirates of the Caribbean, consider a cruise aboard the **Jolly Roger**, Tel. 345/945-7245, an authentic replica of a 17th century galleon. Cruises, starting at US $29 for adults, take families on a rollicking pirate excursion or an elegant dinner cruise.

A sunset cruise may be pure heaven, but one of Grand Cayman's top tourist spots is pure **Hell**. This odd attraction is actually a community named **Hell**, a moniker derived from the devilishly pointed rocks near town, a bed of limestone and dolomite that through millions of years eroded into a crusty, pocked formation locally called ironshore.

Today, Hell trades upon its unusual name as a way to draw tourists to the far end of west Bay. The Devil's Hangout Gift Shop (open daily) is manned by Ivan Farrington, who dresses as the devil himself to greet tourists who come to buy the obligatory postcard and have it postmarked from Hell.

For a look at native birds, animals, and reptiles **Cardinal D's Park**, off Courts Road, Tel. 345/949-8855, is a good stop for families. Over 60 species of exotic birds including Cayman parrots and whistling ducks as well as agoutis, blue iguanas, turtles, miniature ponies, emus, and more are on display. A petting zoo and snack bar make this attraction popular with kids. The park is open daily; guided tours available at 11am and 2pm.

Island Tours

Experienced tour operators offer an in-depth look at the islands. Guides can provide a general overview of the island as well as specialized tours focusing on eco-tourism, plants, history, birding, and shopping.

Overviews of the island range in length from two and a half hours to all day. Typical tours include a drive through look at the capital city of George Town, a photo stop at the Conch Shell House (a private residence made of conch shells), a drive along Seven Mile Beach, a tour of the Cayman Turtle Farm (the world's only such operation), and a visit to the community of Hell where vacationers can stop to mail postcards and have them postmarked from Hell.

Full day tours include the same stops as a brief tour but also take a look at the less visited east side of the island. Tours often drive through Bodden Town, visit the Pirate's Caves, stop for photos of the Blow Holes, and swing around to Rum Point, a popular watersports area overlooking the entrance to the North Sound.

You'll find island tours available from these tour operators:
- Burton's Tours, Tel. 345/949-7222, Fax 345/947-6222
- Elite Limousine Service, Tel. 345/949-5963, Fax 345/949-2058

- Majestic Tours, Tel. 345/949-7773, Fax 345/949-8647
- McCurley's Tours, Tel. 345/947-9626
- Tropicana Tours Ltd., Tel. 345/949-0944, Fax 345/949-4507
- Vernon's Sightseeing Tours, Tel. 345/949-1509, Fax 345/949-0213

Teens and older children with an interest in local flora and fauna will appreciate tours offered by **Silver Thatch Excursions**, Tel. 345/945 6588. Geddes Hislop and his wife Janet are the founders of Silver Thatch Excursions, a company that focuses on the history and ecology of the island. Families with an interest in botany can select from two excursions that include the Queen Elizabeth II Botanic Park. One tour follows the historic route, traveling to the Old Savannah Schoolhouse, to Bodden Town to see the Slave Wall and Cayman style homes, and then to the park for a walk along the Woodland Trail. The Environmental Route includes bird watching stops at the Governor Michael Gore Bird Sanctuary and other birding sites and then a tour of the Botanic Park.

Excursions are offered Monday through Saturday with pick up along West Bay Road starting at 8 am. Participants are provided with snacks including traditional Caymanian foods and beverages. Silver Thatch Excursions also offers specialized bird watching trips. These depart at 6 am on Saturdays and include stops at the Governor Michael Gore Bird Sanctuary, a haven for waterfowl, as well as Meagre Bay Pond, Queen Elizabeth II Botanic Park, and the Willie Ebanks Farm to view endangered West Indian whistling ducks.

Sports & Recreation

There's no doubt that one of the top draws of Grand Cayman is the unparalleled **scuba diving** in its clear waters. With visibility often exceeding 100 feet, this is a diver's paradise with over 130 sites to select from near Grand Cayman. Wall and reef dives, many less than half a mile from shore are available as well from many operators including Bob Soto's Diving, Tel. 800/BOB-SOTO, Don Foster's Dive Cayman, Tel. 800/83-DIVER, Red Sail Sports, Tel. 800/255-6425, Treasure Island Divers, Tel. 800/872-7552, Tortuga Surfside Divers, Tel. 800/748-8733, and many more.

If you would like to introduce your children to the joys of scuba diving, Cayman is the place. Thanks to a new program operated by Red Sail Sports, children as young as four can now have a taste of scuba diving. SASY, or Supplied Air Snorkeling for Youths, is a scuba unit customized for young bodies. Developed in the Cayman Islands by Capt. Wayne Hasson, a father of two young children, the unit combines a regulator so young divers can breath from a continuous air supply and a buoyancy compensator to keep children floating safely near the surface. Units are available for use at Red Sail

Sports (www.redsail.com) locations at the Hyatt Regency Grand Cayman, Westin Casuarina Resort and Marriott Grand Cayman.

"Grand Cayman is the perfect place for kids to learn to use SASY," explains Red Sail Sports Operations Manager Rod McDowell. "The waters here are clear and calm, and there's a lot for them to see. Parents can now take their children along on a dive boat, and together the whole family can explore our underwater world."

The top attraction on Grand Cayman is **Stingray City**, the place for your family to act out Jacques Cousteau fantasies. It's an area where numerous operators (including many of the scuba operators named above) introduce vacationers to one of the most unique experiences in the Caribbean.

Following a short boat ride, visitors don snorkel gear and swim with the stingrays just offshore on a shallow sandbar. Accustomed to being fed, the stingrays (which range in size from about one to six feet across) are docile and friendly, brushing against swimmers and even allowing themselves to be held and petted. About 30 stingrays frequent this area. Even non-swimmers can enjoy the shallowest stop. Use your own judgment on this attraction. We've seen many school age children participating but you should realize that the rays are large and will come close to the children.

Sports fun also exists on dry land. The Links at Safe Haven, Tel. 345/949-5988, Fax 949-5457, is the only championship 18-hole **golf course** in the Cayman Islands. Rates average about US $60 for 18 holes. Shoe and cart rental are available.

If you're looking for a bird's eye view of Grand Cayman take a **flightseeing tour** offered by Seaborne Flightseeing Adventures and Island Air, Tel. 345/949-6029. The 25-minute tour includes a look at Grand Cayman from a 19-passenger Twin Otter aircraft. Tours are scheduled only from December through June.

What Can We Buy?

Duty-free shopping is especially popular in George Town where you can choose from china, perfumes, leather goods, watches, crystal, and more. If you're looking for something uniquely Cayman, check out the Caymanite jewelry. Made from a stone found only on the eastern end of Grand Cayman and on Cayman Brac, Caymanite somewhat resembles tiger's eye.

An excellent shopping spot for families is the museum shop at the Cayman Island Museum in George Town. Look for Caribbean children's books, puzzles, locally made jewelry, crafts, and other inexpensive items with a real Cayman feel.

What Else Do We Need to Know?

Currency. The official currency is the Cayman Dollar, exchanged at a rate of US $1 equals CI 80¢.

Driving. Driving is British style, on the LEFT.

Information. For general information and reservations, call the Cayman Islands Department of Tourism, Tel. 800/346-3313. For hotel and condo rates in the Cayman Islands and for special air-accommodation packages, call Cayman Airways Holidays, Tel. 800/G-CAYMAN.

Information on Island. When on Grand Cayman, visit the Cayman Islands Department of Tourism office at Elgin Avenue in George Town, Tel. 345/949-0623.

Website. Check out the Cayman Islands Website on the Internet at: www.caymanislands.ky for lots of helpful information, current weather, news, and more.

Island Report Card	
Transportation to island	A+
Transportation around island	A
Family Resorts	A
Family Restaurants	A
Friendly atmosphere	A
Activities for kids	A
Weather	A
New cultures to experience	B-
Safety	A+

Chapter 12

CURAÇAO

For family travelers in search of something a little off the beaten path, here it is. Curaçao is a magical destination, favored by those looking for beautiful beaches, good snorkeling, and an exotic atmosphere that combines a Dutch heritage with a strong South American influence and a Caribbean beat for a truly unique getaway.

The island is part of the Netherlands Antilles along with the islands of Sint Maarten, Bonaire, Saba, and St. Eustatius. (The Netherlands Antilles, the island of Aruba, and Holland comprise the Kingdom of the Netherlands.) Ruled by a governor appointed by the Queen, each island has autonomy on domestic affairs. Curaçao is the capital of the Netherlands Antilles, and here you'll find most of the governmental, financial, and industrial positions.

Tucked into the far southern reaches of the Caribbean, less than 40 miles from the coast of South America, Curaçao is very much an international destination. Dutch is the official language, and you'll hear many Dutch-speaking vacationers. Many South Americans also enjoy the island where most residents speak Spanish. We found that most Curaçao residents speak an amazing total of five languages: Dutch, Spanish, English, Papiamento, and either French or German.

Papiamento is the local language spoken on the streets, a veritable cocktail of tongues. Spanish, Portuguese, French, Dutch, Indian, English, and some African dialects combine to form the *lingua franca* of the Netherlands Antilles. Even between the islands the language varies slightly, each with its own slang and accent.

Curaçao

— Primary road
- Secondary road
• Point of Interest

0   4 km   8 km

©1997 MAGELLAN GeographixSM Santa Barbara,CA

That ease with multiple languages also seems to translate into a comfort with many nationalities as well. Over 70 nationalities are represented on the island and, with such a true melting pot on this 184-square mile piece of land, there's a true welcoming spirit for tourists, wherever their homeland. When Curaçaoans says "Bon Bini," they mean welcome in any language.

On one side of the island lies the capital of Willemstad, a truly international city with streets lined with Dutch-style architecture as colorful as a candy store. The city is divided into two sides: Punda, the original settlement, and Otrobanda, literally the "other side." Both sport picturesque harborfront buildings, and are connected by the largest bridge in the Caribbean, a free ferry, and the Queen Emma Pontoon Bridge for pedestrians, locally known as the "Swinging Old Lady" because of the way it moves out of the way for harbor traffic.

Beyond Willemstad, Curaçao becomes a three tiered countryside dotted with tall cacti trimmed with coastlines of the windswept and tranquil varieties. The Atlantic shoreline of the island is rugged and wild, with pounding surf, shady sea caves, and evidence of past volcanic action. Swimming is prohibited in the dangerous waters, but families will find plenty of calm waters along the placid Caribbean side of the island.

Are We There Yet?

By Air

Curaçao International Airport lies just minutes from Willemstad and the nearby resort hotels. Air carriers include American Airlines, KLM, and others. Flying time from Atlanta is about four hour.

Getting Around the Island

Taxis are available but, for a stay at most hotels, rental jeeps are the best option. Traffic is light throughout much of the island, which invites exploration. Hertz, Avis, Budget, National, Dollar, and other firms offer rentals.

When traveling in the downtown Punda area, if you have questions or need directions, look for burgundy-suited men and women, members of the Curaçao Hospitality Service. Stationed throughout the shopping area, these friendly assistants provide help in many languages.

Where Are We Staying?

BREEZES CURACAO, Cornelisbay, Tel. 011/599-9-736-7888, Fax 011/599-9-461-4131, Toll-free reservations 800/GO-SUPER. www.breezescuracao.com. Winter rates from $228-$490, Summer rates from $187-$436. Credit cards accepted.

This super-inclusive resort, part of Jamaica's SuperClubs family, is ideal for families. Unlike the Breezes properties of other islands, which have a minimum age for guests, this property is super-family-friendly.

While parents learn water sports, sample drinks, or try cuisine from around the world, the kids will be having a great time in the Kids' club program. From 9 am to 5 pm, then 6:30 pm to 9 pm, children ages 2-7 can have a great time with other kids their own age. Here is a sample day of activities in the **Kids' Club**:

9 am Meet & Greet
9:30 am Sandcastle Building
10 am Pool Party
11 am Kiddies Tennis
11:30 am Loopy Lion Story
12 noon
1:30 pm Story Time
2 pm Laser Tag
3 pm Crazy Games
3:30 pm Snacks
4 pm Art & Craft
5 pm Super Siesta
6 pm(dinner) Safari Night
7 pm Planet Hop Jungle
9 pm Pick-up

Don't think that Breezes has forgotten about older kids. There is a Teens Club open from 10 am to midnight. The Teens Club schedules activities every day for teens, from tennis to rock climbing.

For kids 0-23 months, the Kids' Club has facilities to watch the babies, and a baby sitter may be hired through the guest relations desk for $7 per hour before midnight and $8 per hour after midnight.

Kids age 14 and over stay at adult prices. For families with kids under age 14, there's a special pricing structure:

•One adult and two children are charged as two adults (double) and one child

•One adult and three children are charged as two adults (double) and two children

•Two adults and one child are charged as two adults (double) and one child

•Two adults and two children are charged as two adults (double) and two children

•Two adults and three children are charged as three adults (triple) and two children

•Three adults and two children are charged as three adults (triple) and two children

CURAÇAO MARRIOTT BEACH RESORT AND EMERALD CASINO, Piscadera Bay, Tel. 599/9-433-7730, Fax 599/9-462-7502. Toll-free reservations Tel. 800/223-6388; www.curacaomarriott.com. Summer rates from $149. Credit cards accepted.

This 248-room resort (formerly the Sonesta) is Curaçao's only AAA four-diamond resort, an elegant resort filled with a Dutch Caribbean style. The three-story hotel. Cool lemon walls contrast with chile pepper-colored roofs, all framed by stately palms. The property is a veritable oasis on this dry island, just down the beach from the desalinization plant (the world's largest), where unsightly smokestacks distract slightly from the view but don't interfere with the enjoyment of this beautiful property

We especially liked the low-rise, open-air quality of this resort, starting with the lobby, where you'll arrive to a view over a cascading fountain across the palm-shaded pool and out to the sea. Every room includes either a balcony or patio (ask for a ground floor room for direct beach access) and at least a partial view of the ocean.

The hotel has many family-friendly features including a year-around children's program, babysitting services, roll-away beds, and cribs.

LION'S DIVE HOTEL AND MARINA, Bapor Kibra, Tel. 011/599-9-341-8888, Fax 011/599-9-434-8889. Toll-free reservations Tel. 866/546-6734; www.lionsdive.com Winter rates start at $138, Summer rates begin at $110. Credit cards accepted.

Especially popular with divers, this hotel has everything scuba enthusiasts could want: a five-star dive center, dive courses, snorkel and dive trips, rentals, and a complete dive shop. Its 72 guest rooms are all air-conditioned, each with a balcony or a patio. The hotel also operates a shuttle to Willemstad and offers free admission to Seaquarium.

The resort also operates an annual Kids' Sea Camp, offered for four weeks. Kids are divided into age groups of 4-8, 9-12, 10-15. The 4-8 age range learns snorkeling and SASY (see the introduction for information on this neat introduction to scuba diving.) Ages 9-12 take part in a Seal Team

Program (as in sea lions) while the 10-15 year olds can take part in the open water course. The most expensive option is the dolphin trainer course, available for all ages. The camp also includes activities such as pizza night on the beach and a treasure hunt.

What Can We Do Now?

This is an island without hasslers or pushy vendors, a place where your family can walk safely along the streets, dine at sidewalk cafes, and be greeted by friendly Curaçaoans.

Start with a visit to **Willemstad**, a historic city that bustles with activity but also takes a slower pace in its shopping district. Here you can take a guided tour aboard an open-air trolley or a self-guided walk for a look at Fort Amsterdam. And you can't miss the historic harborside shops, as colorful as Easter eggs.

Stroll through the streets and alleyways, then walk across the Wilhelmina Bridge to the **Floating Market**, one of Willemstad's most colorful sites. Here Venezuelans sell fresh fish and vegetables (a real commodity on an island without much agriculture). Stroll along the waterway booths and buy exotic tropical fruits or watch fishermen cleaning their catch for a buyer. Behind the stalls, colorful schooners make an excellent photo.

While you're in the city, make time for a visit to **Seaquarium**, Bapor Kibra, Tel. 461-6666, one of the Caribbean's finest marine exhibits and a definite winner with kids. Along with tanks of local fish, coral, and sponges, the aquarium also has several outdoor tanks with larger species—including sharks, sea turtles, and stingrays. Divers and would-be divers can take a dip here and feed the sharks through holes in an underwater Plexiglass wall. Complete instruction and equipment are provided. For those who want a drier look at these toothy denizens, just walk down into the Seaquarium Explorer, a semi-submarine parked by the shark tank.

After the Seaquarium have a dip at the Seaquarium Beach, a full-service beach with watersports, restaurant, bar, and plenty of action. There's a small admission charge. This is the beach where Curaçaoans and visitors come to see and be seen. Waters as calm as a lake make swimming inside the breakwaters easy and popular with families.

Curaçao has over three dozen additional **beaches** from which to choose, all located on the Caribbean side of the island. Some of the most popular are Knip Bay and Barbara Beach.

Curaçao may be a dry island, but you'll find plenty of other natural attractions. One is **Boca Tabla**, a sea cave carved by pounding Atlantic waves. Located on the road to Westpoint, the cave is a short walk off the road (wear sturdy shoes!). Kneeling in the darkness of the sea cave, you'll watch the surge of crystal blue waves as they come within feet of you, roaring into the cave and back out to sea. Above the cave, walk on the volcanic rock (stay on the pebble path) to the seaside cliffs for excellent photos. This stop is not recommended for families with young children but is a good stop for those with kids 10 and older who will stay by parents.

If you'd like to venture into a cavern, take a tour of **Hato Caves**, open daily except Monday. Guided tours take the two of you through the stalactite and stalagmite filled rooms, several of which include pools or waterfalls.

Nature lovers should save time for a visit to **Christoffel National Park**, on the western end of the island. This wildlife preserve includes the island's highest point and 20 miles of trails that wind through local flora and fauna. Don't be surprised to see some native wildlife in the park; it is home to iguanas, donkeys, small deer, rabbits, and many bird species.

For a look at all these attractions, consider an **island tour**. Tours can be booked through hotel desks or call Taber Tours, Tel. 737-6637, for a rundown of their packages which include east and west end tours, Hato Cave tour, jeep safari, and sailing and sunset cruises.

What Can We Buy?

Curaçao's shopping opportunities keep many travelers busy, especially in downtown **Willemstad**. The prime shopping district is in **Punda**, just across the floating bridge. Cross the bridge and continue up Breede Straat, where you'll find most of the shops and boutiques aimed at vacationers, along with some charming sidewalk cafes.

The most obvious shop in Punda is the **J.L. Penha and Sons** department store, housed in a beautiful lemon-tinted colonial building constructed in 1708. You'll find just about everything in this department store, from perfumes to fine jewelry to collectibles.

Down **Breede Straat**, you'll find more appropriate shops for families. Stop by Sunny Caribbee for a look at many Caribbean collectibles, spices, and crafts. The Gomezplein plaza, just a couple of blocks up from the bridge, offers picturesque boutiques and a relaxed shopping atmosphere.

For lower priced purchases, take a turn off Breede Straat and enjoy a stroll down Heeren Straat or Keuken Straat. These streets are filled with electronics, inexpensive clothing, and housewares. It's a fun atmosphere where you'll have a chance to mix with residents.

These streets end at the water, where you'll find an entirely different shopping opportunity: the **Floating Market**. Schooners from Venezuela bring exotic fruits, vegetables, spices, and plants to this open-air market that's very popular with older residents. To reach the floating market, walk across the bridge at Columbus Straat. We highly recommend the market to enjoy a slice of island life and, for the photographers out there, to capture one of Curaçao's most colorful sights.

Americans are allowed to return to the US with $600 worth of purchases (per person) before paying duty.

What Else Do We Need to Know?

Banks. Bank hours are 8am to 3pm. ATMs are available for use with Cirrus network cards.

Currency. The official currency is the Antillean guilder, exchanged at a rate of US $1=ANG 1.77.

Driving. Driving is on the right side of the road.

Electricity. The current is a little different from that found in the United States. Curaçao operates at 110-130 volts alternating current, 50 cycles.

Information. Call the Curaçao Tourist Board, Tel. 800/328-7222. Information on Island: Once you're here, stop by the Visitors Information Booth at the airport (just past customs) for brochures and maps. The tourism office is located at 19 Pietermaai in Willemstad, Tel. 434-8200.

Website. Check out the official Website at: www.curacao-tourism.com.

Island Report Card	
Transportation to island	B
Transportation around island	B+
Family Resorts	B
Family Restaurants	B-
Friendly atmosphere	A+
Activities for kids	B+
Weather	A+
New cultures for kids to experience	A+
Safety	A+

Chapter 13

DOMINICAN REPUBLIC

"Can you see the mosquito?" asked the guide.

We peered at the amber, backlit in the museum display. The insect was frozen in the solidified sap. One day over 50 million years ago, that mosquito had made a fatal mistake: landing on sap from a now-extinct species of pine tree. His slender legs were caught in the sticky substance that over the years had formed a crystal coffin.

The mosquito, along with amber-encased termites, ants, fern, cockroaches, and even a tiny lizard, is found in the Amber Museum in Puerto Plata, Dominican Republic. This Caribbean nation is one of only a few sites on the globe where amber is found. The popularity of *Jurassic Park*, where fiction gave scientists the ability to use DNA found in the mosquito blood to spawn dinosaurs, brings visitors flocking to this museum on the north shore of the island.

Although its history, from the prehistoric amber to Christopher Columbus' first landing in the New World, is fascinating, it is the Dominican Republic's present day situation with which most travelers are familiar. The Dominican Republic shares the island of Hispaniola with Haiti, a tumultuous neighbor that frequently overshadows the popular vacation destination.

The second largest Caribbean island (only Cuba is larger), Hispaniola is a land of rugged mountains, palm-lined beaches, and two diverse cultures. Haitians speak French; Dominicans, Spanish. The leadership of Haiti has frequently been torn by assassinations and military takeovers while the citizens of the Dominican Republic enjoy the relative tranquillity of a stable, freely elected government. And while life has become a struggle for Haitians,

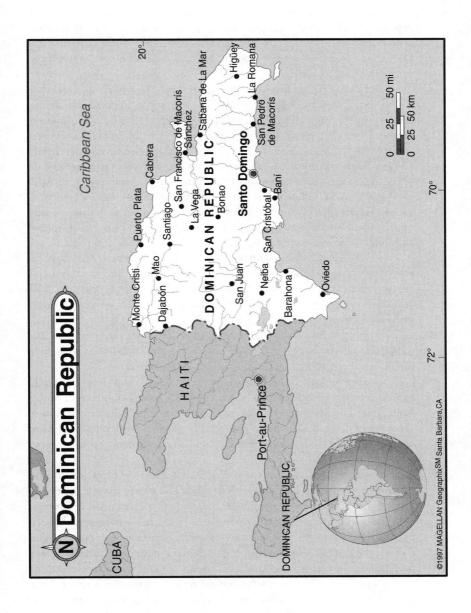

Dominican Republic days are far more carefree, with plenty of time to dance to the throbbing sounds of merengue.

The Dominican Republic has long been heralded as one of the least expensive Caribbean destinations, some sources estimating it to be as much as 50 to 70 percent cheaper than its neighbors. Excepting such resorts as Casa De Campo where jet setters come to relax, the island boasts inexpensive prices and bargain resorts.

Many resorts are found on the Dominican Republic's north side, a region nicknamed the Amber Coast. The Dominican Republic boasts the fastest growing tourism business in the Caribbean, with over two million visitors a year. We found that over 60% of the vacationers are European.

Most visitors arrive at Puerto Plata's La Union International Airport and journey to the resort area about twenty minutes away. A drive past fields of tall sugar cane with a backdrop of lush mountains takes many vacationers to Playa Dorada, a horseshoe-shaped complex containing 14 resorts, a casino, several discotheques, a two-story shopping mall, numerous restaurants, and a Robert Trent Jones-designed 18-hole golf course. Only guests and hotel vehicles are permitted within the Playa Dorada complex.

Playa Dorada is located on the Atlantic side of the island. Although the sea here is choppier that its Caribbean counterpart on the south shore, a gentle breeze makes it popular with windsurfers, boogie boarders, and families that enjoy playing in the surf. Other guests are just content to lie on the beaches lined with majestic palms.

Although Playa Dorada is almost a city within itself, travelers shouldn't miss Puerto Plata. Founded by Nicholas de Ovando in 1504 at the request of Christopher Columbus, this city is rich with history.

Dating back to the 16th century, the Fortaleza San Felipe still stands guard over the city and the harbor. Built by the Spaniards to protect the city from pirates, in this century it was used as a prison. The doors within the fort are only four feet tall, slowing down would-be attackers (and keeping tourists alert). The fort includes a small museum with a collection of period weapons and cannon balls.

Another fort stands at the top of Pico Isabel de Torres, one of the highest points in the Dominican Republic. The dome-shaped fortress is topped with a statue of Christ similar to one that overlooks Rio de Janeiro.

Santo Domingo is located on the island's southern shore. Here history buffs will find a wealth of Spanish Renaissance architecture to explore. The city was the first permanent European settlement in the New World and has been honored for its cultural landmarks by a United Nations proclamation.

Near Santo Domingo is located the nation's most lavish resort: Casa de Campo, as well as a host of other first-rate vacation destinations.

Are We There Yet?

By Air

The Dominican Republic is home to several international airports so make sure you know the location of your resort before booking your air. On the south side of the island, the capital city of Santo Domingo is served by Las Americas International Airport, about a half-hour drive from the city. On the north side of the island, Puerto Plata is served Puerto Plata International Gregorio Luperon Airport. Other airports include Punta Cana International Airport on the far east end, Maria Montez International Airport at Barahona, La Romana International Airport near Bavaro, and Arroyo Barril Airport in Samaná.

Getting Around the Island

With 12,000 miles of roads, getting around the Dominican Republic can be achieved many different ways. You can rent a car from a major agency at the airports and in the larger cities. You'll need your driver's license and a major credit card. You'll also need good reflexes to deal with the frequent displays of driving *machismo* you will encounter. One fortunate thing: driving is (more or less) on the right side.

Taxis are a safer bet, but are fairly expensive and are unmetered; you'll need to negotiate a price before you embark. A variety of buses are also available from luxury lines to those with few creature comforts. The most basic transportation in the DR are the *guaguas,* unregulated taxi/buses which are usually crowded with locals. If you speak Spanish, riding the *guaguas* can be a good way to get the lowdown on what's happening.

Where Are We Staying?

Punta Cana

BARCELO BAVARO BEACH RESORT, Punta Cana, Tel. 809/ 688-3600, Fax 809/221-0921. Toll-free reservations 800/BARCELO; www.barcelo.com. All-inclusive rates for room with two adults, two children $180-$450. Credit cards accepted.

You know that saying, "if you can't say something nice, don't say anything at all" ? Well, we almost heeded that advice and nearly skipped listing the Barcelo, a property we stayed at for four days. The reasons? They range from difficulties on check-in (literally running from resort to resort at the five-property complex—all at 10 pm after a full day of travel) to a buffet that could best be described as sparse.

But then we decided to list this five-in-one hotel complex. Why? Price, price, price. If you have a limited vacation budget, the Barcelo is a wonderful bargain. Yes, the buffet is sparse (but you've now been warned, so pack some snacks). Yes, the service is less than adequate (so pack an extra helping of patience.) Nonetheless, it does offer an all-inclusive program, a huge beach, nice swim complex, and clean rooms. The five properties are connected by an open-air tram that's fun for kids to ride and you'll be able to enjoy dining or playing at the other properties, with the exception of the Barceló Bávaro Palace, which is the most upscale of the five. (If you stay there, you'll have reciprocal privileges at the other four, but not visa versa.)

BREEZES PUNTA CANA RESORT SPA & CASINO, Punta Cana, Tel.809/476-7777, Fax 809/412-2334. Toll-free US phone number Tel. 877/GO-SUPER; www.superclubs.com. Rates from $130-$234. Credit cards accepted.

This all-inclusive resort is a family favorite, both with American and European travelers. Located on Arena Gorda Beach, the 735-room resort is the largest in the chain and offers not only a wide swath of beachfront but also an expansive pool complex (including a kids' pool.)

Children ages 4-12 stay free and can take part in the Miniclub open daily 9 am to 5 pm. Like other resorts in the chain, the club offers everything from arts and crafts to sandcastle building. Kids can also enjoy a separate mini-disco held every night.

For grown-up travelers, there are plenty of diversions as well including a casino, spa, nearby golf, and watersports.

Kids age 14 and over stay at adult prices. For families with kids under age 14, there's a special pricing structure:

•One adult and two children are charged as two adults (double) and one child

•One adult and three children are charged as two adults (double) and two children

•Two adults and one child are charged as two adults (double) and one child

•Two adults and two children are charged as two adults (double) and two children

•Two adults and three children are charged as three adults (triple) and two children

•Three adults and two children are charged as three adults (triple) and two children

CLUB MED PUNTA CANA, Punta Cana, Toll-free reservations 800/CLUB-MED; www.clubmed.com. Summer rates for seven-nights all-inclusive stays start at $840 per adult and $430 per child ages 4-15, $305 for children 2-3. Credit cards accepted.

Parents who have traveled with teens know that the kids' club just doesn't work anymore once kids reach the teen years. It's just too much like babysitting to please independent young teens who want to explore a resort in a far less structured way.

The answer? The Ramp. This is a new teen lounge opened in March 2005 at this all-inclusive property. The two-story teen lounge allows no visitors not in the 14-17 age bracket. While at the open-air lounge, young guests can skateboard, rollerblade, play foosball, and meet other teens. The introduction to the club begins at check-in, when teens get a packet which includes a combination for a personal mailbox at The Ramp. The mailbox provides daily updates and also a way for teens to communicate with one another. The welcome packet also includes a cloth bracelet that provides admission to The Ramp and tokens for The Ramp's photo booth. Other activities for teens range from movie nights to themed dance parties for teens only. Before they check out, participants are invited to "Leave a Mark" at The Ramp with a note or graffiti tag.

For younger members of the family, Club Med offers a kids' club for ages 2-13 with activities ranging from circus fun to arts and crafts.

MELIA BAVARO, Playas de Bavaro, Higuey, Tel. 809/221-2311, Fax 809/686-5427. Toll-free US phone number 800/33-MELIA; www.solmelia.com. Winter rates from $80, Summer rates from $70. Credit cards accepted.

Located in Punta Cana on the eastern end of the island, this 57-acre resort offers rooms in two-story bungalows and a two-story hotel for a total of nearly 600 rooms.

Children's activities are conducted daily, free for hotel guests. Kids under two years stay free with parents; children over two years are charged only 50% of the normal rate.

PUNTACANA RESORT & CLUB, Punta Cana, Tel. 809/959-22627. Toll-free US phone number 888/442-2262; www.puntacana.com. Credit cards accepted. Winter rates from $145, Summer rates from $93. Credit cards accepted.

Located on 15,000 acres with a three-mile beach, this expansive 420room resort is just five minutes from the Punta Cana International Airport. Appealing to both adults and kids, the resort offers a championship P.B. Dye-designed golf course (with a second one designed by Tom Fazio to be added in 2006), a new spa, scuba diving, water skiing, sailing, fishing, windsurfing, and a full-service marina. The resort also offers a daily kids' club for ages 4 to 12. The kids program includes a variety of activities ranging from water skiing classes to horseback riding. A horse ranch is located directly across the street from the resort and includes one-hour, two-hour, and half-day trail rides on the beach. The ranch is also home to a petting farm for kids; on Wednesdays, the ranch offers Western Night with Dominican-style western dishes, horseback and foot races, and more.

Children ages 2-12 years old pay 50% of adult rate in deluxe rooms at the resort.

La Romana

CASA DE CAMPO, La Romana, Tel. 305/856-5405, Fax 305/858-4677. Toll-free US phone number Tel. 800/877-3643; www.casadcampo.com. Winter rates from $353, Summer from $224. Credit cards accepted.

The Dominican Republic's most lavish resort is also one of the most activity-oriented in the Caribbean. You name it, you can do it at the plush resort sprawled over 7000 acres. Here, all children under 18 stay for free in their parents' room, with a maximum of 2 childrend per room.

The hotel operates kids' programs for ages three to five, and six to 12 years. Kidz 'n Casa operates daily from 9 am- 4 pm, and has programs for ages 4-7 and 8-12. Kids get lunch and plenty of activities. There are other kids programs offered for evenings and nights.

IBEROSTAR HACIENDA DOMINICUS, Bayahibe, Dominican Republic. Tel. 809/688-3600, Fax 809/221-0921. Toll-free reservations 888/923-2722; www.iberostar.com. Winter rates from $130, Summer rates from $100. Credit cards accepted.

This expansive all-inclusive resort is located on 30 acres of the Dominican Republic's tropical southern coast. All drinks, meals, and snacks are included in the cost, so families don't have to worry about watching the budget while on the island. While at the Hacienda Dominicus, guests can try scuba diving, sun bathe at the pool, sailing on a catamaran, kayaking, and snorkeling. Land activities include billiards, volleyball, table tennis, and golf.

Most visitors at this expansive resort arrive at nearby La Romana International Airport. From the airport, it's less than a half-hour drive to the resort, a drive past sugar cane fields and across the Chavon River, which served as a backdrop for Apocolypse Now and Rambo 2.

You can star in your own movie—a far more relaxing one—at this seaside resort. Families from the US, Canada, and Italy make up much of the clientele of this resort which opened in November 2001. Families are also welcomed, and parents seeking some quality time alone will find the kids' club offers supervised activities for ages 4-12. The kids' club, part of the all-inclusive program, offers fun activities ranging from arts and crafts to pool fun from 10am to 5pm; the resort also offers a kids' disco for evening excitement. Babysitters are available for evening and nights at an additional charge.

Pastel room blocks line the expansive pool complex. Walk from your room to the shade of a thatched palapa at poolside or head straight for the powdery white sand beach for the day. Active travelers can opt for snorkeling right offshore or sign up for a snorkeling or a dive trip. All nonmotorized watersports are included in the all-inclusive package.

Golfers can test their skills on one of the world's top courses, the nearby Teeth of the Dog. Greens fees aren't included but a quick stop by the Guests Services desk can make the necessary arrangements at this championship course located about 25 minutes from Iberostar. Teeth of the Dog is located near Altos de Chavon, a replica 16th century Mediterranean village.

Evening fun here is family-friendly with numerous restaurants from which to choose including Mexican, Japanese, and international. After dinner, most guests take in the evening show, an extravaganza on a scale that we've seen matched by few resorts in the Caribbean. And don't forget to have a look at the resident flamingos, who range freely in the fountains nearby.

VIVA WYNDHAM DOMINICUS BEACH RESORT, Bayshibe, La Romana, Tel. 809/686-5658. Toll-free US phone number 800/898-9968; www.wyndham.com. Credit cards accepted. For a room for two adults and two children, the all-inclusive rates start at $65 per person per night.

A family favorite, this 530-room resort is set on a wide swath of white sand beach on the island's southeast coast, facing the islands of Saona and Catalina. The family-friendly resort has three pools and four restaurants plus an extensive all-inclusive program that includes everything from kayaking and sailing to introductory dive lessons and archery. A kids' program runs from 9 am to 5 pm daily and babysitting is also available. The kids club is called the Viva Wyndham Kid's Retreat, aimed at children age four to 12 years old. There's also a teen club for ages 12 to 16.

Puerto Plata

BREEZES PUERTO PLATA RESORT SPA & CASINO, Puerto Plata, Tel. 809/320-3600, Fax 809/571-3389. Toll-free US phone number Tel. 877/GO-SUPER; www.superclubs.com. Winter rates from $118-$249. Credit cards accepted.

Located on the north side of the island near the city of Puerto Plata (an area known as the Amber Coast), this resort is favored by families as well as couples. The 466-room resort has undergone recent renovations, adding an extensive pool as well as the resort's large spa and casino.

Kids 12 and under can enjoy the Miniclub (ages 4-12) daily; babysitting service is also available for a charge. This property includes several facilities of special interest to active young travelers including rock climbing, trapeze and trampoline classes, and a mini disco. Families also find a separate children's pool.

Kids age 14 and over stay at adult prices. For families with kids under age 14, there's a special pricing structure:

•One adult and two children are charged as two adults (double) and one child

•One adult and three children are charged as two adults (double) and two children

•Two adults and one child are charged as two adults (double) and one child

•Two adults and two children are charged as two adults (double) and two children

•Two adults and three children are charged as three adults (triple) and two children

•Three adults and two children are charged as three adults (triple) and two children

What Can We Do Now?

The Jurassic Park buffs in your family have come to the right place. Amber-encased specimens were borrowed from the collection of Puerto Plata's **Amber Museum** to make the movie and today you can have a look at amber-encased mosquitoes, termites, ants, fern, cockroaches, and even a tiny lizard. This Caribbean nation is one of only a few sites on the globe where amber is found.

Housed in a two story Victorian structure, the museum features amber mined in the Septentrional mountains along the north coast.

The museum was founded by Didi and Aldo Costa, the Italian consulate in the Dominican Republic. Their collection of amber is the most extensive in the world.

When removed from the geologic layers on the mountainside, amber looks like an unspectacular stone. Cutting and polishing, however, reveals its true nature — not a stone at all but a translucent fossilized sap. Amber ranges in color from pale yellow to dark brown, depending on the surrounding soil. A rare blue tinted amber is colored by volcanic gas. The most treasured pieces of amber are those that have "inclusions" — leaves, insects or even small reptiles trapped in these crystal coffins.

The Amber Museum has numerous displays of amber and provides guided tours in several languages, including English. After a tour of the museum, most visitors head to the shop downstairs (even larger than the museum). Here shoppers find one of the north coast's largest selections of amber jewelry.

Dating back to the 16th century, the **Fortaleza San Felipe** still stands guard over the city and the harbor. Built by the Spaniards to protect the city from pirates, in this century it was used as a prison. The doors within the fort are only four feet tall, slowing down would-be attackers (and keeping tourists alert). The fort includes a small museum with a collection of period weapons and cannon balls.

Another fort stands at the top of **Pico Isabel de Torres**, one of the highest points in the Dominican Republic. The dome-shaped fortress is topped with a statue of Christ similar to one that overlooks Rio de Janeiro.

In Santo Domingo, historic attractions fill the **Colonial Zone**. Tour sites such as the Catedral Santa Maria la Menor, the first cathedral in the Americas and, according to some historians, the final resting site of Christopher Columbus.

Near Iberostar Hacienda Dominicus and Casa de Campo, **Altos de Chavon** is well worth a visit. This re-creation of a 16th century art colony, complete with Spanish wrought ironwork and hushed courtyards, speaks of colonial style in a way no museum ever could.

What Can We Buy?

The most unique purchase in the Dominican Republic is **amber**, available at gift shops along the north coast. Amber prices vary from US $3 for small earrings to US $200 for a mosquito encased in amber to several hundred dollars for large, chunky necklaces or amber set in gold. The color of the amber affects the price as well. Generally the pale blonde amber is the least expensive.

Amber resembles plastic, so avoid buying from street vendors and check your item before purchasing. Amber possesses a slight electromagnetic charge, so genuine amber, when rubbed on a piece of cloth, should attract particles. Better stores, such as the Amber Museum Shop, also have an ultraviolet light for testing. Genuine pieces will glow under the light. Also, amber will float in salt water while plastic will sink.

For teenagers, popular souvenirs are **merengue cassette tapes**, and **larimar**, a blue stone similar to turquoise.

NOTE: Do not exchange more dollars than you will spend in the Dominican Republic. Upon departure, you may only convert 30% of your pesos back to dollars with proper receipts.

What Else Do We Need to Know?

Currency. The Dominican peso (RD) is the official currency. The exchange rate fluctuates but at press time was about RD $18=$1 US.

Electricity. 110 volt/60 cycles is used.

Information. For brochures on Dominican Republic attractions, call the Tourist Information Center, Tel. 888/374-6361 in the US; 800/563-1611 in Canada, on weekdays from 8 to 5, eastern standard time.

Language. Spanish is the official language of the Dominican Republic. In tourist areas, English is spoken but away from the hotels you will need at least a minimal knowledge of Spanish.

Time. Atlantic Standard Time, one hour ahead of Eastern, is used throughout the year. Daylight savings time is not observed.

Website. Get more Dominicana information at www.dominicana.com.do (the first menu will come up in Spanish but select English from the top menu for a translated version).

Island Report Card	
Transportation to island	B
Transportation around island	B-
Family Resorts	B
Family Restaurants	B-
Friendly atmosphere	B
Activities for kids	B
Weather	A
New cultures for kids to experience	A
Safety	B

Chapter 14

JAMAICA

Spanning over 4,000 square miles, the Caribbean's third largest island has a little bit of everything: rivers, mountains, plains, forests, caves, and, of course, a beautiful coastline. Jamaica is an island that appeals to travelers who enjoy its pulsating reggae music, rich history, and bountiful attractions that highlight its lush, tropical beauty. Perhaps more than any other Caribbean island except St. Lucia, Jamaica is incredibly lush and fertile. Fruits, orchids, bromeliads, hardwoods, and ferns all thrive in this rich soil and bountiful environment. Sugar remains a major product.

Jamaica also offers several distinct destinations that lie a few hours' drive apart on roads that twist and wind beside a jagged coast and, on the eastern end, stands the Blue Mountains, with peaks that top 7,500 feet above sea level.

The capital city of Kingston lies on the south shore, a metropolitan area that's visited primarily for business rather than pleasure. Most vacationers head to the resort communities of the north shore. Quiet Port Antonio, once a hideaway for Hollywood stars, lies to the east. Heading west, the garden city of Ocho Rios is a popular favorite with couples. Montego Bay or Mo Bay is the first taste most visitors have of the island as it's home of the north shore airport. To the far west is Negril. Once a hippie haven, today it's the preferred vacation spot for many aging yuppies who have returned with their families to enjoy its laid-back atmosphere and unbeatable sunset views.

We have to admit that Jamaica is not for everyone. Many travelers, including some fellow travel writers, prefer to skip this island because of the problems that inevitably reveal themselves even to the casual traveler. Drugs are a problem on this island, and you will probably be approached by *ganja-*

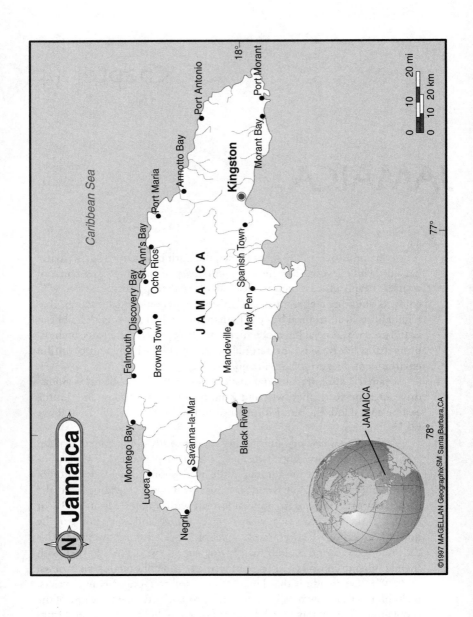

selling entrepreneurs. Although the resorts patrol their grounds and beaches above the high water line, when you step outside the boundaries of the resort be prepared. "I have something special for you" is a frequently used line that you can ward off with a friendly but firm "No, thank you."

Do we take our children to Jamaica? Yes, we have. Do we recommend all travelers take their children to Jamaica? No. If you have older children, especially teens, who insist on exploring on their own, Jamaica may not be the island for you. Teens will be offered drugs for sale if they leave the hotel property or walk along a public beach. If you're not 100% confident of your teen's response, choose another island.

But, in general, we've found that Jamaica has some of the friendliest inhabitants in the Caribbean. Service, even in all-inclusive resorts where tips are not even a question, is excellent. Taxi drivers are proud to tell you about the island, and we've even had drivers jump out of the car and pick herbs and plants along the route in describing their uses in the Jamaican household. We have visited this island more than any other in the Caribbean and it continues to hold a special place in the hearts of our family.

One of the best ways to get an introduction to Jamaica away from the usual tourist scene is to meet its residents in person. Two excellent programs allow visitors to join up with residents with shared interests.

Meet the People is a free program operated by the Jamaica Tourist Board that utilizes the services of over 500 volunteers on the island in different walks of life. Through the years, the program has matched stamp collectors, birders, private pilots, and travelers of many interests with islanders. The program is simple: just give the Jamaica Tourist Board office a call, Tel. 800/294-7687 or 888/995-9999 on the island.

Countrystyle, Tel. 876/962-3725, 876/962-3377 or 800/JAMAICA, Fax 876/962-1461, is another unique service. Owner Diana McIntyre Pike can arrange island experiences tailored just to the visitor's interest. Whether you'd like to visit a school, meet a family with kids the same age as yours, or plan a vacation that includes some home stays in small communities across the island, give Countrystyle a call.

Are We There Yet?

By Air

Service into Montego Bay's Donald Sangster International Airport is available on Air Jamaica, American Airlines, Continental, Air Canada, USAirways, and Northwest Airlines. Service is available from New York, Newark, Baltimore/Washington, Philadelphia, Atlanta, Miami, Orlando, Los Angeles, Tampa, and Toronto.

By Ship

Most cruise ships arrive in Ocho Rios or Montego Bay. Both city's terminals are within easy distance of the craft markets and shopping centers.

Getting Around the Island

Taxis are the easiest mode of travel and can be obtained at any resort. Look for red PPV license plates; these indicate legitimate taxis. Agree on the price with the driver before you depart.

Rental cars are pricey, and are available from most major rental companies. The speed limit is 30 mph in town and 50 mph on the highways, but be warned: Jamaica has some wild drivers! We've often seen two cars passing an auto at the same time, creating a three lane, one way road out of a two lane, two way highway. On top of that, you'll be driving on the left side of the road and dealing with roundabouts at every intersection.

Where Are We Staying?

Montego Bay

HALF MOON, east of Montego Bay, 876/953-2211, Fax 876/953-2731. Toll-free reservations Tel. 876/953-2211; www.halfmoon.com. Winter rates start at $390. Credit cards accepted.

Half Moon is one of Jamaica's top destination resorts, a place you can check into and be perfectly happy until you're ready to depart. In fact, there's no reason not to be: facilities here include a shopping village, hospital, school, dolphin swims, a golf course, and equestrian center. What started out in 1954 as a group of private beach cottages offered for rent during off-season months has blossomed into one of Jamaica's most extensive resorts.

Those beach cottages are still available and—just steps away from the sand as well as public areas—remain a great choice for families. We stayed in the cottages on our last stay and loved the easy proximity both to the public areas and to the beach. Some rooms are a long walk from public areas although a call can arrange for a golf cart pickup. The villas come with a private golf cart for your use.

Half Moon is the Caribbean's only resort with a private dolphin experience. The Dolphin Lagoon is home to four dolphins available for swims and encounters with resort guests only.

The resort also offers a supervised kids' center, available for potty trained children ages three and over. The facility includes a kids' pool, video games, and shaded playground. Babysitting is also available. Other kids' facilities at the property include children's bikes for rent (you'll find bike paths winding through the resort), a game room with a miniature table tennis set, and more. Children are welcomed in all the restaurants; the main Seagrape Terrace restaurant offers a special kids' menu and early seatings. Also, children age 12 and under stay free in their parents' room (except during the week of winter holidays).

HOLIDAY INN SUNSPREE, east of Montego Bay, 876/953-2485, Fax 876/953-2840. Toll-free reservations Tel. 800/HOLIDAY; www.ichotelsgroup.com. Winter rates start at $150 per person; room-only rates begin at $80. Credit cards accepted.

Over a decade ago, we spent our honeymoon at this resort located on the outskirts of Mo Bay. At that time, it was a standard Holiday Inn, albeit one with a private white sand beach, live entertainment every night, and restaurants which introduced us to Caribbean cooking.

But today this hotel has become even better. Following a major renovation, the 516-room Holiday Inn SunSpree Resort is now all-inclusive, offering guests a package that includes all their meals, drinks, non-motorized watersports, tennis, golf, daily activities, theme parties, shopping excursions, and a Great House tour. The Kids Spree Vacation Club accommodates infants through teens.

The Kidspree Centre recently instituted a new program called "Kid E Care" with private nanny. Daytime nannies service the guest room and also take care of the children. Evening nanny services run from 6pm to 1am.

During the Christmas holiday, the resort stages a Mini Miss Holiday Inn Pageant for young girls age 7 to 12. Prizes are offered and hotel management, guests, and local retailers serve as judges.

RITZ-CARLTON GOLF & SPA RESORT, ROSE HALL 1 Ritz Carlton Dr., east of Montego Bay, Tel. 876/953-2800, Fax 876/953-2501. Toll-free reservations Tel. 800/241-3333; www.ritzcarlton.com. Winter from $420. Credit cards accepted.

If you're looking for luxury, you'll be, well, putting on the Ritz at this elegant resort located east of Montego Bay. A favorite with golfers thanks to its lauded White Witch Golf Course (located on the grounds of the historic Rose Hall Great House), the resort has a beachfront location and the highbrow service for which the Ritz is known. There's a fully supervised kids' club for ages 5 to 12. Otehr activities here include a daily high tea, full-service spa, diving, windsurfing, and more.

ROUND HILL HOTEL AND VILLAS, 8 miles west of Montego Bay, Tel. 876/956-7050, Fax 876/956-7505. Toll-free reservations Tel. 800/972-2159; www.roundhilljamaica.com. Winter from $260, Summer rates from $550 per room. Credit cards accepted.

Located eight miles west of Montego Bay, this elegant resort is "old" Jamaica, a reminder of the time when guests came with their steamer trunks, brought the latest European fashions, and stayed for weeks. Today, this is where the rich and famous come to vacation; Ralph Lauren, Paul McCartney, and the Kennedys have been spotted on the guest register at this exclusive resort.

But, for all its luxury, this is also a family-friendly property. Complimentary nanny service is available for up to five hours daily; children under 12 are offered a 50% discount on any meal plan or the all-inclusive package. A special children's menu caters to young tastes.

Kids activities include a free tennis clinic available weekly, a donkey ride at the Monday night beach party, beach fun, glass bottom boat rides, and a weekly sailing trip. Young equestrians can take a pony ride at nearby stables.

SUNSET BEACH RESORT & SPA, west of Montego Bay in Freeport, 876/979-8800, Fax 876/953-6744. Toll-free reservations Tel. 800/234-1707; www.sunsetbeachresort.com. Winter rates start at $340 for a double room; there's a $35 add-on per child.

This expansive all-inclusive resort is a very good value for families if you don't mind mass tourism. With one of Jamaica's best (and most used) lobbies, a waterpark, and excellent beaches on a peninsula jutting out into the bay, the facilities here help to redeem the motel-basic rooms. The resort has three excellent beaches (one nude, although it remains out of sight) plus a new waterpark, four restaurants, four tennis courts, spa, and more. A children's program accommodates young visitors from infants to age 12.

WYNDHAM ROSE HALL, North Coast Highway, east of Montego Bay, Tel. 876/953-2650, Fax 876/953-2617. Toll-Free reservations Tel. 800/996-3426; www.wyndham.com. Summer rates from $250. Credit cards accepted.

Families can enjoy Wyndham Rose Hall on either a room-only basis or as an all-inclusive property. This sprawling resort is just a short drive from the airport, a real boon to those on a short vacation or traveling with restless kids. And once you arrive there's no need to worry about those kids remaining restless for long: Wyndham Rose Hall is home to a massive waterpark, a recent addition to the property.

This 110,000-square-foot, $7 million water complex is called Sugar Mill Falls and comes complete with lagoons and a towering waterslide. Guests can enjoy lazy river rafting among waterfalls scattered throughout the park. Kids can also take part in the supervised Kids Klub.

This resort recently underwent a major upgrade, equipping its guest rooms with new furniture, carpeting, 27-inch TVs, movie channels, and more.

Falmouth
STARFISH TRELAWNY BEACH AND FUN RESORT, Falmouth, Tel. 876/954-2450, Fax 876/954-2149. Toll-free reservations Tel. 800/ 659-5436; www.starfishresorts.com . Winter rates from $72.50. Summer rates from $ 109. Credit cards accepted.

See Chapter 3, "Best Places to Stay," for a detailed write-up.

Negril
BEACHES NEGRIL, P.O. Box 12, Negril, Jamaica. Tel. 876/957-9270, Fax 876/957-9269. Toll-free US phone number 888/BEACHES; www.beaches.com. Winter rates from $670 per person for two nights in a deluxe room, Summer rates from $650 per person for two nights in a deluxe room, all-inclusive. Credit cards accepted.

See Chapter 3, "Best Places to Stay," for a detailed write-up.

BEACHES SANDY BAY, Norman Manley Boulevard, Negril, Tel. 876/957-5100, Fax 876/ 957-5229. Toll-free reservations Tel. 800/BEACHES; www.beaches.com. Winter rates from $255, Summer rates from $265.

Located along Negril's Seven Mile Beach, families will find everything they could need in a vacation spot at Beaches Sandy Bay (formerly Poinciana) although this resort is not as extensive as its sister property, Beaches Negril. This all-inclusive resort has two pools, tennis, snorkeling, scuba diving and a fitness center. Guests have their choice of rooms ranging from a Deluxe with one king or two double beds, with a maximum occupancy of 4 people, to a luxurious Beachfront 2 Bedroom Suite, a two-level suite with kitchenette, living area, a double pullout sofa, two twin beds, and one queen bed. These suites have a maximum occupancy of 5. All guest rooms include air conditioning, telephone, satellite television, and private bath. Kids 2-15 stay here for $80 per child, per night, and children under 2 stay free.

The Kid's Kamp here will the children busy all day. Kids 4 years to teen will have a great time with arts and crafts, ice cream parties, face painting, sand castle building, movie watching, treasure hunts and much more. There is also a nursery for the kids under 4. Here is a sample day for kids in the nursery, and Kid's Kamp. Like other members of the Beaches family, this resort features Sesame Street characters and fun. There's also an Xbox Oasis with all the hottest games (and no tokens!)

Activities for Nursery: 0-3 years
9 am Registration/Orientation
10 am Shell Painting
11 am Nature Walk
12 pm Lunch
1:30 pm Rest Time/Cartoons

3 pm Snack Time
4 pm Face Painting
5 pm Musical Games
6 pm Dinner
7 pm Sing A Long
9:30 pm Pick-up Time

Activities for Kid's Kamp: 4 and older
9 am Registration/Orientation
10 am Talk Jamaica
11 am Treasure Hunt
12 pm Lunch
1 pm Sega Contest
1:30 pm Reggae Dance Class
2:30 pm Pool Games
3:30 pm Snack Time
4:30 pm Head Band Making
5 pm Kiddies Olympics
6 pm Dinner
7 pm Movie Hour
8 pm Talent Show

Parents who are planning on taking advantage of the Kid's Kamp should make sure that their kids have bathing suits, sunglasses, sunscreen, hats, extra diapers, wipes, bottles, formulas and security objects.

Teens have their own program, which includes activities like Reggae dancing, boat cruises, tennis clinics, karaoke, dance parties, and movie watching.

Baby sitters are also available for an additional cost.

Activities for kids: 4-8 years
Sunday
9am Registration & Orientation
10am Beach Volleyball
11am Island Bracelet
12pm Lunch
1pm Charades
1:30pm Musical Games
2:30pm Pool Games
3:30pm Snack
4pm Ping Pong
5pm Caribbean Fun Time
6pm Dinner

7pm Caribbean Story Time
8pm Pyjama Party
9:30pm Pick-up Time

Monday
9am Registration & Orientation
10am Rock Design
11am Picnic on the Beaches
12pm Lunch
1pm Patois Class
1:30pm Tye & Dye
2:30pm Reggae Dance Class
3:30pm Snack
4pm Tennis
5pm Cocktail Party
6pm Dinner
8pm Reggae Dance Night
9pm Crab Hunt
9:30pm Pick-up Time

Tuesday
9am Registration & Orientation
10am Pom Pom Making
11am Shoot-out
12pm Glass Bottom Boat Ride
12:30pm Lunch
1:30pm Face Painting
2:30am Head Band Making
3 pm Pool Aerobics
4pm Water Balloon Rama
5pm Shell Hunt
6pm Dinner
7pm Treasure Hunt
8pm Musical Night
9:30pm Pick-up Time

Wednesday
9am Registration & Orientation
10am Hat Making
11am Fashion Show Rehearsal
12pm Lunch
1pm Art & Craft
2pm Fashion Show

2:30pm Beach Walk
3:30pm Snack
4pm Tennis
5pm Nature Walk
6pm Dinner
7pm Kampers Challenge Quiz
8pm Talent Show
9:30pm Pick-up Time

Thursday
9am Registration & Orientation
10am Treasure Hunt
11am Pool Volleyball
12pm Lunch
1pm Riddle & Giggle
1:30pmTwister
2:30pm Board Games
3:30pm Snack
4pm Beach Games
5pm Headband Making
6pm Dinner
7pm Pictionary
8:15pm Magic Show
9:30pm Pick-up Time

Friday
9am Registration & Orientation
10am Beach Volleyball
11am Nature Walk
12pm Lunch
1pm Art & Craft
1:30pm T-Shirt Painting
2:30pm Dance Contest
3:30pm Snack
4pm Shell Hunt
5pm Soccer on the Beach
6pm Dinner
7pm Dance Contest
8pm Beach Party Night
9:30pm Pick-up Time

Saturday
9am Registration & Orientation

10am Paper Art
11am Sandcastle Design
12pm Lunch
1pm Face Painting
1:30pm T-Shirt Cutting & Design
2:30pmPool Games
3:30pm Snack
4pm Shoot Out
5pm Hoola Hoop Contest
6pm Dinner
7pm Movie Hour
8pm Soca Night
9:30pm Pick-up Time

Activities for kids: 9-12 years
Sunday
9am Registration & Orientation
10am Volleyball
11am Treasure Hunt
2pm Musical Games
3pm Pool Tournament
4pm T-Shirt Painting
5pm Beach Games
7pm Camping
9:30pm Pick-up Time

Monday
9am Registration & Orientation
10am Basketball
12pm Glass Bottom boat ride
2pm Reggae Dance Class
3pm Work-out Time
4pm Table Tennis
5pm Beach Games
7pm Crab Hunt
9:30pm Pick-up Time

Tuesday
9am Registration & Orientation
10am Pom Pom Designs
11am Treasure Hunt
2pm Banana Boat Ride
3pm Pool Volleyball

4pm T-Shirt Designs
5pm Beach Games
7pm Crazy Dress Style
9:30pm Pick-up Time

Wednesday
9am Registration & Orientation
10am Hat Making
11am Picnic on the Beach
2pm Talent Show rehearsal
3pm Know Jamaica
4pm Musical Games
5pm Beach Walk
7pm Quiz Competition
9pm Talent Show
9:30pm Pick-up Time

Thursday
9am Registration & Orientation
10am Head Band Making
11am Fashion Show Rehearsal
2pm Fashion Show
3pm Pool Aerobics
4pm Body Painting Comp.
5pm Talk Back
8pm Magic Show
9:30pm Pick-up Time

Friday
9am Registration & Orientation
10am Beach Volleyball
12 pm Glass Bottom Boat Ride
2pm Tye & Dye
3pm Pool Games
4pm Lawn Tennis
5pm Soccer on the Beach
8pm Beach Party Night
9:30 Pick-up Time

Saturday
9am Registration & Orientation
10am Nature Walk
11am Bracelet Designs

2pm Board Games
3pm Table Tennis
4pmJamaican Game
5pm Movie Hour
7 pm Soca Night
9:30pm Pick-up Time

NEGRIL GARDENS BEACH RESORT, Norman Manley Boulevard, Tel. 876/957-4408, Fax 876/957-4374. Toll-free reservations Tel.
800/327-1991. Winter rates from $165-$190, Summer rates from $115-
$140. Credit cards accepted.

This 65-room hotel, under Sandals management, sports a new, lively
look that's especially appealing to families.

We enjoyed a stay in one of the beachside rooms (less expensive
accommodations are available across the road). Like other guests, we sunned
on the hotel's stretch of Seven Mile Beach, watching the continuous
procession of traffic. Hair braiders, a cappella singers, craftsmen, and more
worked their way along the beachfront (although they are only permitted
within a few feet of the water's edge). Children age two and under stay free.

SUNSET AT THE PALMS RESORT AND SPA, Norman Manley
Boulevard, Tel. 876/957-5350, Fax 876/957-5381. Toll-free US phone
number 800/234-1707; www.sunsetatthepalms.com. Summer from $300.
Credit cards accepted.

Negril is bordered to the east by the Great Morass, a swampland rich
with peat, a substance that was considered as a possible energy source in the
1970s when scientists studied the feasibility of mining this resource.
Environmental concerns about the possibility of damaging Negril's famous
Seven Mile Beach put a stop to the mining plans.

During the study of the Morass, these researchers lived in cabins in
Negril. Today, Sunset at the Palms (formerly Negril Cabins) utilizes those
original structures plus several new buildings and operates as a resort for
those who want to combine the luxuries of a hotel with the natural
experience of camping.

Families enjoy Swiss Family Robinson-style accommodations in
cabins perched on stilts. Lush grounds are filled with indigenous Jamaican
flora and fauna and dotted with colorful hummingbirds. The hotel offer
tours to the Royal Palms Reserve, located directly behind the property.

The hotel, which reopened in early 2005 after a major renovation, is
a favorite with ecotourists. It was the world's first hotel to receive Green
Globe Certification for environmentally sustainable tourism, and the management works to maintain that status. Rooms here are in treehouse-like
cottages amid towering royal palms. Open and airy, they have floral

bedspreads, gauzy curtains, natural-wood floors, and high ceilings. The beach is located across the street, along with activities including non-motorized watersports. Nature buffs can also take a walk with the resort's resident gardener.

Ocho Rios

   BEACHES BOSCOBEL RESORT & GOLF CLUB, Ocho Rios, Tel. 876/975-7777, Fax 876/975-7622. Toll-free reservations 800/BEACHES; www.beaches.com. Winter rates from $295, Summer rates from $315.

   Long a favorite with families (for years this was a SuperClubs property), Boscobel is now part of the Beaches family but still boasts many visitors who have vacationed here for generations. This all-inclusive resort, located 10 miles east of Ocho Rios, provides guests with free ground transfers to and from the airport. The 224-room property has a variety of activities, all of which are included in the cost of the stay. The resort's Boutique Spa has four massage rooms, sauna and steamroom, and offers massages, reflexology, facials, aromatherapy, and a full service beauty salon pampering everything from hair to toe. The resort also has a full fitness center, sports like volleyball, basketball, shuffle board, tennis, and the Sandals Golf & Country Club is not far away. Kids can join parents for complimentary golf (Children under 16 must be accompanied by an adult, and children under 10 must tee off after 12 noon). Watersports range from scuba diving and kayaking, to aqua trampolines and glass bottom boat rides. There are four freshwater pools, and a kid's pool with a waterslide.

   Besides the kids pool, there are plenty of activities for the kids to participate in. The Kids Kamp is open daily from 9 am to 10 pm, and breaks the kids up into age groups: infants 0-3, toddlers 4-7, pre-adolescent 8-12, and teens 13 and older. The age groups allow the children participate in fun and games with others in their age group, and make some friends. There is a nursery on-site at an additional charge, and private babysitters can also be hired for a fee.

   Kids will also enjoy the Xbox Game Oasis with the latest and greatest games at no charge. Like other resorts in the Beaches chain, this property features the Sesame Street characters in all types of activities and shows.

   Also at the resort is a petting zoo that kids of all ages can enjoy. Guests can interact with rabbits, goats, turtles, pigs and chickens, and can watch the birds at the on-property aviary.

   Schedule of Events, Kids Ages 4-7
   Friday
   8:45am Kids Kamp Orientation
   9am Welcome

9:15am Mousercise
10am Card making
11am Water sports
Noon Lunch
12:30pm Cool Down
1:30pm String craft
2:30pm tram games
3:30pm Awards Presentaiton
4:15pm Free Play
5pm Shower Break
6pm Dinner
7pm Movie
8:30pm "Best" of Kids Talent Show
9pm Showtime-Adults
10pm Kids Kamp closes

Saturday
8:45am Kids Kamp Orientation
9am Welcome
9:15am Tennis
10am Fun & Games
11am Pool Games
Noon Lunch
12:30pm Cool down
1:30pm Face painting
2:30pm Electronic games center
3:30pm Beach games
5pm Shower break
6pm Dinner
7pm Movie
8:30pm Party
10pm Kids Kamp closes

Sunday
8:45am Kids Kamp Orientation
9am Welcome
9:15am Mousercise
10am Nature Walk
11am Sand castle contest
Noon Lunch
12:30pm Cool down
1:30pm Arts and Crafts
2:30pm Sand craft

3:30pm Pool games
5pm Shower break
6pm Dinner
7pm Movie
10pm Kids Kamp closes

Monday
8:45am Kids Kamp Orientation
9am Welcome
9:30am Mousercise
10am T-shirt painting (bring your own shirt)
11am Sun, sea, and sand
Noon Lunch
1:30pm Bracelet making
2:30pm Fashion show rehearsal
3:30pm Sing-a-Long
4:15pm Soca dance class
5pm Shower break
6pm Dinner
7pm Movie
8:30pm Storytelling/Reading
10pm Kids Kamp closes

Tuesday
8:45am Kids Kamp Orientation
9am Welcome
9:30am Tennis
10am Arts and Crafts
11am Glass bottom boat ride
Noon Lunch
12:30pm Cool down
1:30pm Nature walk
2pm Pool games
3:30pm Fashion show
4:15pm Ring toss
5pm Shower break
6pm Dinner
7pm Movie
8:30pm Clowning around
10pm Kids Kamp closes

Wednesday
8:45am Kids Kamp Orientation

9am Welcome
9:30am Mousercise
10am Let's bake
11am Watersports
Noon Lunch
1:30pm Ring ding
2:30pm Electronic games center
3:30pm Magic, magic, magic
4:15pm Talent show rehearsal
5pm Shower break
6pm Dinner
7pm Movie
8:30pm Pajama party
10pm Kids Kamp closes

Thursday ("Jamaica Day")
8:45am Kids Kamp Orientation
9am Welcome
9:15am "Jamaica Say" (Talk "Jamaican")
10am T-shirt printing
11am Pool games
Noon Lunch
12:30pm Cool down
1:30pm Sports day
3:30pm Talent show
4:15pm Reggae dance class
5pm Shower break
6pm Dinner
7pm Games evening
8pm Movie
10pm Kids Kamp closes

Kids Kamp Activities: 8-12 years
Friday
8:45am Kids Kamp Orientation
9am Welcome
9:15am Tennis
9:45am Card making
10:45am Sun, sea, and sand
Noon Lunch
1pm Chill out
2pm Team games
3:30pm Awards presentation

4pm Pool games
5pm Shower break
6pm Dinner
7pm Movie
8:30pm Kids' Talent Show
9pm Guest and Staff Talent Show
10pm Kids Kamp closes

Saturday
8:45am Kids Kamp Orientation
9am Welcome
9:15am Sand craft
10am Pool Olympics
Noon Lunch
12:30pm Chill out
1:30pm Treasure hunt
2:30pm Basketball
3:15pm Watersports
4:15pm Electronic games center
5pm Shower break
6pm Kids dinner
7pm Movie
8:30pm Bingo party
10pm Kids Kamp closes

Sunday
8:45am Kids Kamp Orientation
9am Welcome
9:15am Tennis
10am Nature Walk
11am Pool games
Noon Lunch
12:30pm Chill out
2pm T-shirt cutting and design
3pm Sand castle contest
4pm Sun, sea, and sand
5pm Shower break
6pm Dinner
7pm Movie
8:30pm Welcome party
10pm Kids Kamp closes

Monday
8:45am Kids Kamp Orientation
9am Welcome
9:15am String craft
10:15am Snorkeling lessons
11am Snorkeling
Noon Lunch
12:30pm Chill out
1:30pm BoscoBall
2:30pm Pool games
3:30pm Sing-a-Long
4:15pm Fashion show rehearsal
5pm Shower break
6pm Dinner
7pm Movie
8:30pm Party
10pm Kids Kamp closes

Tuesday
8:45am Kids Kamp Orientation
9am Welcome
9:15am Jewelry making
11am Watersports
Noon Lunch
12:30pm Chill out
1:30pm Scavenger hunt
2:30pm Electronic games center
3:30pm Fashion show
4:15pm Dance class
5pm Shower break
6pm Dinner
7pm Movie
8:30pm Clowning around
10pm Kids Kamp closes

Wednesday
8:45am Kids Kamp Orientation
9am Welcome
9:15am Tennis
9:45am T-shirt printing
11am Glass bottom boat ride
Noon Lunch
12:30pm chill out

1:30pm Nature walk
2:30pm Pool Olympics
3:30pm Magic, magic, magic
4:15pm Talent show rehearsal
5pm Shower break
6pm Dinner
7pm Movie
8:30pm Fun & Games at poolside
10pm Kids Kamp closes

Thursday
8:45am Kids Kamp Orientation
9am Welcome
8:15am "Jamaica Say"
10am Boscoball
11am Watersports
Noon Lunch
12:30pm Chill out
1:30pm Jamaica Play
3:30pm Talent show
4:15pm Jamaica Sway
5pm Shower break
6pm Dinner
7pm Movie
8:30pm Island fashion show
9pm Jamaica Way
10pm Kids Kamp closes

Teen Activities: 13-17 years
Sunday
10am String Craft
11am Scavenger Hunt
12 noon Fashion Show Rehearsal
3:30pmBanana Boat Ride
4:30pm Boscoplay
5:30pm Pool Tournament
7pm Break
8:30pm Showtime

Monday
10am Orientation
10:30am Pool Volleyball
11:30am Water Sports

Lunch
2pm Pool Games
3:30pm Fashion Show Rehearsal
4pm Pool Basketball
5pm Chill Craze
7pm Break
7pm Teens Dinner
8pm Karaoke Party
9pm Showtime

Tuesday
10am Orientation
10:30am Jewellery Making
11am Signature Hunt
11:30am Hobie Cat/ Banana Boat/Tricycle Rides
1pm Lunch
2pm Lunchtime Spin
3:30pm Fashion Show
4:30pm Ping Pong
7pm Dinner break
8:30pm Clowning Around

Wednesday
10am Orientation
10:30am Tie-Die Class
11:30am Water Sports
12:30pm Pool Games
1pm Lunch break
2pm Lunch Time Spin
3pm Pool Tournament
4:30pm Guess the Music/Ring Toss
7pm Dinner Break
8:30pm Fun & Games at the Poolside

Thursday
10am Orientation
10:30am Pool Volleyball/Art& Craft
11am Glass Bottom Boat Ride/ Water Sports
12 noon Lunch
2pm Lunchtime Spin
2:30pm Talent Show Rehearsal
3:30pm Jamaica Sway
4pm Chill Time

5pm Pool /Tennis Tournament
7pm Teens Dinner
8:30pm Island Fashion Show

Friday
10am Orientation
10:30am Scavenger Hunt
11:15am Water Sports
12noon Lunch
2pm Pool Basketball
3pm Electronic Games/Soccer
4pm Shuffle Board
5pm Basketball Match
7pm Teens Dinner
8:30pm Talent Show

Saturday
10am Orientation
10:30am WaterSports/Art & Craft
11:30am Basketball Match
12:30 pm Lunch Break
1pm Table Tennis Tournament
2pm Crazy Pool Games
3:30pm Shuffle Board
4:30pm Teens Say
6pm Dinner
8:30pm Pajama Party/Movie

FDR PEBBLES, Trelawny, Jamaica, Tel. 876/617-2500-4, Fax 876/ 617-2512. Toll-free US reservations number Tel. 888/FDR-KIDS, www.fdrholidays.com. Winter rates $810-$1140 for three nights, per person; Summer rates from $810-870 for three nights, per person. Credit cards accepted.

FDR Pebbles is a great place for families who want to make sure that their vacation is fun for every member. At this all-inclusive resort, there are separate programs for children and teens, so that the kids can make friends in their own age group.

The Children's Center is open from 7:30 am until 10 pm and provides many activities to keep the young ones busy. Pebbles' Vacation Nannies supervise the kids while they watch movies, play video games, do arts and crafts in the Small World Kids Club, and take part in the scheduled activities. Other activities include, fishing, shell-collecting, beach games, talent shows, playground time, water sports, Pebbles' special Bubblemaker Scuba Diving program, sports, board games, and a visit to the nearby crocodile farm.

Teens can enjoy activities with kids in their own age group at the Teens Club. Here, they can play games like ping pong, pool, and checkers. The Sports Program teach kids basketball, tennis, volleyball, windsurfing, sailing, and snorkeling. This program also takes kids on local hikes. The Discover Scuba Diving Program is a half-day course that teaches diving in a pool and takes kids out on their first dive. In the teen program, kids can also play beach volleyball, take glass bottom boat rides, kayak, play beach games, participate in reggae tie-dye, bar-b-que, take boat trips, cook-out, fish, enjoy ocean trampolines, go camping, use the Cyber Café, play computer games, take reggae dance lessons, get to know other visitors of their age from around the world, and many more things.

FRANKLYN D. RESORT (FDR), P.O. Box 201, Main Street, Runaway Bay, St. Ann, Jamaica. Tel. 876/973-4591, Fax 876/973-4600. Toll-free reservations Tel. 800/654-1FDR or 888/FDR-KIDS; www.fdrholidays.com. Rates from $560 in summer, from $600 in winter. Credit cards accepted.

See Chapter 3, "Best Places to Stay," for a detailed write-up.

ROOMS OCHO RIOS, Main St. Tel. 876/ 974-6632, Fax 305/666-5536. Toll-free US phone number; www.roomsresorts.com. Winter rates from $94-$143. Credit cards accepted.

Adjacent to Sunset Jamaica Grande Resort, this SuperClubs-owned hotel isn't an all-inclusive resort like those you'd expect from SuperClubs but, instead, is just, well, rooms. It's mostly a base for business travelers but provides a good location for families, too, who don't want to be locked into an all-inclusive plan. The room rate includes Continental breakfast. For long-time Jamaica travelers, this property was formerly Club Jamaica. The family-friendly hotel offers wireless internet access; rooms have ocean views and all the basics, decorated in tropical tones. It's definitely an economical choice for independent-minded travelers who would rather sample the town's many restaurants without being tied to an all-inclusive plan.

SUNSET JAMAICA GRANDE RESORT, Tel. 876/974-2201, Fax 876/974-5378. Toll-free US phone number 800/234-1707; www.sunsetjamaicagrande.com. Winter rates from $320.. Credit cards accepted.

Jamaica's largest conference hotel (formerly the Renaissance Jamaica Grande), is right in Ocho Rios and bustles with groups thanks to its expansive conference center. It was closed for a major renovation through much of 2004 but has reopened with rooms brightened with tropical colors.

Guest accommodations are divided between two high-rise towers; the best views are found in the north tower. The beach here is small, so most guests spend their time at the huge pool, which is built as a replica of Dunn's River Falls. Kids are kept busy in the complimentary supervised program.

What Can We Do Now?

Montego Bay

Several great houses, which once oversaw huge sugar plantations, are today notable visitor attractions. **Rose Hall**, Tel. 876/953-2323 one of the best-known and is an easy afternoon visit for Montego Bay guests. This was once the home of the notorious Annie Palmer, better known as the White Witch. According to legend, Annie murdered several of her husbands and her slave lovers. Readers who would like to know more about the tales of Rose Hall can read the novel The White Witch of Rose Hall. The guided tour is excellent for older children but the recounting of the murders (including the burying of a live baby up to his neck near an ant hill) is too grisly for those under 10.

Jamaica may be the land of sun and fun but it's a birders' paradise as well. Bird lovers find one of the Caribbean's most unique sites at the **Rocklands Feeding Station**, Tel. 876/952-2009, in the village of Anchovy. This was the home of the late Lisa Salmon, Jamaica's best-known ornithologist. Her home is a veritable bird sanctuary surrounded by clouds of grassquits, saffron finches, and, most especially, hummingbirds.

Salmon moved to the verdant hillside in April 1952 and found the site, located a short drive from the beaches of Montego Bay, filled with feathered friends. Through the years, Salmon worked as a bird advocate, achieving a limit on Jamaica's bird hunting season. In 1959 she opened the bird sanctuary and since that time travelers from around the world have hand-fed the regular guests of this bird diner. Tiny finches flutter around outstretched palms filled with birdseed while fast-as-lightning hummingbirds drink from a hand-held bottle of sugar water.

Visitors are invited between 3:30 and 5pm daily.

Next to Half Moon, **Rocky Point Stables**, Tel. 876/953-2286, offers horseback rides and lessons as well as pony rides.

Negril

Negril visitors don't have to venture all the way to Ocho Rios to enjoy waterfalls. Western Jamaica has a much quieter alternative in **Y.S. Falls**, www.ysfalls.com. These spectacular waterfalls cascade in steps through tropical forest. As spectacular (and far less crowded) as Dunn's River Falls, Y.S. is a Jamaican attraction that has remained untouched by hassling vendors and long lines. At the top, swimmers enjoy clear waters under a canopy of fern.

Nearby in the community of Black River, enjoy the **Black River Safari Cruise**, Tel. 876/965-2513, a popular day trip for Negril vacationers looking for a little respite from sun and sand. This hour and a half long tour takes travelers up the Black River, at 44 miles the longest river in Jamaica. The waters here are home to snook and tarpon, some reaching as large as 200 pounds. You may see spear fishermen with a snorkel, mask and speargun, swimming in the dark water stained by peat deposits. The fisherman's canoes are hand-hewn and burned out using a generations-old technique. Among their catch are tiny brine shrimp, sold by women in the St. Elizabeth parish along the roadside. Highly salted and spiced, these are a popular snack with locals and visitors.

The biggest attraction on the Black River are the **crocodiles**. Once hunted, these crocodiles are now protected but still remain wary. These reptiles can live as long as 100 years, so long that some have become known by local residents. One 15-foot-long specimen named Lester is seen nightly.

For a look at the countryside around Negril the way it used to be, consider at day at **Belvedere Estate**, Tel. 876/694-1004, one of the first sugar cane plantations on the island. Located an hour from town, this estate is set up as a living museum with costumed guides to show you the ruins of the 1800's great house, the sugar factory, and the boiler where the juice of the cane is made into brown sugar. In the craft village, watch a weaver make coconut palms into baskets, talk to an herbalist about Jamaica's bountiful herbs, visit a canoe maker, and have a taste of island bread at the bakery. A traditional Jamaican lunch is included with the tour.

Ocho Rios

In Ocho Rios, the most popular attraction (one that just about every cruise ship passenger and resort guest enjoys—sometimes what seems like must be all at one time) is **Dunn's River Falls**. This spectacular waterfall is actually a series of falls that cascade from the mountains to the sea. Here you don't just view the falls, but you climb up the cascading water. Led by a sure-footed Jamaican guide (who wears everyone's cameras slung around his neck), groups work their way up the falls hand-in-hand like a human daisy chain. Be prepared to get wet and have fun, but don't expect a quiet, private getaway. This is Jamaica for the masses, and, no matter what day of the week, the masses do come. At the end of the climb, you'll be deposited into a hectic market for another opportunity to buy crafts, carvings, and the ubiquitous T-shirt.

Or how would your family like the chance to swim with dolphins? **Dolphin Cove** (876/974-5335, www.dolphincovejamaica.com), adjacent to Dunn's River Falls, offers dolphin swims as well as lower-priced dolphin encounters for ages 8 and up, dolphin touch programs for ages 6 and over, or simple admission the grounds, which also include a short nature walk. Advance reservations are required.

An excellent stop in Ocho Rios for families looking to get off the beaten path is **Cranbrook Flower Forest**, west of Ocho Rios at Laughlands, one mile off North Coast Highway (sign on left one mile past Chukka Cove), Tel. 876-770-8071. This beautiful park, a recent addition to this area's tourist offerings, is a must-see for anyone who wants to experience the lush beauty away from the crowds. The park is the private creation of Ivan Linton, who has pampered the plants of this former plantation for over two decades. The day we journeyed here, children were playing in the river as their mothers did the weeks' laundry in the shallow water of the river. Other activities include bird watching, pond fishing, croquet, donkey rides and volleyball. (Be sure to wear good walking shoes for the hike at Cranbrook. On our recent visit, we hiked up to the waterfalls over very slippery rocks. It's well worth the hike.) Kids can fish in the park's ponds or even take donkey rides.

West of Ocho Rios in the town of Oracabessa, 007 fans can visit the **James Bond Beach**. Located near Ian Fleming's home, Goldeneye, the beach has plenty of options for a day of activity: waverunners, helicopter tours, and horseback rides as well as beach bar and grill.

If you're serious about horseback riding, check out the **Chukka Cove Equestrian Centre**, Tel. 876/972-2506, between Runaway Bay and Ocho Rios. Well known for its world-class polo matches, the center also offers guided horseback trips along the beach and in the mountains. The polo horses were exercised in the sea, an activity the tourists saw and wanted to take part in so today visitors can ride on horseback right into the sea.

Beyond horseback riding, Chukka has expanded and now offers a whole range of adventure tours. From its location outside of Montego Bay, **Chukka Blue Adventure Tours**, Tel. 876/953-5619, www.chukkablue.com, offers both biking and ATV tours. There's a minimum age of 16 on the ATV tours. The noisy ATVs jostle and splash their way along trails on a 10-mile ride through the hills before returning so visitors can take a dip in the sea. Also in Montego Bay, Chukka Blue offers a popular canopy tour, allowing visitors to zipline high in the trees.

For visitors in Ocho Rios, **Chukka Cove Adventure Tours**, Tel. 876/ 972-2506, www.chukkacaribbean.com, offers a half-day bike tour through St. Ann and the village of Mt. Zion with several stops and even snorkeling at the end. They also offer an ATV tour. There's a minimum age of six for biking, 16 for ATVs.

For something a little quieter, **Coyaba River Garden and Museum**, Shaw Park, Tel. 876/974-6235, is a good place to bring your young history buff. Exhibits start with pre-Columbian history and follow through the development of the island.

What Can We Buy?

This island has a wealth of **arts and crafts**, everything from colorful paintings to folk art wood carvings, not to mention batik T-shirts and crocheted tams in Rastafarian colors (yellow, red and green). Shopping at the roadside stands or on the beach involves negotiating of price. It's part of the fun.

Our favorite purchases are the **woodcarvings**, both freestanding and bas relief of local animal life, faces, fish, and just about everything else you can imagine. The finest pieces are carved from lignum vitae, or wood of life, a pale hardwood that is so dense it won't float. If you get a woodcarving, don't forget to ask the artist to sign it for you. The craftsmen have great pride in their work and most are happy to oblige. Prices range from about $5 for very small carvings to $20 for masks, more for larger items.

Montego Bay is also home of the **Craft Market**. Many travelers avoid the market because of fears of high-pressure sales, but we have found the market delightful. A friendly "good morning," abstaining from photos until a purchase (no matter how small) is made, and general good manners will go far with the salespeople. On a recent visit, one cheerful vendor gave us a small basket as a gift. After shopping, take a break with a soft drink or "sky juice" (like our snow cone) sold from pushcarts beneath the shade trees.

Some small purchases include small straw baskets, perfect for a youngster's jewelry and prized possessions ($2), tiny straw purses ($4), friendship bracelets in rasta colors ($1), coffee bean necklaces ($2), and bamboo bangles ($4).

For fixed prices, head to the **shopping centers**. In Montego Bay, the top shopping centers are City Centre, a block-long collection of duty-free shops, the new (and high-priced) Half Moon Shopping Village, and our favorite, the Holiday Village Shopping Centre near Holiday Inn SunSpree. Look for Bob Marley T-shirts, rasta tams, woodcarvings, straw baskets, and more.

In Negril, the Hi-Lo Shopping Center offers a good selection of souvenir, liquor, music, and sportwear stores. The Hi-Lo grocery itself is an excellent shopping stop; pop in to purchase spices, hot sauces, and Blue Mountain coffee at prices far lower than you'll see in the hotel gift shops.

Ocho Rios is home to the Taj Mahal Shopping Centre, a complex of fine duty-free shops and other stores that sell souvenir items, liquor, and Blue Mountain coffee.

In every resort area, be prepared for numerous offers by higglers, Jamaica's word for peddlers. Also be prepared for offers of "something special." Ganja or marijuana is widespread, but purchase or use of the drug is strictly illegal. Talk with your teens before a trip to Jamaica. Teenagers—especially boys—will be approached by salesmen in the larger resort areas.

A very legal agricultural product is **Jamaican Blue Mountain coffee**, considered one of the finest coffees in the world. Gift shops at the resorts and the airport sell the coffee in small burlap gift bags for about $1 US per ounce (less than half the price found in American coffee shops). You can find the coffee even cheaper at local markets.

What Else Do We Need to Know?

Banking. Know before you go that ATM cards from US and Canadian banks are not accepted by Jamaican machines. You can obtain a cash advance on major credit cards at the banks, but this is a slow process (it took us close to two hours to obtain money in Negril recently). Banks are open 9am to 2pm Monday through Thursday, 9am to 4pm Friday.

Currency. The Jamaican dollar is the official tender; its exchange rate fluctuates frequently but at press time was about $1US=48. US dollars are accepted throughout the island.

Driving. Driving is British style, on the left.

Electricity. The island uses 110volts/50 cycles, although 220 is used in some of the hotels. Adapters are not required for North American appliances.

Information. For questions or brochures, call the Jamaica Tourist Board, Tel. 800/233-4JTB.

Island Report Card	
Transportation to island	A+
Transportation around island	B
Family Resorts	A+
Family Restaurants	A
Friendly atmosphere	A
Activities for kids	B+
Weather	A
New cultures to experience	A
Safety	B

Information on Island. You will find several tourist offices across the island: Black River (Hendricks Building, 2 High Street, Tel. 876/965-2074), Kingston (64 Knutsford Blvd., Tel. 876/929-9200), Montego Bay (Cornwall Beach, Tel. 876/952-4425), Negril (Coral Seas Plaza, Tel. 876/957-4243), Ocho Rios (Ocean Village Shopping Centre, Tel. 876/974-2582), and Port Antonio (City Centre Plaza, Tel. 876/993-3051).

Language. English is the official language, although you'll frequently hear the Jamaican patois on the street, a combination of several languages.

Time. Jamaica is on Eastern Standard Time and does not observe Daylight Savings Time.

Website. Get more Jamaica information at: www.visitjamaica.com.

Chapter 15

PUERTO RICO

Puerto Rico is an easy destination for families. It's a short airplane ride, just 2-1/2 hours from Miami and under four hours from New York. As a commonwealth of the US, travel here is easy and hassle free. No money to be exchanged. No immigration lines to endure.

And yet Puerto Rico has a culture as vast and exotic as those found anywhere in the Caribbean. The island can give young travelers a chance to try out their Spanish phrases. Or it can provide an opportunity to sample some Old World dishes spiced with a New World flavor. And best of all, this island offers a full menu of attractions to please every member of the family with fun that ranges from shopping to snorkeling, from historic forts to heady rainforests.

Your visit to Puerto Rico will likely begin in the capital city of San Juan. Pulsating with a big city atmosphere, San Juan is one of the most modern cities in the Caribbean and a hub for American Airlines. It's so large that it's divided into several districts. Tourists typically visit Condado, Isla Verde, and Old San Juan, the historical heart of the city. Here you'll find buildings so old and quaint they look more like part of a movie set than part of a modern downtown district.

But beyond the boundaries of San Juan, the sounds change to the slap of waves on the honey-colored shore or the peek of the tiny coqui (co-kee), a frog that's a national symbol of Puerto Rico. (It's said that the coqui can survive only on the island, so to be as Puerto Rican as a coqui is a declaration of national pride.) Here over 200 miles of coastline welcomes families with a hearty "Buenos dias."

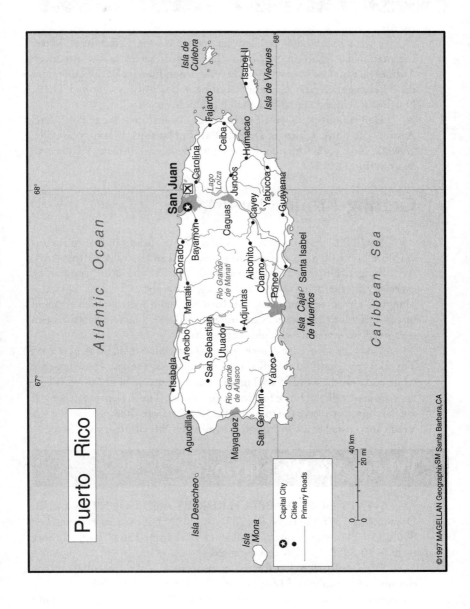

Puerto Rico

Atlantic Ocean

Caribbean Sea

Isla Desecheo

Isla Mona

Isla de Culebra

Isabel II

Isla de Vieques

Fajardo

Humacao

Ceiba

Carolina

San Juan

Lago Loiza

Juncos

Yabucoa

Cayey

Guayama

Caguas

Bayamón

Dorado

Aibonito

Coamo

Santa Isabel

Manatí

Rio Grande de Manati

Adjuntas

Ponce

Isla Caja de Muertos

Isabela

Arecibo

San Sebastián

Utuado

Rio Grande de Añasco

Yauco

Aguadilla

Mayagüez

San Germán

Capital City
Cities
Primary Roads

40 km
20 mi

©1997 MAGELLAN GeographixSM Santa Barbara,CA

68°

67°

68°

68°

Are We There Yet?

By Air

Puerto Rico boasts excellent air service via the Luis Muñoz Marin International Airport in San Juan. The airport serves as the American Airlines hub for Caribbean flights. Service to San Juan is also available from the other major carriers. Carnival, Continental, USAirways, United, Delta, Northwest, United, and TWA each have flights to San Juan.

Daily nonstop service to San Juan is available from Atlanta, Baltimore, Boston, Charlotte, Chicago, Dallas, Detroit, Hartford, Miami, Nashville, Newark, New York, Orlando, Philadelphia, Raleigh-Durham, Tampa, and Washington D.C.

Getting Around the Island

You'll find that you have many of the same options in Puerto Rico as you do at home. Rental cars from the major agencies are available from AAA, Avis, Budget, Discount, Hertz, National, Thrifty, and other companies, especially in the San Juan area. Driving is on the right and signage is bilingual. However, realize that San Juan is a major metropolitan area and just as difficult to maneuver as any other city its size. The Old San Juan area is especially congested, with old, narrow streets.

Taxis are a popular choice, especially within San Juan. A new Taxi Turisticos program sets specified rates within certain zones. These taxis are white and bear the words Taxi Turisticos and a drawing of El Morro. These taxis are an excellent choice for first-time visitors. The drivers have received special training to serve the tourist zones. A drive from the airport to the Isla Verde area costs $8; a trip from the airport to Old San Juan runs $16.

Where Are We Staying?

HYATT DORADO BEACH RESORT AND COUNTRY CLUB, Dorado, Tel. 787/796-1234, Fax 787/796-2022. Toll-free reservations Tel. 800/233-1234; www.hyatt.com. Winter rates from $365-$640, summer from $170-$450. Credit cards accepted.

For families looking for the comfort of a resort that offers classic elegance and simplicity, Hyatt Dorado Beach fits the bill. With its low rise buildings overlooking a wide stretch of palm-lined beach, Hyatt Dorado Beach exudes a 50s feel in the finest tradition of Laurance Rockefeller's former Rockresorts.

The simple guest rooms are decorated in West Indian style, with furniture inspired by Caribbean antiques including an armoire/TV center, daybed that folds out to a double sleeper, and, in second floor rooms, carved four poster beds with white linens. Standard amenities include AC, cable TV, minibar, in-room safe, direct dial telephone, electronic locks, and a marble bath and dressing area with sit-down vanity. Rooms open out to a balcony or a patio with views of the ocean, golf course, or, in the older three-story section, the swimming pool. Seventeen casita rooms feature split-level elegance that includes a private lawn and marble shower beneath a clear skylight.

Nature walks on the property, featuring 600 species of tropical plants, are available. The resort features two 18-hole golf courses designed by Robert Trent Jones Sr. Seven tennis courts, some lit for night play, are available. A tour desk arranges excursions into Old San Juan, El Yunque Rain Forest, Rio Camuy caves, shopping in the nearby town of Dorado, and other tours. At night, activity centers around the casino.

PARADISUS PUERTO RICO, Rio Grande, Tel. 787/809-1770, Fax 787/809-1785. Toll-free reservations Tel. 888/95-MELIA; www.paradisus-puerto-rico.com/. Winter and summer from $460-$635. Credit cards accepted.

Paradisus Puerto Rico is the first all-inclusive resort in Puerto Rico. Packages begin with one of the resort's 500 suites, all housed in low-rise, two-story buildings. Junior suites offer a combined living and sleeping area as well as a private terrace or verandah. Cool marble flooring leads from the living area into the marble bath, which has a soaking tub and separate shower. All suites have an in-room safe, coffee maker, minibar and satellite TV.

Want to upgrade? Your family can be super pampered with the Royal Service. An exclusive concierge helps book tours and answer questions. You'll also have a private lounge, butler service, a daily newspaper, exclusive check-in and check-out, and what has to qualify as the dreamiest of all room amenities: a pillow menu. No more of that Princess and the Pea feeling from sleeping on a too fluffy hotel pillow if that's not what you want.

And for pampering with plenty of elbow room, there are five garden villas, 12 honeymoon suites and is a Presidential Suite with its own swimming pool.

Puerto Rico is well-known for its golf courses, and this new property fits right into the island's offerings thanks to its neighboring Coco Beach Golf and Country Club. The 48,000-square-foot ocean view clubhouse (the Caribbean's largest) has a lawn with views of El Yunque rainforest. Two championship courses designed by Tom Kite and Bruce Besse offer special greens fees for resort guests as well as preferred tee times, private lessons and storage of clubs.

Landlubbers find plenty of other diversions on property: volleyball, table tennis, tennis, bicycles, billiards and more.

THE VILLAS AT PALMAS, Humacao, Puerto Rico. Tel. 787/852-6000, Fax 787/852-6370. Toll-free reservations Tel. 800/PALMAS-3; www.palmasresort.com. Winter rates from $249 for double occupancy, summer from $160-$195. Credit cards accepted.

For vacationers looking to getaway from the glitz of San Juan, the Villas at Palmas is an excellent choice. Located 45 minutes from the capital city, the resort lies tucked on the Caribbean side of the island near the town of Humacao. Actually a compendium of resorts that range from standard hotel rooms to a bed and breakfast inn to luxury condominiums, Palmas is a city in itself, with a staff of over 500 employees.

Although three and a half miles of groomed beach (plus another six miles of nearly deserted beach) tempt vacationers to soak up sun and sometimes rolling surf, the sports facilities offer plenty of opportunities to stay busy. The Golf Club features a championship course designed by Gary Player with holes offering views of El Yunque rain forest, the sea, and the nearby island of Vieques. The largest tennis center in the Caribbean has classes for players of every level.

Children 3-13 find plenty of fun at the Palmas Adventure Club. The daily program offers a full slate of activities: Olympic beach games, swimming, kayaking, miniature golf, water sports, hikes, talent shows, arts and crafts, pony rides, fishing, tennis, and a play ground. The program is available on a half or full day basis. Drop your child off in the morning or afternoon for the half day or the full day program (it's cheaper to buy a 5-day package, if the vacation lasts longer than a few days). Babysitting is also available by appointment only.

WESTIN RIO MAR BEACH RESORT AND CASINO, Rio Grande, Tel. 787/888-6000, Fax 787/888-6600. Toll-free US reservations Tel. 800/4-RIOMAR; www.westinriomar.com. Winter rates from $399, summer rates from $399. Credit cards accepted.

One of Puerto Rico's most lavish hotels, the Westin is a 600-room resort located on the northeast coast. You name it, you'll find it here: two championship golf courses, a casino, 13 tennis courts, two oceanfront swimming pools, watersports, 11 restaurants, and more.

Club Iguana is named for the first residents of the Westin Rio Mar's two golf courses. This supervised children's program is housed in a three-room camp center with a TV room (which converts to a sleeping room for late night campers), an arts and crafts room, and a playroom. Fun includes arts and crafts, sailing clinics, tennis clinics, beginner through advanced golf lessons, horseback riding, volleyball, and beach activities.

The camp is available as a full- or half-day session. The full-day program runs from 9am to 3pm and includes lunch and a T-shirt. The half-day program runs in three-hour blocks, from either 9am to noon or noon to 3pm, and includes snacks. The Night Time Fun program runs from 5 pm to midnight, and lets kids enjoy a good dinner, arts and crafts, ice cream, movies, talent shows, and more.

Recently the Westin Rio Mar added the Rio Mar X-Perience, aimed at pre-teens and teens ages 11-17. "As a popular destination for families, we've had plenty of opportunities to see that teenagers and parents sometimes need a break from each other – especially when trying to relax on vacation," said Drew Toth, Director of Marketing & Sales for The Westin Rio Mar Beach Golf Resort & Spa. "X-Perience is a great way to guarantee teens and their parents alike will enjoy their Caribbean getaway."

The program offers on-site fun as well as off-site adventure including rain forest power walks/hikes, river kayaking, snorkeling, horseback riding and much more. On property, the program is headquartered in a teen center that combines the atmosphere of a game room and cafe, including plasma televisions, music videos, karaoke, pool, ping pong, X-Box (monitors and games), sports equipment, and teen essentials like smoothies, sodas, lattes, snacks and more at X-Perience "bar." The club is open Wednesday through Saturday from 4 pm to 10 pm.

WYNDHAM EL CONQUISTADOR RESORT & COUNTRY CLUB, 1000 El Conquistador, Tel. 787/863-1000, Fax 787/863-6586. Toll-free reservations Tel. 800/WYNDHAM; www.wyndham.com. Winter rates $395-$495, Summer from $215. Credit cards accepted.

Perched atop a 300-foot cliff, this is one of the grandest resorts in the region. With 918 guest rooms, it's not the place for those looking for privacy and to get away from the crowds, but you'll find just about everything else at this $250 million resort. Choose from an 18-hole championship golf course, a private marina with rental boats and charters for deep-sea fishing, scuba facilities, six swimming pools, seven tennis courts, a nightclub, casino, fitness center, salon, and luxurious shops. Not to mention a 100-acre private island, Palomina, where guests can be whisked on complimentary ferries. On secluded Palomina, families can enjoy snorkeling, nature trails, and siestas in hammocks stretched between tall palms.

The kids' program, Camp Coqui, is designed for kids age three to nine and nine to 13. This program is one of the most unique in the Caribbean. The kids' program is located on Palomino Island, just offshore and accessible by water taxi. With its own nurse located on the island and always in touch with the mainland by radio, the kids' program includes activities such as watersports, nature hikes, and island crafts. Special overnight programs are also available and give kids the chance to feel like Robinson Crusoe. The fee for the full-day program includes lunch, a travel journal, a duffel bag, and a T-shirt; a half-day program runs from 9-1, and does not include lunch.

What Can We Do Now?

Old San Juan is dotted with museums and historic sites. The best known is **Fuerte San Felipe del Morro** or **El Morro**, Old San Juan, Tel. 787/ 729-6754. This fort, one of the most photographed sites in the Caribbean, contains a museum and is administered by the National Park Service. On its grounds, the Cuartel de Ballaja, once Spanish troop quarters, now houses the Museum of the Americas.

The park is open daily from 9am to 5pm; there is no admission charge. Start with a video on the site then take a self-guided tour. You'll find a map at the entrances, and exhibits throughout the park are posted in both English and Spanish. Even if you're not a history buff, this site is a family place where you can look out on the sea and enjoy a gentle tradewind. Bring along your camera for this scenic stop.

Nearby, **Casa Blanca**, 1 Sebastian Street, Old San Juan, contains exhibits on 16th and 17th century life and on its most famous residents: Ponce de Leon and his family. (Actually Ponce de Leon died before the home was completed.) Built in the 1520s, the home was the city's first fortress and is now open for tours Wednesday through Sunday.

Puerto Rico is also rich in natural attractions, including what is called one of the finest cave systems in the world. The **Rio Camuy Cave Park**, Route 102, Tel. 787/898-3100, located 2-1/2 hours west of San Juan, was formed by large underground rivers. Today the park includes a new visitors center with reception area and cafeteria and a theater with AV presentation. Visitors reach cave level by trolley then follow walkways on a 45-minute guided tour.

Another natural attraction is **El Yunque National Forest**, Highway 3 east between San Juan and Fajardo to Route 191 near Luquillo, Tel. 787/ 888-1810, the only tropical rainforest in the US National Forest Service. Forty-five minutes east of San Juan, the rainforest boasts 240 species of trees and flowers, including 20 varieties of orchids and 50 varieties of ferns. Walking trails carve through the dense forest, and guided tours are available.

Kids also enjoy the **Children's Museum or Museo del Niño**, 150 Cristo, San Juan, 787/722-3791. Young visitors enter the museum through the legs of a large wooden figure then enjoy hands-on displays and activities from a village of playhouses to a "Visit the Dentist" exhibit where children can play dentist.

Sports & Recreation

If your interests run more toward eco-tourism, you're in luck in Puerto Rico as well. One of our favorite excursions is a snorkel trip out to **Monkey Island**. More fun than a barrel of monkeys, this island of curious primates is located off the southeast coast of Puerto Rico. It's a sanctuary for hundreds of monkeys, and access to the island is prohibited. Visitors cannot actually step on land, but you can snorkel around the fringes of the island while excited primates hoot and holler at the intrusion. We found the snorkeling here excellent as well, full of colorful fans and bright corals.

Baseball buffs are in the right place. Watch major league stars during the Winter League, from November through January. The games take place nearly nightly in San Juan's Hiram Bithorn Stadium and tickets are just $6 and under.

What Can We Buy?

Shopping is a major activity for Puerto Rico visitors. Duty-free shopping is found at the Luis Muñoz Marin International Airport and at factory outlet shops in Old San Juan.

If you're looking for jewelry or factory outlets, check out the shops on Calle Christo and Calle Fortaleza in Old San Juan.

If you're looking for an island product, popular purchases are cuatros (small handmade guitars), mundillo (bobbin lace), and santos (hand carved religious figures).

What Else Do We Need to Know?

Currency. The US dollar is the official currency.

Doctors. In an emergency, call 911. The doctors in Puerto Rico meet the same standards as those on the mainland of the United States.

Driving. Driving is on the right side. Most road signs are in both English and Spanish.

Electricity: The island uses 110 volts, 60 cycles.

Language. Both Spanish and English are the official language of Puerto Rico. You'll find plenty of English spoken in the resort areas and in San Juan but in the smaller communities most conversation is in Spanish.

Information. Contact the Puerto Rico Tourism Company, Tel. 800/866-7827 in US, 800/667-0394 in Canada. Island Information: The Luis Muñoz Marin International Airport has an excellent tourist information booth near the baggage claim area.

Time. Puerto Rico is located in the Atlantic Time Zone, one hour ahead of Eastern. The island does not observe Daylight Savings Time.

Website. Get more information on Puerto Rico at www.gotopuertorico.com.

Island Report Card

Transportation to island	A+
Transportation around island	A-
Family Resorts	A
Family Restaurants	A-
Friendly atmosphere	A
Activities for kids	B+
Weather	A
New cultures for kids to experience	A
Safety	B+

Chapter 16

ST. KITTS & NEVIS

They're often referred to as "the way the Caribbean used to be." Life is quiet and unspoiled on this two island nation where most guests stay in small, locally owned plantation inns that recall the heritage of the Caribbean with period antiques, wide porches to pick up gentle trade winds, and an atmosphere that appeals to travelers who are independent and ready to strike out on their own.

Rugged and tropical, both islands are excellent destinations for hikers, birders, and nature lovers. St. Kitts is the larger of the two, spanning 68 square miles. The island covers 23 miles in length and at its widest point five miles across. For its size, St. Kitts offers varying terrains that range from semiarid to rain forest, from flat to nearly impassable. Most of the population lives on St. Kitts with a large percentage in the capital city of Basseterre (pronounced bos-tear). Modern life and ancient history live hand-in-hand as the island is sprinkled with historic sites that date back both to pre-history and to the days of colonization.

Development has, thankfully, been slow on St. Kitts. Although the island has one all-inclusive property, most hotels are locally owned and managed and provide a genuine Caribbean experience. They're found sprinkled throughout the island, both at seaside destinations and high in the hills overlooking fields that were formerly part of plantations.

The most noticeable feature of St. Kitts is Mount Liamuiga (pronounced Lee-a-mweega), usually fringed with a ring of clouds. This dormant volcano, elevation 3,792 feet, is home of the island's tropical rain forest and an excellent destination for eco-travelers. Guided tours take visitors to the far reaches of the forest for a look at this ecosystem.

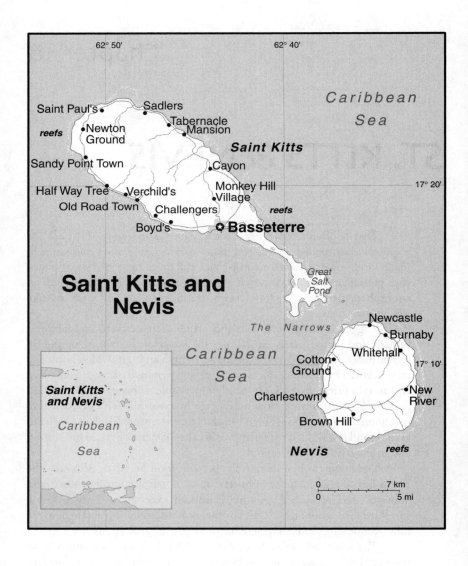

One area presently being eyed for development is the Southeast Peninsula, a site that, until a few years ago, could only be reached by boat. Since the days when the British and the French fought for domination of the small island of St. Kitts, the Southeast Peninsula remained impenetrable. Although it was blessed with white sand beaches and palm-fringed coves, this rugged area was inhabited only by a few die-hard residents who traveled by boat and by troupes of green vervet monkeys and shy white-tailed deer. Today the Dr. Kennedy Simmonds Highway, a $14 million road, links this final frontier with the rest of the Caribbean island.

Just two miles away from St. Kitts lies the tiny island of Nevis (pronounced NEE-vis), covering a total of 36 square miles. Columbus first named this island because of the ever-present cloud that circled Mount Nevis, giving it almost a snow-capped look. Today the cloud still lingers over the mountain peak. Home to only 9,000 residents, this country cousin has a charming atmosphere all its own, plus a good share of plantation houses where guests can enjoy a look back at Caribbean history.

Recently the citizens of Nevis voted for independence from St. Kitts so the coming months and years may bring some changes in the political structure to this tiny isle.

Monkeys

Ownership of the Caribbean islands frequently flipped between countries during the early days of European settlement. When the former government left, it was not uncommon for the new country to be left with reminders of the earlier residents in the form of architecture, forts, and city names. But when the French were deported from the islands of St. Kitts, they left more than Gallic names at cities such as Basseterre. They also left behind their monkeys.

The French had imported a few vervet or green monkeys from Africa as pets during their century of rulership. When the British took over the island, they deported their enemies. However, they refused to allow the monkeys on the ships, and the primates were turned loose on the mountainous island. The tropical climate, miles of untamed rainforest, and plentiful vegetation agreed with the furry creatures, so much in fact, that today the monkey population is estimated to be two and a half times larger than the human population in this twin island federation.

The monkeys do not have a prehensile tail, so they're often seen on the ground, scampering across a lawn in search of a fallen mango. Social like other monkeys, the green monkeys often travel in groups of 30 or 40. Early mornings and late evenings are the best times for spotting the most common resident of St. Kitts and Nevis.

Are We There Yet?

By Air

Most visitors first arrive at St. Kitts' Robert Llewelyn Bradshaw International Airport (formerly Golden Rock Airport) with daily jet service from the USAmerican Airlines providing daily service from the Caribbean hub in San Juan.

From St. Kitts, air service to Nevis' small Newcastle Airport is served by commuter flights from St. Kitts. Air St. Kitts Nevis, Tel. 869/465-8571 on St. Kitts, Tel. 869/469-9064 on Nevis, whisks visitors from island to island in less than 10 minutes.

By Ship

St. Kitts' new $16.25 million cruise ship terminal is located in Basseterre. Visitors arrive just off Pelican Mall, a new establishment with 26 shops that feature tropical clothing, locally made goods, and tourist items. Kittitian architecture makes this mall different from the typical mall you might see back home.

Nevis is presently constructing a new cruise port in Charlestown.

By Ferry

To reach Nevis, most travelers travel by ferry rather than air. Ferry service is available several times daily between the two islands aboard The Caribe Queen; the journey takes about 45 minutes and costs $10 EC (about US $4) round trip. Departure is from Basseterre, St. Kitts and arrival is in Charlestown, Nevis. An excellent family option is a catamaran cruise between two islands.

Getting Around the Island

Getting around St. Kitts can be accomplished by taxi or rental car (on the left side of the road), depending on your independence and the frequency with which you wish to travel around the island. If you think you'll be journeying down to the Southeast Peninsula and buzzing around the island beyond an island tour, it's worth it to rent a car for your stay. Rentals are readily available.

Taxi rates are fixed. Within Basseterre, you can journey from one point to another for about $3 US. Rates increase between the hours of 11 p.m. and 6 a.m.

Only 35 square miles, Nevis is circled by just one road that works its way from the capital city of Charlestown to communities such as St. George and Newcastle.

Rental cars are available on Nevis, but be advised that, here too, driving is on the left side of the road. Excellent taxi and mini-bus service is also available on Nevis. Taxi prices rise 50% between 10 pm and 6 am or 20% extra after 6 pm.

Where Are We Staying?

St. Kitts

BIRD ROCK BEACH HOTEL, Tel. 869/465-8914, Fax 869/465-1675. Toll-free reservations 888/358-6870; www.birdrockbeach.com. Rates start at $100 during winter months, from $85 during summer and fall. Credit cards accepted.

Scuba divers especially enjoy Bird Rock, a property just five minutes from the airport or from Basseterre. The hotel is home of St. Kitts Scuba and divers can head right off the dock on the dive boat. The hotel is simple and clean and rooms include cable TV, air conditioning, telephone, and balcony or patio. Facilities include restaurant, dockside BBQ grill, pool, bars, tennis, fitness center and scuba.

OCEAN TERRACE INN FISHERMAN'S WHARF, Basseterre, Tel. 869/465-2754, Fax 869/465-1057. Toll-free reservations Tel. 800/524-0512; www.oceanterraceinn.com. Rates from $190 winter, $150 summer. Credit cards accepted.

We love this small hotel just steps from downtown Basseterre. Just a short walk from Fisherman's Wharf restaurant (a property under the same ownership), Ocean Terrace Inn or OTI is a favorite with returnees to St. Kitts and with business travelers. The hotel has views of Basseterre Bay and Nevis; many of the recently renovated guest rooms overlook a pool with swim up bar and a hot tub. Beautiful landscaping and walks made of stone divided with low growing grass connect the hotel with two bars. Families can take a complimentary shuttle to Turtle Bay on the island's southeast peninsula for a day of watersports and beach fun then enjoy an evening at the hotel that might include a solo guitarist nightly in the Harbour View Restaurant or a show by the Coronets Steel Orchestra on Friday nights.

Kids under 12 stay free here when they share a room with their parents. There is a charge of $45 per person, per night for an extra person.

ST. KITTS MARRIOTT RESORT & THE ROYAL BEACH CASINO, Tel. 869/466-1200, Fax 869/466-1201. Toll-free reservations

800/223-6388; www.stkittsmarriott.com. Rates start at $239 during winter months, from $164 during summer and fall. Credit cards accepted.

The newly opened St. Kitts Marriott Resort and The Royal Beach Casino, with close to 650 rooms, offers a full menu of activities ranging from golf to sailing, diving to rainforest wlaks. The resort includes three pools as well as a kids' club for ages 5-12. For teens, a game room offers video and arcade games daily from 10 am to 10 pm.

Nevis

FOUR SEASONS NEVIS, Pinney's Beach, Tel. 869/469-1111, Fax 869/469-1040. Toll-free reservations Tel. 800/332-3442 US; 800/268-6282 Canada; www.fourseasons.com. Rooms start at $575 per night during the winter season. Credit cards accepted.

This resort is the most luxurious accommodation on Nevis and indeed one of the top resorts in the Caribbean. Boasting a championship golf course, 10 tennis courts, two outdoor Jacuzzis, 24-hour room service, and more, this resort is for those looking for a little pampering. Children enjoy the Kids for All Seasons complimentary program with supervised activities.

When word went out that the Four Seasons was coming to Nevis, doomsayers predicted the end of the quaint atmosphere for which Nevis is known. However, during the hotel's construction, Hurricane Hugo hit the island and the Four Seasons' bosses stopped building and put crews to work cleaning up the island. Today, the tiny island inns coexist peacefully with this corporate giant.

The Four Seasons Nevis sprawls across grounds dotted with coconut palms and other carefully tended fauna. Guests can enjoy a round of golf, scuba, windsurf, or just sun around the pool, cooled by Evian sprayed on guests by mindful pool attendants.

MONTPELIER PLANTATION INN & BEACH CLUB, Tel. 869/469-3462, Fax 869/469-2932; www.montpeliernevis.com. Winter rate $460, Summer rate $260; additional guests are $70. Children under 12 stay for $45 per night, Children's rates apply only when the child shares the room with two adults. Children over 8 welcome. Credit cards accepted.

Travelers may have heard of this classic plantation inn because of one of its most famous guests: Princess Diana. When Diana and her children visited Nevis, they opted for this hotel's quiet seclusion. Both royalty and honeymooners are offered peace and quiet in this very British hotel located on the slopes of Mount Nevis.

The late Princess Diana focused the eyes of the world on Montpelier, but it was hardly the property's first brush with royalty. On March 11, 1787 Admiral Horatio Nelson married Fanny Nisbet in front of a royal audience right on these grounds.

Today the plantation includes a 16-room inn that exudes a dignified British air appreciated by travelers who come to the Caribbean for peace and quiet. The inn provides shuttle service to the beaches and evenings here are spent at the open-air restaurant that features classical cuisine with many local ingredients. The rooms are decorated in a tropical style and include telephone, ceiling fan, hair dryer, tea and coffee maker and patio; electricity is 220 volts with a 110 volt shaver adapter. Facilities include swimming pool, tennis court, restaurant and bar.

The inn also has a private stretch of beach along Pinney's Beach with lounging facilities. Complimentary transportation to the beach is available daily. Montpelier closes annually from late August through early October.

MOUNT NEVIS HOTEL AND BEACH CLUB, Tel. 869/469-9373, Fax 869/469-9375. Toll-free reservations Tel. 800/75-NEVIS; www.mountnevishotel.com. Rates from $250 during high season, $35 per person per night for extra people. Credit cards accepted.

Those looking for a simpler accommodation will find some of the island's best views at this cozy hotel. This family-operated property sits perched high atop Round Hill estate with a view of the Caribbean and of nearby St. Kitts. The view is best enjoyed from the open air restaurant, a facility that's well-known for its innovative cuisine. Rooms here offer a telephone, air conditioning, cable TV, and video players. Facilities include a pool, with a good view of the sea, that helps travelers cool off on hot days, and the hotel also has a beach facility. The Mount Nevis Beach Club has a restaurant and beach pavilion.

NISBET PLANTATION BEACH CLUB, Tel. 869/469-9325, Fax 869/469-9864. Toll-free reservations Tel. 800/742-6008; www.nisbetplantation.com. Winter rates from $400-$620, Summer rates from $400-$535. Children under 12 stay for $50 nightly; under 5 for $25 nightly. Children under 2 are free. Seven night minimum stay is required for arrivals during peak Christmas holiday week. Credit cards accepted.

This plantation was the former home of Admiral Nelson's bride, Fanny Nisbet. The plantation today is a 38-room inn boasting one of Nevis's most striking vistas: a quarter-mile palm-lined walk from the greathouse to one of Nevis's finest beaches. Guests stay in lemon-tinted bungalows scattered throughout the property. Today the greathouse of this former coconut plantation is home to an elegant restaurant and bar. Other facilities include beach, pool, and tennis courts.

OUALIE BEACH HOTEL, Tel. 869/469-9735, Fax 869/469-9176; www.oualiebeach.com. Rates start at $245 in the winter months, $195 in the summer. Credit cards accepted.

Families will find one clear choice on Nevis: Oualie Beach Hotel. Home of Nevis's only dive shop and windsurfing operator, this hotel also offers a fine stretch of sand, 22 charming Caribbean bungalows with screened seaside porches and a comfortable atmosphere. Oualie (pronounced Wally) is the old Carib Indian name for Nevis and translates as land of beautiful water. Cribs are available as well as a kids' menu.

Rooms here are spacious and perfect for quick dashes to the beach. Four units include full kitchens. All rooms include a minibar, hair dryer, electronic safe, direct dial telephone, cable TV; air conditioning is offered in the deluxe and studio units. Facilities include SCUBA, deep sea fishing, windsurfing and sailing. They are available for guests and non-guests alike.

Kids under 12 stay free in their parents' room, with a maximum of 2 kids.

What Can We Do Now?

St. Kitts

A day's worth of sightseeing is found on St. Kitts, more if you're especially interested in historic sites. Budget a day for an overall look at the sights, which range from historic homes and museums to natural formations and Indian petroglyphs.

Don't miss the **petroglyphs**, located near Romney Manor, carved many years ago by the Carib Indians. While you're stopped here, check out the handicrafts sold next door by a neighbor who creates turtles and bird feeders from coconut shells. (Kids love the coconut shell turtles—their heads bob up and down on a spring.)

Just beyond the petroglyphs lies **Caribelle Batik**, Romney Manor, Tel. 869/465-6253, a stop worth making even if you don't want to shop. Here you can watch batik in progress and buy the finished product in the form of shirts, wraps, and wall hangings. (Even if you don't want to buy, it's worth a trip to Romney Manor just to visit the ruins of the stately greathouse and the grounds shaded by trees that date back hundreds of years.) The closest thing that St. Kitts has to a botanical garden, these grounds are home to many tropical plant species. You can't miss the huge Saman tree, said to be the largest tree in the Caribbean. On the drive to Caribelle Batik, look for the historic aqueducts along the side of the road, a reminder of the island's early water system.

Continue around the island and don't miss a visit to **Brimstone Hill Fortress National Park**, Tel. 869/465-2609, one of the top historical attractions in the Caribbean. From over 800 feet above sea level, you'll enjoy one of the best views found on any of the islands. On a clear day, you can view Nevis, Montserrat, Saba, St. Martin, and St. Barts.

Brimstone Hill is nicknamed "The Gibraltar of the West Indies," and is one of the most amazing attractions in the Caribbean, a mandatory stop for anyone interested in military history. The structure took over a century to construct of volcanic stone and is named for the faint sulfur smell sometimes encountered here. At this site, the French and the British fought for control of the island, a battle first won by the French and the next year won back by the British.

Wear good walking shoes and bring along drinking water for your look at Brimstone Hill. (At the parking level, you'll find a small concession that sells water, soft drinks, and snacks.) And a safety tip: At Brimstone Hill, visitors can climb upstairs for additional views. Families with young children, however, **be careful**. There are no railings on the second level and, between glare, wind, and a floor that is black with hundreds of years of weathering, it can be tough to see just where the second level opens into the first floor courtyard. Keep young children by the hand here.

Your first stop should probably be the brief film that gives an overview of the site and its rich history at the Visitors Orientation Centre.

From the parking level, walk up the cobbled path to the citadel. Here a view of up to 70 miles makes neighboring islands seem just a stone's (or a cannonball's) throw away. From this lofty peak, it's easy to imagine the British forces keeping an eye on the seas over two centuries ago.

The citadel has two levels. Museums featuring Amerindian artifacts, British and French memorabilia, and St. Kitts items are located in the stone rooms. The fort is open daily from 9:30 to 5:30. Admission is $5, children get in for $2.50.

For familes who want to get a sense of the history of the island, jump aboard the **St. Kitts Scenic Railway National Tour,** Tel. 800/582-6208. This is one of St. Kitts' newest attractions. The Scenic Railway takes guests on a tour of the island on the same railway that was built in 1912 to deliver sugar came from the plantations to the sugar mill in Basseterre, and has been in constant operation since then. The trail leaves Needsmust Station in Basseterre and heads north, along the coastline. Riders can see some on St. Kitts' villages, farms, and other sites on the voyage, which is narrated by the Railway Conductor. Tours leave twice a day, at 8:20 am and 1:10 pm, and arrive back at the station at 11:30 am and 4:20, repectively. Tickets cost $89.50 US for adults and $44.75 US for children, and include a seat in the lower cabin and in the observation deck, refreshments, and entertainment.

Nevis

Nevis has two spectacular beaches custom made for families. **Pinney's Beach** is one of the island's best, the waters here are protected by reefs and popular with snorkelers, swimmers, and sunbathers. **Oualie Beach** is the most active beach on Nevis, with watersport operations.

The main community in Nevis is the city of **Charlestown**. On Tuesday, Thursday, and Saturday mornings, the place to be in Charlestown is the **Market Place**. Here kids can experience a real slice of Caribbean life at a market that bustles with locals shopping for Caribbean fruits, vegetables, and seafood.

In Charlestown, save some time for a stop at the **Museum of Nevis History**. This small museum includes exhibits on indigenous people, Nevis's first residents approximately 4,000 years ago. Other displays include the island's political history, slavery, home crafts, churches, and more. The museum is housed in the home that was the birthplace of Alexander Hamilton, first Secretary of the US Treasury. Exhibits recall the life of this famous Nevis resident. The museum is open Monday through Saturday. If you visit one of Nevis's museums, admission to the second (see Horatio Nelson Museum, below) is half price. Admission is US $2 (children under 12, $1).

Another excellent stop is the **Nelson Museum**, next to Governor's House, Belle Vue. The name Horatio Nelson is heard throughout the Caribbean as a naval hero. Today his life is remembered at the Nelson Museum, the largest collection of Nelson memorabilia in the Western hemisphere. Paintings, china, figurines, and remembrances of the naval leader are found here along with displays on Nevisian history. The finest museum in St. Kitts and Nevis, it is well worth a visit. The museum is run by the Nevis Historical and Conservation Society; hours are Monday to Friday 9am to 4pm and Saturday 9am to noon. Admission is $2 for adults, $1 for children.

Ready for a little ghost story? Time to make a stop at the **Eden Brown Estate**. These ruins, formerly an estate of a wealthy planter, were the site of a true tragedy. The legend goes that on the eve of his wedding a bridegroom planter and his best man got into a duel and both men were killed. The bride-to-be went mad and is said to haunt the ruins today. The site is grown over and is little more than a few stone walls, but for those with an active imagination it's an interesting stop.

Sports & Recreation

Once the last Kittitian frontier, the **Southeast Peninsula** is now accessible by a modern highway. Some of St. Kitts most beautiful sights and beaches are located along this area, which is also home to many vervet monkeys. (Look for them in the early mornings and late evenings.) **Turtle Beach** is the most popular beach on the peninsula (actually the only one where you might have a little company). On the drive, you'll pass a salt pond with a distinct pink hue, the result of many tiny kroll shrimp. Birders will enjoy this region for its unspoiled opportunities to spot some of the island's species.

With its towering volcano, lush rainforests, and beautiful beaches, St. Kitts offers a full menu of **hikes**. You'll find plenty of soothing walks along powdery beaches for families but also lots of rugged walks and hikes for those with older children and teens.

Guided tours of the rainforest are a popular option, most combining a guided ride with a hike. A far more strenuous hike is to the crater rim of Mt. Liamuiga, an all day excursion only for those ready for a challenge.

Rainforest and volcano tours are available from several operators. **Greg's Safaris**, Basseterre, St. Kitts, West Indies, 869/465-4121, offers a half day guided Rainforest Safari through mountain trails into the Oceanic Rainforest. Visitors have a chance to look for birdlife, cross springs, identify exotic wildflowers, and enjoy the mist shrouded forest.

Greg's Safari's also offers a full day Volcano Safari. This strenuous trip includes a rugged hike up the volcano to view the mile-wide crater rim, and a chance to see the cloud forest and steaming sulphur vents in the volcanic region. The hike is a tough one, so come prepared with very good walking shoes.

Kriss Tours, Tel. 869/465-4042, offers half and full-day tours of the rainforest and, a full-day tour, of the volcanic rim.

These two islands also offer plenty of diving fun. The most common dive sites are found on the western side of the island in the calmer Caribbean waters. Here visibility runs as much as 100 feet.

The Nevis Equestrian Centre, Cole Hill, Tel. 869/469-8118, offers guided tours of the Saddle Hill area, the historic plantations, Nelson's Lookout, historic Gingerland, and other scenic points. Many of the trails offer good views of neighboring islands. Rides last about 1 1/2 hours.

The Hermitage, Tel. 869/469-3477, has an equestrian center and offers 1 1/2 hour trail ride through historic Gingerland. Escorted trail rides are English style and taken at the pace of the least skilled rider. Headgear is provided. For riders over 250 pounds, two Belgian horses are available. Riding lessons are also available at The Hermitage. And for those who'd rather let someone else take the reins, plantation carriage rides are offered. The relaxing two or three mile ride travels through historic Gingerland on hilly backroads where vacationers can witness traditional West Indian life. The carriages are authentic Creole adaptations of mid 19th century Victorian styles and are constructed of West Indian mahogany.

What Can We Buy?

The best shopping stop is St. Kitts' **Caribelle Batik** at Romney Manor. Here you can watch **batik** in progress and hear an explanation of the step-by-step process involved. You can buy the finished product in the form of shirts, wraps, and wall hangings. Prices are reasonable and the batik makes a colorful souvenir of your island visit. We purchased a batik of a string band that brings back good memories of our island stays. (Even if you don't want to buy, it's worth a trip to Romney Manor just to visit the stately greathouse and the grounds shaded by trees that date back hundreds of years. The grounds here are some of the most beautiful in the Leeward Islands.)

In Basseterre, duty-free devotees will find plenty of selection at **Pelican Mall** on the waterfront. This two-story mall, designed with Kittitian architecture and tropical colors, features duty-free shops selling everything from china to liquor to Cuban cigars. Twenty-six shops make this a popular stop, especially for cruise ship passengers who come in from the new cruise ship berth adjacent.

Stamp collectors will be familiar with Nevis because of its often-sought stamps. Stop by the Philatelic Bureau in Charlestown for the best selection. While you're in Charlestown, stop by the **Handicraft Cooperative**. Located near the Bureau of Tourism, this little shop is a must for arts and crafts shoppers and anyone looking to bring back a Nevisian souvenir. Look for wood carvings, small artwork, and even Nevisian honey here. It's a terrific place for kids to shop with just a few dollars and to pick up a special souvenir that's Nevisian-made.

One of the best stops is **Nevis Pottery** in Newcastle, where artisans craft the local clay soil into various vessels. The pots are finished over a fire of coconut shells behind the shop. The shop is open Monday through Friday and is located near the Newcastle Airport.

What Else Do We Need to Know?

Currency. The Eastern Caribbean (EC) dollar is legal tender. It is exchanged at a rate fixed to the US dollar: $1 US=2.7 EC.

Driving. Driving is British style on both islands, on the LEFT side of the road.

Information. For brochures and maps of the islands, contact the St. Kitts Tourism Office, Tel. 800/582-6208 or 212/535-1234, Fax 212/734-6511, In Canada, Tel. 888/395-4887 or 416/368-6707, Fax 416/368-3934.

For information on Nevis, contact the Nevis Tourism Authority, Tel. 866/55-NEVIS, or visit them on Main Street in Charlestown, Nevis Tel. 869/469-7550, Fax 869/469-7551.

Information on Island: While on St. Kitts, stop by the Basseterre office on the first floor of Pelican Mall for assistance, brochures, and maps. In Nevis, the tourism office is located in Charlestown.

Website. An excellent source of St. Kitts and Nevis information is the Web page for the islands, accessible at www.stkittstourism.kn for St. Kitts, and www.nevisisland.com for Nevis.

Island Report Card	
Transportation to island	B
Transportation around island	B+
Family Resorts	B
Family Restaurants	B
Friendly atmosphere	A+
Activities for kids	B
Weather	A
New cultures for kids to experience	A
Safety	A+

Chapter 17

ST. LUCIA

Jagged peaks clothed in velvety tropical plants, honey-colored beaches shaded by towering palms, and everywhere, colorful blooms and greenery: this is a true garden of Eden.

This is St. Lucia, one of the most beautiful islands in the Caribbean. Orange, lime, lemon, mango (over 100 varieties, we learned), breadfruit, plum, and coffee trees cover the landscape. Pineapples sprout alongside the highway. Spices like vanilla, nutmeg, and cinnamon grow in thick profusion.

But most evident are the bananas. Not just banana trees, but banana plantations. Miles of bananas that stretch to the horizon.

Along with its reputation as a drive-through grocery market, St. Lucia is also abloom with color from a million blossoms: tall flame flowers, orchids, hibiscus, shrimp plants, and more.

The famous sights are the Pitons, mountains located in the southwest region of the island. Gros Piton, the shorter but fatter of the two, and Petit Piton are among the Caribbean's most recognizable landmarks.

Are We There Yet?

By Air

Unlike most Caribbean islands, St. Lucia is served by two international airports, so pay close attention here. More than one family has booked flights into one airport only to discover that their hotel was across the island, over an hour's (expensive) taxi ride away.

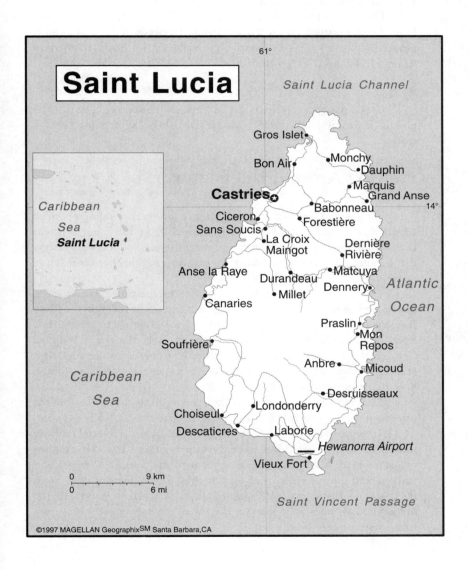

Saint Lucia

Saint Lucia Channel

Caribbean
Sea
Saint Lucia

Gros Islet

Bon Air
Monchy
Dauphin

Castries
Marquis
Grand Anse

Ciceron
Babonneau
Sans Soucis
Forestière

La Croix
Maingot
Dernière
Rivière

Anse la Raye
Durandeau
Matcuya
Millet
Dennery
Atlantic
Canaries
Ocean

Praslin
Mon
Repos

Soufrière
Anbre
Micoud

Caribbean

Sea
Londonderry
Desruisseaux

Choiseul
Descaticres
Laborie
Hewanorra Airport

Vieux Fort

Saint Vincent Passage

0   9 km
0   6 mi

©1997 MAGELLAN GeographixSM Santa Barbara,CA

The main airport is Hewanorra, located on the southern end of the island. It's the larger of the two airports, with jet service from American Airlines, Air Canada, BWIA, and several European carriers. Hotels near the Pitons are only a short taxi ride from the Hewanorra terminal.

On the northern end of the island lies Vigie International Airport, located in the city of Castries. This is closest to the bulk of the island's hotel properties, but it is served primarily by smaller carriers such as American Eagle, LIAT, and BWIA with daily service from New York and Miami.

By Ship

Cruise passengers arrive either in Castries or Soufriere. The Castries port is in easy walking distance of duty-free shopping and the Castries market.

Getting Around the Island

For years, St. Lucia was known for its poor roads, winding potholed terrors that made travel slow and uncomfortable. In 1995, however, the island completed a major road refurbishment project, and we're glad to say that we found travel from one end of the island to the other both speedy and easy.

Taxis are the most common means of transportation for vacationers, but be advised that a journey from the north end of the island to the Piton region is an expensive one: about US $50 one way. Rental cars are available from the airports and the major hotels; look for Avis, Budget, or National Car Rental. You'll need to obtain a local license from the immigration desk at either airport, police station, or from the larger rental dealers. You will also need to present your local driver's license.

Taxis can also be rented by the hour for a private tour. Work out the price with the driver before you leave, but estimate about US $20 per hour.

Tour companies also offer a wide array of guided full- and half-day tours of the island. Visit the rain forest in a open-air jeep (book early for this one since space is limited), take a bus tour to the volcano, the botanical gardens, and the waterfalls, or enjoy a combination tour with a drive down the coast and a catamaran ride back. Sunlink Tours offers a good selection of tours and we found the guides very knowledgeable about everything from island vegetation to history.

Where Are We Staying?

ANSE CHASTANET, Soufriere, Tel. 758/459-7000, Fax 758/459-7700. Toll-free reservations Tel. 800/223-1108; www.ansechastanet.com. Winter from $455 (including breakfast and dinner), summer from $245. Credit cards accepted.

For vacationers looking to put as little as possible between the Caribbean and themselves, St. Lucia's Anse Chastanet offers a place where the barriers between guests and the great outdoors are frequently as minimal as three exterior walls. Not for families with young children due to open walls and steep walks, this resort works best for school-age and older kids.

The vision of architect Nick Troubetzkoy, this hillside resort rises from a quiet bay and palm-lined beach to offer views of St. Lucia's spectacular twin Piton mountains. The architect-owner designed this singular resort to scale the hillside with guest accommodations that offer unique features that offer visitors open-air showers, trees that sprout right up through guest rooms, and open walls where views are uninterrupted by windows or screens.

The resort atmosphere is pure St. Lucian. Anse Chastanet's owners work to preserve the island's natural and cultural resources. "Our allegiance is to the island," points out Troubetzkoy. The resort utilizes island-made furnishings, cloths, foods, and artwork both to offer the guests a genuine island experience and to nurture the culture and economy of St. Lucia. Although it has long been considered one of the most romantic resorts in the Caribbean, Anse Chastanet also is a family experience for families with children five years and older. (Open walls and steep walkways make it inappropriate for families with infants and toddlers.)

Marine biology classes are held two times a week for children age 5 to 11. Children 12 and older can participate in a Learn to SCUBA course to lead to certification. Another choice for children 12 and over and adults is the "Dive 'n' Discover" course to introduce non-certified divers to the reef.

The simple guest rooms are decorated in West Indian style, with furniture that is produced on St. Lucia, usually from the Soufriere region. Beds, chairs, and couches are covered in a simple madras, the national cloth of St. Lucia, and covers are changed every three months to provide a different look for frequent return guests. Rooms are all oversized, ranging from 900 to 1,600 square feet.

Amenities include hair dryers, refrigerators, coffee makers, and ceiling fans. Although they're not always necessary, for guests' convenience mosquito nets are provided, along with electric mosquito coils. Telephones are not available in rooms; an outdoor bank of phones for guest use is located near the main office. Guests check for messages on a chalkboard posted nearby.

CLUB ST. LUCIA, Castries, Tel. 758/450-0551, Fax 758/450-0281. Toll-free US and Canadian reservations Tel. 800/777-1250; www.splashresorts.com. Winter rates from $190 for family room and $40 for children 2-11, summer from $210 for family room and $40 for children 2-11. Credit cards accepted.

Located on 50 acres in the northern tip of St. Lucia, this all-inclusive resort is a favorite with families. Over 370 guest rooms include standard, ocean view, and family rooms, with an air-conditioned bedroom with king size bed, a separate living room with ceiling fan and convertible couch that can sleep two children, and a patio area.

Family activities range from use of five swimming pools (one with a shallow children's area), sandy beach, two tennis courts, sunfish sailing, snorkeling, water-skiing, canoeing, and windsurfing as well as beach cricket, golf clinics, bicycling, volleyball, and classes in everything from local dancing to coconut carving.

The all-inclusive program includes all meals, beverages, taxes, service charges, evening entertainment, daily sports and recreational activities, watersports, tennis, and the daily supervised children's program.

Children age four to 12 are welcome at the kids' club, which operates daily. Activities include field trips, videos, face painting, T-shirt designing, cooking classes, and games. Special activities are also organized for teenagers.

WINDJAMMER LANDING VILLAS BEACH RESORT, Tel.758/456-9000, Fax 758/452-0907. Toll-free reservations Tel. 800/958-7376; www.windjammer-landing.com. Winter rates from $220, summer rates from $160. Credit cards accepted.

The two-bedroom Junior Suite is a good choice for families staying at this resort. This suite includes two bedrooms connected by stairs, to give parents and kids plenty of privacy. There is a queen bed on the upper level of the suite and the second bedroom comes with one queen or two twin beds.

Sports offered here include sailing, windsurfing, kayaking, snorkeling, paddle boast, tennis, and banana rides, all included in the cost of the stay. There are other sports that guests can try for additional costs. Windjammer also offers a full service Serenity Spa, which includes treatments from facials to body wraps.

While Mom and Dad relax, kids can have a ball in the Children's Program, which offers supervised activities for kids 4-18 years old. The Jacquot Fun Club is for kids 4-12, and offers games, snacks, and many other fun activities. Guests ages 13-18 have their own set of daily activities including aqua volleyball, soccer, snorkeling, karaoke, movies and many more.

Babysitting and nanny services are also available for parents wanting some time alone.

What Can We Do Now?

St. Lucia has one of the most unique children's programs in the Caribbean. "**Safari Summer**", designed by the National Trust, is designed for family vacationers to learn more about St. Lucia's heritage and to have fun.

The program is for kids 5-14. Programs last for two weeks, and participants can see various natural and cultural sites. Young people can get to know the island, and understand St. Lucia's natural envirnoment. Call the National Trust, Tel. 758/452-5005, for scheduling and costs.

On the northern reach of the island lies **Pigeon Island**, a 35-minute drive from Castries. No longer a true island but connected to the main island by causeway, Pigeon Island has a long history as everything from a pirate hideout to a military fort. The ruins of the fort can still be seen at Pigeon Island National Park, a popular day trip for north shore vacationers and the site of many of St. Lucia's festivals.

Most guests stay on the northeast section of the island near **Castries**, the island's largest city with a population of 60,000. This capital city was destroyed by fire several times, but some colonial period wooden structures still remain. You'll see several of them as you head south on Government House Road. This twisting, climbing slice of road is slow going but offers you a great view. Save time for a stop across from the Governor's House for a panoramic look at the city. From atop Morne Fortune, hill of good luck (not such good luck for the French soldiers who resided here in the 18th century; they were plagued with yellow fever), you'll have a postcard view over Castries Harbour, Vigie Peninsula and Pigeon Island.

Continuing south, the road soon drops into a veritable forest: the first of several **banana plantations**. Driving past this display of the island's number one crop, you'll see blue plastic bags hanging from many trees. These cover the bananas themselves to shield the crop from insects and bruising by the banana leaves. The banana plant yields only one crop during its lifetime, a process that takes nine months to bear fruit.

Marigot Harbour, located just off the main road, is the next stop. This magical harbor, often considered to be the most beautiful in the Caribbean, is dotted with yachts from around the globe. If you don't have your own, don't worry. The Moorings, a company headquartered in the British Virgin Islands, can rent you a yacht with or without a crew to enjoy a sailing vacation of your own. Landlubbers will enjoy the scenic harbor as well, and may recognize it from the movie Dr. Doolittle.

South of Marigot, the road passes through many small communities and fishing villages. Make time for a walk around **Anse La Raye** (Beach of the Ray), a traditional St. Lucian fishing village. Enjoy a walk along the waterfront to view the hand-crafted fishing canoes painted in bright primary colors and the various fishing nets and traps used in these waters. In town, stroll past traditional Caribbean homes with lawns outlined in conch shells, past the large Roman Catholic church, and make a stop in the authentic Creole bakery for a treat.

The **Soufriere** region is the heartland of the island's many attractions. There's no denying that the most scenic part of the island is this south-central region. Starting with the rain forest and continuing down to the Pitons, this spectacular region is the breadbasket of the island. Every tropical fruit and vegetable thrives in this rich region, which is sparsely populated.

For many families, the most fascinating area is the **rain forest**. You'll need a guide to enter the restricted rain forest region, so sign up for a guided tour with one of the island's tour operators. Hiking tours are available with guides from the Forestry Department. You'll walk through the dense foliage, swim in a tropical waterfall, and learn more about the plants that make up this fragile ecosystem. And, if you're lucky, you may have the opportunity to see the rare St. Lucian parrot.

This area is also home to a unique **Sulphur Spring volcano**, often called the "drive-through volcano." Actually, visitors cannot drive or walk through the volcano anymore (a few years ago a Rasta guide fell through a weak part of the crust—and fortunately received only severe burns). Groups walk only to the edge of the volcano which last erupted two centuries ago. With the smell of sulphur heavy in the air, you'll see jets of bubbling water black with ash and bubbling with gases released from deep in the earth's core. (Leave your silver jewelry back at the hotel for this trip. The gases can cause silver to tarnish.)

Sports & Recreation

Another major attraction of St. Lucia is its **scuba diving**. Anse Chastanet is considered to be the top dive spot on the island and one of the best in the Caribbean. The reason? Extraordinary fish life, coral formations, and sponge growth right off shore. Divers and snorkelers can enjoy spectacular underwater exploration just yards from the beach.

St. Lucia's **beaches** run from golden brown to a salt-and-pepper mixture of sand and volcanic elements. Some of the most popular beaches are Anse Chastanet, Anse Cochon, and Reduit Beach. Sunbathers take note: topless and nude sunbathing is prohibited throughout St. Lucia.

For fun away from the water, Trim's National Riding, Tel. 758/450-8273, offers **horse and carriage rides**. All levels of riders are accommodated on guided rides along the Caribbean or Atlantic beaches.

What Can We Buy?

Castries, the island's largest town, is also its top shopping area. Here you'll have a choice between malls and markets for everything from fine jewels to handmade crafts that capture the island spirit.

Pointe Seraphine is the island's duty-free port. Here you'll find well-known chains such as Little Switzerland, Colombian Emeralds and Benetton. (Remember to bring your passport and return airline tickets to take advantage of the duty-free shopping. Items can be taken with you at point of purchase.) Pointe Seraphine is open weekdays, and on Saturdays, until 1pm only. Like most shops in St. Lucia, the mall is closed on Sundays.

Outside of Castries, make a stop at **Caribelle Batik** for handmade batik shirts, wraps, and scarves. In Choiseul, stop by the **Choiseul Arts and Crafts Center**. This town is known as the crafts center of the island, and here you'll find straw, wood, and clay handcrafts, all manufactured locally.

For teens, another local item that's a good reminder of your vacation is perfume. **Caribbean Perfumes**, located in Castries, captures the scents of the islands with perfumes for both men and women. Caribbean Perfumes are sold at shops across the island, including most resort gift stores.

What Else Do We Need to Know?

Currency. The Eastern Caribbean (EC) dollar is the official currency. The exchange rate is fixed to the US dollar at US $1 equals EC $2.65.

Electricity. The current on the island is 220 volts, 50 cycles. Some hotels offer 110 volts, 60 cycles. Also, socket styles vary, although most are the three-pin style with square plugs (UK).

Hospitals. Four hospitals are available on the island. Most hotels have a doctor on call that will make "house" calls.

Island Report Card

Transportation to island	A-
Transportation around island	B
Family Resorts	A-
Family Restaurants	B
Friendly atmosphere	A-
Activities for kids	B
Weather	A
New cultures to experience	A-
Safety	B

Information. Contact the St. Lucia Tourist Board, Tel. 800/456-3984 or 212/867-2950, Fax 866/363-4300. In Canada, Tel. 416/362-4242, Fax 416/362-7832. Information on island: Contact the Tourist Board at Pointe Seraphin in Castries, Tel. 758/452-4094.

Website. Check out the official site of the St. Lucia Tourist Board for up-to-date information on the island: www.stlucia.org.

Chapter 18

ST. MARTIN/SINT MAARTEN

This island calls itself "a little European and a lot Caribbean." It's a fitting description of a most unusual political situation: two nations sharing a single, small piece of land. The smallest mass on the globe shared by two nations, it's a peaceful neighboring of French and Dutch that offers vacationers twice the cultural experience. Travelers can enjoy fine French food, topless French beaches, Dutch architecture, and Dutch casinos that ring with baccarat and roulette all in an atmosphere that's definitely West Indian.

Although the border is almost superficial, there are distinctions between the two countries. Mention "St. Martin" and many visitors will immediately think of fine dining and charming sidewalk cafes. French is heard in the markets and there's no mistaking that this is la partie francaise.

The Dutch influence is felt far less strongly in Sint Maarten than the Gallic influence in St. Martin. Although the official language taught in the schools, Dutch is rarely heard on the street. And although it falls under the government of the Netherlands Antilles and the Kingdom of the Netherlands, the US dollar reigns here. The atmosphere is strictly West Indian with an eye toward American commerce. US dollars are accepted freely and shopping on the Dutch side is more American-style than in St. Martin, which features more European-style shops.

Are We There Yet?

By Air

Air service is available at two airports on the island: Princess Juliana International Airport on Dutch St. Maarten and L'Esperance Airport in Grand Case on the French side. The French airport is served only by a few commuter flights from St. Barts and Guadeloupe and private planes. Most travelers arrive in Dutch Sint Maarten.

Travel time to the island from is 2 1/2 hours from Miami, 3 1/2 from New York, 4 1/2 from Dallas, 5 from Montreal, and 8 hours from Paris.

Princess Juliana is a major airport and a Caribbean hub for inter-island travel. Service is available from American Airlines, Continental, USAirways, Northwest Airlines, and others from Europe.

By Boat

In Philipsburg, Sint Maarten, the $2.5 million Captain Hodge Wharf, can accommodate up to 600 passengers an hour (triple the size of the former tender pier). It's the first step in a $60 million master improvement plan for the area.

The wharf includes a Tourist Information Center and is now the disembarkation point for over 650,000 cruise ship passengers annually. The site is named for Captain Arsene Hodge who, beginning in 1938, operated the first government ship delivering mail, passengers, and goods between St. Maarten and Saba, Statia, and St. Kitts.

The wharf regularly welcomes cruise passengers from Carnival, Costa, Norway, Cunard, Club Med, and other lines.

In Marigot, the cruise pier is located at the market and is used to tender cruise passengers to this area. It sports a new look, thanks to renovations that occurred during the filming of the movie *Speed 2: Cruise Control.*

Getting Around the Island

Taxis are one of the best ways to get around the island, especially for the first time visitor. Steep, winding roads combined with plentiful traffic can be challenging the first day or two, so consider a taxi for the first part of your stay. Taxis travel freely to both sides of the island.

If you'll be traveling extensively during your stay, however, a rental car can be a good investment. Taxi rates from end to end of the island quickly surpass rental rates. You'll find that most rental companies offer free pickup and delivery service. To rent a vehicle, you'll need a valid driver's license and a major credit card. Driving throughout the island is on the RIGHT side of the road.

Public buses are available and offer an inexpensive and colorful (although not fastest) way to travel the island. Buses run from Marigot to Philipsburg, other routes travel to Mullet Bay, Simpson Bay, Cole Bay, and Grand Case. Buses run from about 6 a.m. to midnight and can be flagged down anywhere. They leave every hour from Grand Case.

When a cruise ship is in port in Philipsburg, you can often find cheap transportation to Orient Beach. Look for taxi drivers holding an Orient Beach sign; vans shuttle back and forth for about $5 per person.

Where Are We Staying?

French St. Martin

ESMERALDA RESORT, Orient Beach, Tel. (59) 05 90 87 36 36, Fax (59) 05 90 87 35 18; www.esmeralda-resort.com. Rates start at $300 in low season. Credit cards accepted.

From the action packed waters off Orient Beach, the green roofs of Esmeralda Resort are easy to spot. Fifteen villas, accommodating 54 guest rooms, are sprinkled across the low rise hills that rise up from Baie Orientale. Each villa includes its own swimming pool; accommodations offer air-conditioning, satellite TV, telephones, fully equipped kitchenettes, and private terraces. A poolside restaurant, L'Astrolabe, offers continental cuisine.

LE MERIDIEN L'HABITATION LE DOMAINE, Anse Marcel, Tel. 011/590-590-87-6700, Fax 011/590-590-87-3735. Toll-free reservations Tel. 800/543-4300. Summer rates run from $140-340. Credit cards accepted.

L'Habitation Le Domain, is located on the island's northeast coast, tucked into Marcel Cove. Surrounded by a 150-acre nature preserve, the resort is landscaped with bougainvillea, hibiscus, and oleander. Guest rooms, with bright Caribbean colors, include 251 rooms at L'Habitation with garden or marina views and 145 rooms and suites at the newer wing, Le Domaine. Facilities include swimming pools, private white sand beach, shuttle service to casinos, Philipsburg, and Marigot. Watersports activities are deep sea fishing, marina activities, motorboat, sail, power, and glass bottom boating, sailing and catamaran boating, scuba diving, water skiing, canoeing, jet skiing, kayaking, and more. Horseback riding, racquetball, squash, fitness center, and tennis also available.

Villas

Several villa rental companies offer families the option of staying in a fully furnished villa, complete with cooking facilities and plenty of room. Contact these villa rental companies for information: **Carimo**, Tel. 011/590-590-87-57-58 or **West Indies Immobilier**, Tel. 011/590-590-87-56-48.

Dutch Sint Maarten

DIVI LITTLE BAY, Philipsburg, Tel. 011/599-54-22333, Fax 011/599-54-25150. Toll-free reservations Tel. 800/367-3484; www.diviresorts.com. Rates start at $181 in winter, from $127 in summer. Credit cards accepted.

Perched on a peninsula between Great Bay and Little Bay, this property offers spectacular views. The 235-room resort offers typical hotel rooms as well as studios and one-bedroom units. Facilities include a restaurant, pool, and water activities center.

Facilities for children include a children's program, where kids can get to know other visiting children and have fun participating in supervised activities. Babysitting, cot rental and crib rental are available for an additional fee.

GREAT BAY BEACH HOTEL, Philipsburg, Tel. 011/599-54-22446, Fax 011/599-54-23859. Toll-free reservations Tel. 800/223-0757; www.greatbayhotel.com. Winter rates start at $160 per person for double occupancy; summer rates start at $130 per person with double occupancy. Credit cards accepted.

Located 10 minutes from downtown Philipsburg, this 285-room hotel offers visitors 24-hour fun. Daytime activities include watersports (wave runners, sailboats, windsurfing, snorkeling, paddleboats), tennis, beach, and two swimming pools. Rates are all-inclusive and include transfers, three meals daily, drinks by the glass, sunset cruise, sightseeing tour, windsurfing, snorkeling, and sailing, scuba clinic, and more.

PELICAN RESORT CLUB, Pelican Key, Tel. 011/599-54-42503, Fax 011/599-54-42133. Toll-free reservations Tel. 800/550-7088; www.pelicanresort.com. Winter rates from $225, Summer from $85. Credit cards accepted.

This all-suites property is located on the beach and is a good choice for families. Rooms include fully equipped kitchens; families can select from hillside, poolside, or beachfront accommodations. Five swimming pools (not to mention the beach) keep waterlovers happy. A children's pool is available, along with a children's playground and baby-sitting. Adults find plenty of activity as well including tennis, watersports, spa, and a shopping arcade.

SONESTA MAHO BEACH HOTEL AND CASINO, Simpson Bay, Tel. 011/599-545-2115, Fax 011/599-545-3604. Toll-free reservations Tel. 800/SONESTA; www.sonesta.com or www.mahobeach.com. Winter rates from $424, summer from $370 for all-inclusive. Credit cards accepted.

This 600-room hotel, recently taken over by the Sonesta chain, is a high-rise built around a sprawling freshwater pool. The Sonesta chain has long been one of our favorites so we're glad to see them reenter the Caribbean market with this family-friendly resort. Rooms are divided among two towers and families find plenty of dining option as well as a supervised kids' club on site.

Villa Rental Companies

These rental companies handle a variety of island properties:
- Caribbean Destinations, Tel. 800/888-0897
- Caribbean Resorts and Villas, Tel. 800/955-8180
- Coral Shore Villas, Tel. 800/942-6725
- Island Properties, Tel. 800/738-9444

What Can We Do Now?

There's no denying that St. Martin's beautiful **beaches**, nearly 40 in all, are one of this island's top assets. Whether you're looking for pulsating action or blissful privacy, you'll find it somewhere on the island. On the French side, topless sunbathing is standard and nudity is permitted on the nude beach at Orient Bay, so prepare your children first if you plan a visit to this bustling beach.

Kids enjoy the **St. Maarten Zoological and Botanical Garden** (sxmzoo.networkidl.net), located near Philipsburg on the Dutch side of the island. The zoo emphasizes the flora and fauna of the Caribbean with an eye toward conservation. Over 60 species are on display here including mammals, birds, and reptiles. The zoo is open daily from 9:30 am to 6 pm.

Another top stop with families is the **St. Martin/St. Maarten Butterfly Farm** (sxmzoo.networkidl.net), located on the French side of the island near Orient Bay. You'll walk among free-flying butterflies in this fascinating display which is open daily from 9 am to 3:30 pm.

Sports & Recreation

Horseback riders will find plenty of action on both sides of St. Martin. Bayside Riding Club, Tel. 011/590-873664, Fax 011/590-873376, offers beach rides, riding lessons, pony rides, and even horse leasing. Beach rides follow the surf and, if you're on the island at the right time, full moon rides can be a unique experience. Bayside Riding Club is located next to Orient Bay on the road to Le Galion Beach.

Caid and Isa, Tel. 011/590-87-32-79, at Anse Marcel (near Le Meridien) offers two rides daily at 9am and 3pm except on Sunday. Six paso finos are stabled and available for hire for an hour excursion that goes over the hills of Anse Marcel to the beach of Petites Cayes, also known as Anse de la Pomme d'Adam or Adam's Apple Cove.

St. Maarten offers **scuba diving** for first timers and advanced divers. Visibility ranges from 75 to 125 feet in these waters which are home to a wide array of marine life. Waters are warm year around, averaging 70 degrees.

Good visibility makes **snorkeling** popular around St. Maarten's beaches. The top snorkel spot is Little Bay Beach, with good reefs and calm waters except during a southeast wind.

For many travelers, a good day's adventure is **sailing** around the island, a little snorkeling, and a deck picnic or perhaps an elegant sunset sail to watch the lights come out in Dutch Sint Maarten.

Day Excursions

Explore neighboring St. Barts with a quick trip aboard the Voyager 2, Tel. 011/590-590-27-54-10, which departs from Marigot to Gustavia, St. Barts at 9am and 6:15pm daily (reservations required for Sunday departure). The hour and a half trip aboard the high-speed boat is comfortable, air conditioned, and includes a stocked bar. Round trip is $57 for adults and $32 for kids under 12, children under 5 are free. A package including lunch and an island tour is available for $49 and, considering the dining prices on St. Barts, is a real bargain. Car rental is available for day trippers as well for $49.

From Grand Case, St. Barth Commuter offers day trips to nearby St. Barts. Additional flights are available to Anguilla, Antigua, Barbuda, Guadeloupe, Nevis, St. Kitts, and Statia. For information, contact St. Barth CommuterTel. 011/590-590-27-54-54.

Sint Maarten's proximity to other islands give vacationers the opportunity to visit St. Barts and Saba (take a day trip to Anguilla from Marigot in French St. Martin). For information or reservations on either trip: Tel. 011/ 544-2640.

What Can We Buy?

French St. Martin

On the French side, the best shopping is in the capital city of Marigot. A crafts market near the cruise terminal offers jewelry, T-shirt, souvenir items, carvings, and paintings (we were especially taken with the Haitian artwork available here). We've bought lots of inexpensive children's gifts in this market: wooden turtles that open to hold jewelry or small treasures for $10, painted wooden animals from Haiti for $3, and for teens inexpensive silver jewelry starting at about $10 and pareos for about $10.

Marigot also is home to boutique shops open 9am to 12:30pm and 3 to 7pm.

Dutch Sint Maarten

In Philipsburg, shops line Frontstreet, the narrow boulevard nearest the waterfront. In these duty-free stores, electronic goods, leather, jewelry, and liquor (especially guavaberry liqueur) are especially good buys. (For the best prices, shop on days when the cruise ships are not in port.) No duties are charged in or out of port (one of the few such ports in the world), so savings run about 25-50% on consumer goods at this popular duty-free stop. Shop carefully, though, and know prices on specific goods before you leave home. Some items are not such bargains.

Most shops are found on Philipsburg's Frontstreet. Typically, shops open at 8 or 9am and remain open until noon, then reopen from 2 to 6 daily. When cruises ships are in port, most shops remain open through the lunch hours.

What Else Do We Need to Know?

Currency. The official currency for the French side is Euro; the Dutch side uses the Netherlands Antilles guilder. However, you'll rarely see either currency. US dollars are used almost exclusively on both sides of the island.

Information. For information on Sint Maarten, call Tel. 800/ STMAARTEN for information on the Dutch side of the island including transportation, accommodations, and activities. For information on the French side, call "France On Call," Tel. 900/990-0040. This is a toll call and provides information on all lands which are part of France. Information on Island: While on the Dutch side, you'll find an information center at the cruise terminal in Philipsburg: Vineyard Office Park, WG Buncamper Rd.,

Island Report Card	
Transportation to island	A
Transportation around island	A-
Family Resorts	B
Family Restaurants	B
Friendly atmosphere	B
Activities for kids	B+
Weather	A
New cultures for kids to experience	A+
Safety	B

#33, Tel. 011/599-542-2337. Fax 011599-542-2734. On the French side, stop by the St. Martin Tourist Office near the waterfront in Marigot; the office is open Monday through Friday 8:30 to 1, 2:30-5:30 and Saturday from 8 to noon.

Websites. Check out the Dutch Sint Maarten Website at this address: www.st-maarten.com. The French Martin site is located at www.st-martin.org.

Chapter 19

TRINIDAD & TOBAGO

Trinidad and Tobago may share membership in the same independent republic. They may share the Trinidad-Tobago currency, the TT dollar. And they may both enjoy the same idyllic climate, located south of the hurricane zone and rarely disturbed by the storms that can ravage other Caribbean islands in the summer and fall months.

But that's where the similarities between these two islands stop. Like city and country cousins, Trinidad and Tobago each have their own unique personalities and their own distinct attributes.

Trinidad is by far the largest, both in terms of population and size. This anvil-shaped island bustles with activity in Port of Spain, the capital city that's also a capital in the world of Caribbean commerce. Here you'll hear accents from residents who have relocated from around the world to work in this modern metropolis. The Indian influence is stronger here than anywhere else in the Caribbean, and is seen in the faces of islanders, the architecture, food, and religion of the island, where nearly one quarter of all residents are Hindu.

Both islands are especially popular with nature lovers and are veritable gardens of Eden for families to enjoy.

Are We There Yet?

By Air

Trinidad's Piarco International Airport is served by American Airlines

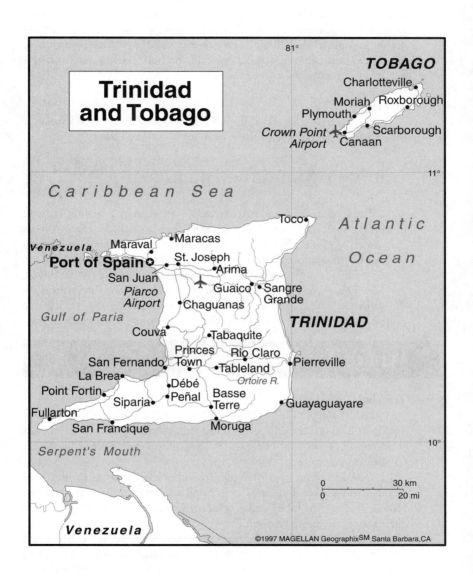

Trinidad and Tobago

81°

TOBAGO

Charlotteville
Moriah Roxborough
Plymouth
Crown Point   Scarborough
Airport Canaan

11°

Caribbean Sea

Atlantic

Toco

Maracas

Venezuela Maraval
Port of Spain St. Joseph
Arima
San Juan
Piarco Guaico Sangre
Airport Chaguanas Grande

Gulf of Paria **TRINIDAD**

Couva Tabaquite

Princes Rio Claro
San Fernando Town Tableland Pierreville
La Brea *Ortoire R.*
Point Fortin Débé
Siparia Peñal Basse
Fullarton Terre Guayaguayare
San Francique Moruga

Ocean

10°

Serpent's Mouth

0   30 km
0   20 mi

Venezuela

©1997 MAGELLAN GeographixSM Santa Barbara,CA

and BWIA. The airport is located about a half hour drive from Port of Spain, a taxi ride of about $20 US.

You can reach Tobago's Crown Point International Airport, near the town of Scarborough, on American Eagle from San Juan or via a 20-minute flight on Air Caribbean, Tel. 868/623-2500. Air Caribbean passengers should reconfirm their flight arrangements the day before flying; these interisland hops are very popular especially on holidays and weekends and many passengers are wait-listed for seats.

By Ferry

Ferry service connects Trinidad and Tobago. The journey, a six-hour trip, is usually taken only by those bringing autos to Tobago.

Getting Around the Island

Taxis are a common means of transportation on both islands. Driving in Port of Spain is a little like participating in a stock car race, so most vacationers opt for a cab. Inexpensive options are the maxi taxis, vans which cover different areas of the island (locations are designated by the color of the stripe on the side of the vans). Maxi taxis stop anywhere along their routes.

In Tobago, taxis also frequent Scarborough's streets, but visitors on the north end of the island may find rental cars a better option. Thrifty Car Rental and several local companies offer rentals from Crown Point airport.

Where Are We Staying?

Trinidad

HILTON TRINIDAD & CONFERENCE CENTRE, Port of Spain, Tel. 868/624-3211 ext. 6040, Fax 868/624-4485. Toll-free US phone number Tel. 800/HILTONS; www.hilton.com. Rates from $125. Credit cards accepted.

Conrad Hilton's personal project still exudes an air of comfort and elegance amid a bustling city. This hotel is known as the "upside-down Hilton" because the lobby and ground level make up the top floor and the guest rooms are located downhill.

Visitors are met by walkways of smooth teak, grown on the island and used in furniture and railings throughout the hotel. Rooms are similar to those found in other traditional business-oriented hotels, but all include a private balcony overlooking Queen's Park Savannah. Carnival is held directly across the street from the hotel, so during that time come prepared to party—like it or not.

Kids under 18 stay free in their parents' room, and kids under 5 eat free. Kids 5-12 get a free breakfast and half off all other meals when the eat with and adult. Families staying three nights or longer get one night of babysitting for free for up to four hours. Kids will be happy to receive a free gift when they check in.

THE NORMANDIE HOTEL & RESTAURANT, Port of Spain, Tel. 868/624-1181, Fax 868/624-0108. Toll-free reservations Tel. 800/223-6510; www.normandiett.com. Winter and summer rates from $135. Credit cards accepted.

The Normandie Hotel is small (53 rooms) and is an intimate place in which to enjoy the downtown region in a setting much like a country inn. This property may be small in size, but, it has a large number of amenities to offer its guests: an excellent shopping arcade and cultural events scheduled every month. Rooms here are simple, and for the most room consider a split level loft, perfect for families. A freshwater pool is available.

Tobago

BLUE WATERS INN, Speyside, Tel. 868/660-4341, Fax 868/660-5195. Toll-free US phone number 800/742-4276; www.bluewatersinn.com. Winter rates from $160, summer rates from $100. Credit cards accepted.

This beachfront hotel is casual and fun. Situated on the edge of Batteaux Bay, this resort is perfect for families who plan to spend time enjoying nature, either on the resort's 46 acres of tropical foliage or in the clear waters best known as the home of giant manta rays. Activity is the name of the game here, and it comes in forms such as scuba diving, snorkeling, windsurfing, glass-bottom boat tours of the reef, deep sea fishing, tennis, and more.

COCO REEF RESORT AND SPA, Coconut Bay, Tel. 868/639-8571, Fax 868/639-8574. Toll-free reservations Tel. 800/221-1294; www.cocoreef.com. $203-$259 for rooms ($417-$1622 for suites) in summer and fall. Credit cards accepted.

From an entrance highlighted by a Classic Rolls Royce Silver Cloud parked beneath a columned porte-cochere to a breezy, open-air public area filled with wicker furniture, the mood here is one of elegance combined with a relaxed Caribbean atmosphere. The hotel requests no jeans, T-shirts, or shorts in public areas after 7pm.

Europeans make up the bulk of Coco Reef's clientele, led by Germany and England, each with 35% of the guest list. Americans, mostly from the Northeastern states, compose 18% of the Coco Reef's visitors. Coco Reef's guests include honeymooners, couples, and families with children. Supervised activities are available for children when the resort has many children staying, and families can have the services of a nanny during their stay.

One hundred ocean view rooms make up the bulk of the property, each with Saltillo-tiled patios or balconies. Other categories include superior rooms with no ocean view, six suites, five villas, a presidential suite, and the sunset villa, with a private lawn and decks overlooking the sea.

All rooms include air conditioning, satellite TV, a mini-refrigerator, direct dial telephone, hair dryer, and twice daily maid service. Wicker furniture and walls decorated with hand stenciling emphasizing the pineapple, the theme of the hotel and the symbol for hospitality, complete a cozy look for the rooms.

Coco Reef is located between two top Tobago beaches, but the hotel itself is situated on a small man-made beach. Protected by a breakwater, the calm waters are excellent for young swimmers. Snorkeling, windsurfing, and Sunfish sailing are offered nearby. Pool lovers will also find a freshwater pool or, for more active recreation, two Har-Tru tennis courts are lit for day or night play; lessons are available from the resort pro. Guests also have complimentary access to a fitness center, part of a complete spa facility.

GRAFTON BEACH RESORT, Black Rock, Tel. 868/639-0191, Fax 868/639-0030; www.grafton-resort.com. Winter rates from $168, summer from $140. Credit cards accepted.

Grafton Beach Resort exudes fun. At the 114-room property all rooms include TV, minibar, and air conditioning. Families enjoy a freshwater pool as well as watersports and squash on property. Activities also include deep sea fishing, horseback riding, sailing, and kayaking.

HILTON TOBAGO, Scarborough, 868/660-8500, Fax 868/660-8503. Toll-free reservations 800/HILTONS; www.hilton.com. Rates from $215. Credit cards accepted.

This 200-room property offers good deals for traveling families, starting with a gift for kids at check-in as part of the V.I.C. (Very Important Children) program. Children under 18 stay for free in the same room as their parents. Kids under five get all meals free, and kids 5-12 get a free breakfast and 50% off on all their other meals that they eat with their parents. Families staying three or more nights here get one night of free babysitting for up to four hours.

Hilton Tobago's Learning Centre is open for kids 5-17, and provides kids with toys, games, and other fun and educational activities. Meals are child-friendly, too; Hilton Tobago's executive chef prepares a daily lunch for the Learning Centre with dishes like Oodles of Noodles, Loaded Boats (potato skins), Mini Burgers and Banana Splits. Daily activities are scheduled including arts and crafts, hikes, beach games, glass-bottom boat rides, lunch and classes on the rain forest and marine biology. The Learning Centre is open daily from 9 am to 5 pm.

LE GRAND COURLAN RESORT & SPA, Black Rock, Tel. 868/639-9667, Fax 868/639-9292. Toll-free US phone number Tel. 800/468-3750; www.legrandcourlan-resort.com. Winter rates from $318. Credit cards accepted.

Tobago's most elegant resort features a new spa with a teak floor for aerobics, massage rooms, juice bar, hot and cold Jacuzzis. Based upon the Eastern philosophy that right angles create stress, the spa walls are curved.

PLANTATION BEACH VILLAS, Black Rock, Tel. 868/639-9377, Fax 868/639-0455; www.plantationbeachvillas.com. Winter rates $545 (for four people). Credit cards accepted.

For villa lovers, these two-story homes are a dream come true. They lie just steps from the sea and from both Le Grand Courlon and Grafton Beach Resorts. The villas, with a full kitchen, living and dining room, and three bedrooms, are filled with locally crafted furniture. Perfect for families, each home tempts residents with wide porches across the back of the homes, overlooking a tropical garden. A freshwater pool is available for guests' use and is adjoined by a bar.

Housekeeping services are provided daily, and cooking and baby-sitting are also available.

REX TURTLE BEACH, Courland Bay, Tel. 868/639-2851, Fax 868/639-1495. Toll-free US phone number 800/255-5859; www.rexcaribbean.com. Winter rates from $320 per person all-inclusive, summer rates from $270 per person. Children under 2 stay free, children 3-12 are $25 per child per day. Credit cards accepted.

The Rex hotel chain is well known among UK travelers, but its offering should also be a favorite with North American vacationers. Like its name suggests, this hotel is located right on a beach favored by turtles as a nesting site. The atmosphere here is casual and fun, enjoyed by an international array of visitors who come to soak up Tobago's sun. The hotel offers 125 rooms, each with oceanview.

What Can We Do Now?

Nature tours definitely rank as a top attraction on Trinidad. The **Asa Wright Nature Centre**, Tel. 868/667-4655, is the island's top spot for naturalists and birders, who can enjoy guided walks on nature trails or go off on their own in search of multi-color hummingbirds and many of the island's other tropical species. Near Port of Spain, the **Caroni Swamp**, Tel. 868/645-1305, is a sanctuary that's home to the scarlet ibis, and in the sunset hours the sky turns truly scarlet as these birds come in to roost in the mangroves. Boat tours are available for a closer look at these beautiful birds.

Although Trinidad is not known for its beaches, **Maracas Bay**, located on the north shore, is a popular spot with both tourists and residents. About an hour from Port of Spain, the drive to this area is a treat in itself, winding through the Northern Range with views of forests where species such as howler and capuchin monkeys, ocelot, Amazon parrots, and wild pigs can be found. Make a stop at the Hot Bamboo Hut for a taste of spicy mango slices in pepper and a beautiful view of the coastline. Nearby, Maracas Bay offers a full day of fun, with complete changing facilities, chair rentals, watersports, and local food such as "shark and bake," a fast food snack made with fresh shark encased in a pancake sandwich.

In Port of Spain, the **Queen's Park Savannah** is a top stop. This central park, encircled by what's termed the world's longest roundabout, is home to cricket fields, botanical gardens, and tall trucks selling green coconuts. Enjoy a walk around the Savannah, which is lined with grand historic homes, and stop for a drink of coconut water.

Nature attractions are also a big draw on Tobago. Of special interest are the **leatherback turtles** who come to nest on the leeward side of the island between March and August. Come out after sunset between 7pm and 5am for the best chance of viewing these large marine turtles when they come ashore to lay between 80 and 125 eggs in the sand. The tiny offspring make their run for the sea about two months later.

When it comes to festivals, no island can beat Trinidad at **Carnival**. This is more than a festival; it's a way of life. Held the Monday and Tuesday prior to Ash Wednesday, this pre-Lenten blowout is preceded by weeks of parties, balls, competitions, and calypso shows. J'ouvert, Carnival Monday, starts at 2am as Trinidadians take to the streets in costume. Partiers practice Carnival dances: chipping (a slow shuffle down the street), jumping up, and wining. Soca music pulsates from giant trucks while steel pans deliver traditional calypso sounds.

Should you visit Trinidad during Carnival? Only if you're looking for pulsating action around the clock. Otherwise, stick to other weeks for a visit to this island. Tobago is quiet during Carnival but it's traditional for merrymakers to recuperate with a Tobago vacation following Carnival festivities, so crowds are larger than usual during that time as well.

Sports & Recreation

Cruising Tobago's calm waters is a fun a way to look at the island's beautiful coast. The Loafer, Tel. 868/639-7312, a 50-foot catamaran, departs from Buccoo Reef, the most popular beach on the island for all day

Information. Contact the St. Lucia Tourist Board, Tel. 800/456-3984 or 212/867-2950, Fax 866/363-4300. In Canada, Tel. 416/362-4242, Fax 416/362-7832. Information on island: Contact the Tourist Board at Pointe Seraphin in Castries, Tel. 758/452-4094.

Website. Check out the official site of the St. Lucia Tourist Board for up-to-date information on the island: www.stlucia.org.

cruises as well as sunset sails and full moon dinners. The all-day trip includes a swim at the **Nylon Pool**, a calm, shallow area in the sea formed by a sandbar close to the surface where guests of all swimming levels enjoy a swim.

Divers often head straight to Speyside, located on the northern tip of the island. Here they might have the opportunity to swim with giant manta rays; dolphins, turtles, whale sharks and porpoises are sometimes spotted. This area is especially rich, with a profusion of coral growth and marine life, because of Venezuela's Orinoco River. The river's nutrients flow through the Guyana current that brushes Tobago and provides the island with some of the Caribbean's best diving.

What Can We Buy?

The best purchase on Trinidad and Tobago for children are **steel pans**. Child-size drums are available for under $10 and are marked with the notes; some also come with simple song books. The magical sound of the pan will bring back the vacation memories for months to come and is just about indestructible.

You can find steel pans for sale at the Piarco International Airport in Trinidad. Here duty-free shops tempt those departing with local liquor, electronics, watches, jewelry, and more. There's also a good selection of locally made items ranging from hot sauces to copper jewelry to tiny steel pans.

Port of Spain is also home to several sprawling **malls**. The newest and most complete is the Grand Bazaar, an open-air extravaganza with fine shops much like you'd find at home offering clothing, jewelry, Indian clothing, the ubiquitous T-shirt, and spices in a large supermarket.

Non-shoppers will love Tobago: it's tough to spend money on this island. The most colorful shopping is found in Scarborough's **open-air market**, where tropical fruits and vegetables explode in an artist's palate of colors. Sample a few items (watch out for the fiery Scotch Bonnet peppers!) and buy a bottle of homemade hot sauce and packaged curry, some of the island's top buys.

For more traditional shopping, check out the shops at Coco Reef. Here you'll find jewelry, clothing, and small souvenir items.

What Else Do We Need to Know?

Currency. The official currency is the Trinidad-Tobago dollar. The exchange rate fluctuates but at press time the rate was $1US equals about 5.98TT.

Driving. Driving is on the LEFT on both islands.

Information. Call the Trinidad and Tobago Tourist Office, Tel. 888/535-5617. Information on Island: In Trinidad, contact the Tourism and Industrial Development Company of Trinidad and Tobago, 10-14 Phillips Street, Port of Spain, Tel. 868/675-7034. On Tobago, stop by the tourism offices at IDC Mall in Scarborough, Tel. 868/639-4333.

Website. Check out the official Website at: www.visittnt.com.

Island Report Card	
Transportation to island	B
Transportation around island	B+
Family Resorts	B
Family Restaurants	B-
Friendly atmosphere	A
Activities for kids	B+
Weather	A+
New cultures to experience	A+
Safety	B

Chapter 20

TURKS & CAICOS

We really don't want to write about the Turks and Caicos.

No, it's not a case of, as our mothers always told us, "If you can't say something nice, don't say anything at all." And it's certainly not that we didn't fall in love with the miles of endless beaches or the almost palpable sense of tranquillity in these islands just off the tip of the Bahamas.

It's just that we feel we've discovered a slice of paradise. And we just don't want the rest of the world to know about it. But, as our mothers also always warned, "Share and share alike." Others searching for their own piece of paradise may find that this archipelago of nearly 40 islands, most uninhabited, will fit the bill.

The Turks and Caicos (pronounced Cay-cos) are located 1-1/2 hours from Miami, tucked halfway between the tip of Florida and Puerto Rico. This British crown colony, ruled by a governor appointed by the Queen, is better known to the world of banking than among travelers. With its tax-free status, use of the English language and the US dollar as official currency, and with the stability of the British government backing the islands, the Turks and Caicos have been a popular off-shore banking center for American corporations for many years.

We found that the same attributes that make these islands so attractive to businesses also make them appealing to travelers. A trip to the islands is quick thanks to daily jet service from Miami. Once there, travel around the islands, although on the left side of the road, is easy, and we didn't need to take time to learn a foreign currency or exchange rate. And the political stability of this government has brought a sense of security to the Turks and Caicos, resulting in an incredibly low rate of crime. Beaches are safe and

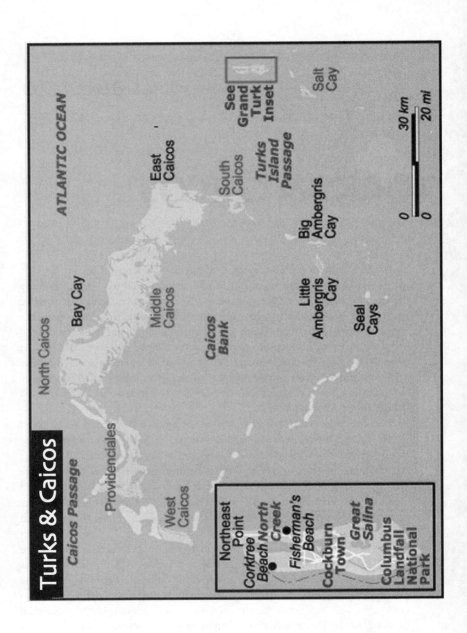

uncrowded, and tourists can enjoy late night walks from property to property on the beaches of the main island, Providenciales.

Just how uncrowded these islands are is very obvious when arriving in Providenciales, better known as simply Provo. Although this island boasts the largest portion of the Turks and Caicos population of 15,000, it is still open and unsettled. This sickle-shaped island is dotted with scrubby growth, short palms and climbing sea grapes. Chalky limestone roads wind across the flat island, connecting settlements like Blue Hills and The Bight.

But the traveler to Provo will soon realize that its desert terrain is just a backdrop to the beaches and clear waters that are the main attractions. On some parts of the island the beaches stretch for miles, dotted only with the footprints of iguanas or shorebirds. You won't find beach vendors or hagglers on these shores, just a few tourists and locals enjoying snorkeling or a swim in the gentle surf. High rises are forbidden, with resorts built no taller than three stories.

For most visitors, the real attraction of Provo is the luxury of being able to do nothing at all. Days are spent on the beach or in water so clear that it is often cited as one of the top scuba destinations in the world. Visibility averages 80 to 100 feet or better, and the water temperature ranges from 82-84 degrees in the summer and 75-76 in the winter months. Beneath the calm waves swim colorful marine animals as exotic as hawksbill turtles, nurse sharks, and octopus. With a one mile vertical coral wall located offshore, Provo is a diver's paradise.

To protect the ecology of the islands, the Turks and Caicos have established an extensive national park and nature reserve system. Over 31 national parks dot the islands: Provo's Princess Alexandra National Park, with 13 miles of protected beaches; the NW Point Marine, with spectacular wall diving; and Chalk Sound, with small boat sailing on the west end of the island, just to name a few. National park rules make it illegal to hunt or fish, remove any animal or coral, moor vessels over 60 feet except on fixed buoys or drive boats within 100 yards of the shoreline.

One of the most protected treasures around the islands is JoJo the dolphin. This wild dolphin has been sighted for 12 years along the north coast of Provo, the only case ever documented of prolonged interaction between an individual wild dolphin and humans. Often spotted swimming along the north shore or near boats, JoJo is protected and the government has declared him a national treasure.

Although it is a rarity to spot JoJo, vacationers are certain to spot wildlife on daytrips to nearby Water Cay. Located northeast of Provo, this small island is the home of numerous iguanas that greet boat passengers and happily pose for photos just yards away. Snorkeling cruises take visitors from Provo to this island most every afternoon. But snorkeling, scuba diving, golfing, and even iguana watching take a back seat to Providenciales' real draw: pure relaxation.

Although the chain is composed of nearly 40 limestone islands, only eight are considered destinations. Providenciales or Provo is home to about 6,000 residents and to most of the tourist industry. The capital of the Turks and Caicos is the island of Grand Turk, a short hop from Provo. This seven-mile square island has some historic buildings and the national museum, a must-see for history buffs.

Other inhabited islands include North Caicos, the most verdant island in the chain; South Caicos, a fishing center; Middle Caicos, home of several sea caves; and Salt Cay, a tiny island of only 300 residents that was once the world's largest producer of salt.

Are We There Yet?

By Air
Visitors to the Turks and Caicos arrive on Providenciales. Service from Miami is available from American Airlines, Air Jamaica, Delta, British Airways, Turks and Caicos Airways, and others. Flying time to Providenciales is about 80 minutes from Miami or two and a half hours from Atlanta.

To island hop, book a seat aboard an inter-island charter flights with InterIsland Airways, Tel. 649/946-4181.

Getting Around the Island

Rental cars are available, but they can be tough to obtain and expensive — about $45 a day for a full-size. Once you have a rental car, you'll find that gasoline prices are equally expensive: about $2.50 a gallon. Taxi service is easier. (Check out the neckties hanging from every taxi driver's rear view mirror. They're required attire for drivers picking up a fare at the airport.)

Where Are We Staying?

BEACHES TURKS AND CAICOS, Providenciales, Tel. 649/946-8000, Fax 649/946-8001. Toll-free reservations Tel. 800/BEACHES; www.beaches.com. Summer and winter rates from $345. Credit cards accepted.

Part of the Sandals family of resorts, this all-inclusive is a favorite with families. Located on the 12-mile beach at Grace Bay, this 453-room resort is open to singles, couples and families.

For kids, the focal point of this resort is its massive Pirates Island Waterpark which includes everything from a full-size "pirate" ship to waterslides, a kids' pool, a self-serve ice cream machine, swim-up soda bar, diner, six big screen TVs, a jungle games room, and video center.

Like other members of the Beaches chain, this resort features Sesame Street characters in a variety of special shows and activities throughout the day (see our "Beaches and Sesame Street" sidebar.) Also, the resort has an Xbox Oasis Game Room with the latest from Xbox, EA Sports, Sega, Activision, Midway, Ubi Soft and many more. For teens, there's also a special teen disco.

Dining includes a variety of restaurants. Reflections is the main dining room and features buffet servings of breakfast, lunch and dinner. Sapodilla's and Schooners serve adults only while families are welcome in the Arizona Bar and Grill for Tex-Mex cuisine or the Teppanyaki restaurant Kimonos, which has family seating from 6 to 7 nightly.

Watersports include snorkeling and scuba diving (a resort course is offered for all guests 12 years and older), aqua trikes, windsurfing, kayaking, sailing, hobie cats, and view boards for a peek at what lies beneath the sea's waves. Two swimming pools cool down guests once they leave the beach, and a special Toddler's Pool and Activity area keeps young visitors happy.

Children are also kept entertained at the supervised areas. A nursery is available for infants and toddlers while the Cuda Kids Club keeps older children happy at the children's pool, kids gazebo, playground, table tennis, pool table facilities, and at classes in everything from sandcastle building to reggae. Video game buffs will love the Sega Center with state-of-the-art video games (all complimentary). Teens also have special activities including disco nights, movie nights, sports tournaments, and more.

COMFORT SUITES TURKS AND CAICOS, Grace Bay, Tel. 649/946-8888, Fax 649/946-5444. Toll-free Reservations 888/678-DIVE; www.comfortsuitesci.com. Summer rates from $99. Credit cards accepted.

For families who don't necessarily have to be right on the beach but would like to keep an eye on the budget, there's Comfort Suites, adjacent to Ports of Call shopping center. The 99-room property offers accommodations with either a king or two double beds; rooms include a sofa bed and small refrigerator as well. There is no restaurant on site although a complimentary continental breakfast is served daily at several restaurants are located at Ports of Call. The hotel has a pool and pool bar. We stayed here recently and found the property pleasant and well-located. For the price, it's very convenient, just a short walk to the beaches at Grace Bay. Kids under 16 stay free in a room with adults (with a maximum of four persons in the room.)

OCEAN CLUB, Providenciales. Tel. 649/946-5880, Fax 649/946-5845. Toll-free reservations Tel. 800/457-8787; www.oceanclubresorts.com. Winter rates begin at $225 for studio suite, Summer rates are $180. Credit cards accepted.

Starting as a small hotel, the property has grown to full resort status with a small shopping arcade, convenience store, watersports concession, restaurant, beach grill, two bars, and more. The all-suite Grace Bay property still has the feel of a quiet getaway, but now takes its place alongside other full service resorts on this 12 mile stretch of beach.

Expansive rooms greet even those guests who chose the smaller accommodations at Ocean Club. With white tile floors, wicker furnishings, sliding glass doors opening to screened patios and balconies, and numerous windows, suites here are sunny and styled in a casual beachfront decor. Every room includes air conditioning, fully equipped kitchens or kitchenettes, cable TV, direct dial phones with voice messaging, in-suite washer and dryer, and daily maid service. Family-friendly features such as rollaway beds, baby cribs, and high chairs are available.

The resort's white sand beach is one of its top assets, located just steps from the suites. Water lovers can also choose from two freshwater pools, including a freeform pool that's a favorite with young vacationers. Art Pickering's Provo Turtle Divers, located at the resort, offers dive excursions and watersports including snorkel trips, bonefishing and deep sea fishing, parasailing, scuba certification, and more.

Guest facilities include a fitness center with stationary bikes, universal station, stair climbers, and free weights. There are also massages and aromatherapy at the fitness center or in-room with Ocean Club's licensed massage therapist. Tennis is available day and night on a lighted court.

A dining shuttle operates nightly for drop-offs at island restaurants; a shopping shuttle runs three days a week, primarily to the island supermarket so guests can stock their kitchens. The front desk staff arranges for rental cars, scooters, bicycles, and baby-sitters as well as island tours and day sails aboard private sailing charters such as the Beluga, a 37-foot catamaran.

TURTLE COVE INN, Turtle Cove, Providenciales, Tel. 649/946-4203, Fax 649/946-4141. Toll-free US phone number 800/887-0477; www.turtlecoveinn.com. Winter rates from $85, Summer from $75. Credit cards accepted.

When divers come up for air, many head to this resort where they find an on-site dive center and packages including two tank morning dives. Located directly off the marina, rooms here are simple but include telephone, cable TV, and a private balcony. A freshwater pool is available for guests along with a casual restaurant and bar. Kids under 10 sharing a room with a full-price paying adult stay free.

What Can We Do Now?

With the number of tourists relatively low, you'll find that the number of attractions are equally sparse. Don't expect the shopping of St. Thomas or the reggae clubs of Jamaica or the submarine rides of Grand Cayman at this destination. For most families, the real attraction is being able to do nothing at all. Days are spent on the beach or in the water that's so clear it's often cited as the world's top scuba destination.

One unique attraction is the **Conch Farm**, Providenciales, Tel. 649/946-5643, the only farm in the world that raises Queen conch, the shellfish that's become a favorite meal throughout much of the Caribbean. On a guided tour, you'll see conch in various stages, from the larvae in the hatchery to juveniles about 4mm in length, to adulthood. In Provo, the product of this unique farm is served at the Anacaona Restaurant and the Tiki Hut.

History buffs will find reason enough to take a day trip to Grand Turk to visit the **Turks and Caicos National Museum**, Grand Turk, www.tcmuseum.org; Tel. 649/946-2160. We think this is one of the most fascinating museums in the entire Caribbean. The main exhibit features the Molasses Reef shipwreck, which occurred in the Turks and Caicos nearly 500 years ago. The Spanish caravel hit the reef and quickly sank in only 20 feet of water where it remained until the 1970s. Once excavated, it was recognized as the oldest European shipwreck in the New World.

The museum, located in a 150-year old house on the island's main street, features artifacts from the wreck with interactive displays, video presentations, and scientific exhibits.

The name of this wrecked ship was never learned because, like drug-running planes of today, this was a ship with an illegal booty. Kept off the official records of Spain, the ship was carrying slaves probably bound for the plantations of nearby Hispaniola.

Sports & Recreation

Scuba diving and **snorkeling** are the top attractions of these islands. Visibility ranges from 80 to 100 feet or better and water temperatures hover at about 82 degrees in the summer and 75 or so in the winter months. Beneath the calm waves swim colorful marine animals as exotic as hawksbill turtles, nurse sharks, and octopus. With a one mile vertical coral wall located offshore, Provo is a diver's paradise.

You'll find top **dive operators** here as well. In Provo, call Dive Provo, Tel. 800/234-7768. In Grand Turk, check with Blue Water Divers Tel. 649/946-2432, and Sea Eye Diving, Tel. 649/946-1407; in Salt Cay call Salt Cay Divers, Tel. 649/946-6906.

From December through April, ecotourists journey to Salt Cay for a chance to spot **humpback whales**, watching for the giant mammals from shore or in the water in scuba gear.

Families can enjoy bird watching on North Caicos or watching gentle rock iguanas on **Little Water Cay**, home of a new nature trail program, one of 33 nature reserves and refuges in the Turks and Caicos. Kids enjoy watching the iguanas in their natural habitat from raised boardwalks and observation towers. Trips to Little Water Cay are offered by several operators who also schedule full-day excursions to the inhabited but sparsely developed islands of North and Middle Caicos for viewing a pink flamingo colony, talking with local residents, and a enjoying a beach barbecue.

Monthly "**glow worm**" cruises are another unique experience for travelers. Scheduled from three to six nights after a full moon, these cruises take visitors to the Caicos Bank for a look at a phosphorescent marine worm that lights the waters about an hour after sunset in a unusual mating ritual.

What Can We Buy?

There is a shopping complex in Provo called Ports of Call, designed to resemble an old Caribbean seaside town. Look for restaurants, crafts and art in this new development near Grace Bay.

Conch (pronounced Konk) shells make a wonderful souvenir from these islands. Stop by the Conch Farm to purchase a beautiful shell.

What Else Do We Need to Know?

Currency. The US dollar is the official currency.
Driving. Driving is on the LEFT.
Information. Call the Turks and Caicos Tourist Board,
Tel. 800/241-0824.
Website.www.turksandcaicostourism.com

Island Report Card	
Transportation to island	A
Transportation around island	B+
Family Resorts	B
Family Restaurants	B-
Friendly atmosphere	A
Activities for kids	B+
Weather	A
New cultures to experience	B
Safety	A+

Chapter 21

U.S. VIRGIN ISLANDS

License plates proudly proclaim that this is "America's Paradise." It's the United States' own vacationland, a place to dance to a Caribbean beat, swim in some of the region's clearest waters, or do some "limin'," the Virgin Islanders' word for just kicking back and enjoying a taste of paradise.

The US Virgin Islands offer three distinct vacations for families. **St. Croix** boasts some of the best of the other US Virgin Islands: the bustle of St. Thomas and the eco-tourism of St. John. In St. Croix's cities of Christiansted and Frederiksted, duty-free shopping is on a smaller scale than St. Thomas' Charlotte Amalie, but you'll still find enough jewelry, leather goods, perfume, and china to keep even the most dedicated shopper happy. On the island's far reaches, eco-tourists can hike through a sultry rain forest or enjoy an unparalleled snorkeling trail where fish as bright as gumdrops swim among century-old coral.

On the south shore, Frederiksted is the quieter of the island's two cities, a sleepy port that springs to life when a cruise ship pulls into town. After Hurricane Marilyn wrecked havoc on St. Thomas, the popularity of this cruise destination soared and several new shops popped up on the city's waterfront streets.

Nature lovers, set your sights for tiny **St. John**. This is the eco-tourism capital of the Caribbean, an island where the family, from the luxury of a beautiful resort or a posh villa or the inexpensive accommodations of a tent or cabin, can hike, snorkel, and tour an island where two-thirds of the land is preserved as a national park.

The stewardship of the island's natural beauty began with Laurance Rockefeller. Developer of Caneel Bay Resort, the multi-millionaire donated

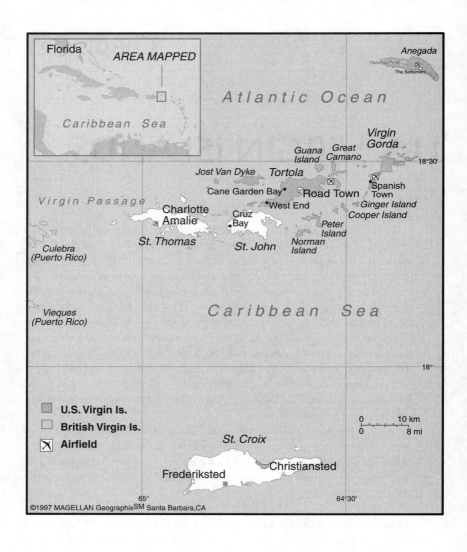

Florida

AREA MAPPED

Atlantic Ocean

Caribbean Sea

Anegada

Flamingo Pond
The Settlement

Virgin Gorda

18°30'

Guana
Island

Great
Camano

Jost Van Dyke   *Tortola*

Cane Garden Bay   Road Town   Spanish
Town

Virgin Passage   •West End   *Ginger Island*
Cooper Island

Charlotte
Amalie   Cruz
Bay   Peter
Island

St. Thomas   *St. John*   Norman
Island

Culebra
(Puerto Rico)

Vieques
(Puerto Rico)

Caribbean   Sea

18°

U.S. Virgin Is.

British Virgin Is.

Airfield

0   10 km
0   8 mi

St. Croix

Frederiksted   Christiansted

©1997 MAGELLAN GeographixSM Santa Barbara,CA

65°   64°30'

much of the island to the National Park Service in the 1950s. Today, preservation of this island's resources lies in the hands of the park service and a developer named Stanley Selengut, a leader in the world of eco-tourism who operates several eco-friendly properties on the island. St. John leads the world in sustainable tourism resorts where guests make a minimal impact on nature.

St. John may be the smallest of the US Virgin Islands but it is a giant in the world of eco-tourism. Along with lavish hotels such as the Westin St. John and Caneel Bay, St. John also offers camping designed to allow vacationers to bring down the walls that separate hotel guests from nature.

Four campgrounds invite visitors who are ready to rough it in varying degrees. At Cinnamon Bay Campgrounds, located in the national park, campers select from bare sites, canvas tents, and screened shelters. At Maho Bay Camps, guests enjoy screened tent cottages, connected by a network of raised boardwalks. Nearby, Harmony Resort offers camping luxury with kitchens, balconies, and ceiling fans. A closer inspection reveals, however, that this is no ordinary resort. Running on solar energy, the cabins are built entirely of recycled materials. Sawdust and trash bags assume a new life as sturdy deck materials; recycled cardboard now serves as siding.

Now Stanley Selengut, founder of both Maho and Harmony, has gone a step further in offering an ecological choice for St. John guests. Concordia eco-tents feature high-tech reflective materials that keep the interior cool beneath the Caribbean sun, solar energy that powers appliances and heats showers, and compost toilets that minimize waste. And, in keeping with the Rockefeller connection with eco-tourism, Laurance's niece, Abby, heads the work on waste management at the resort.

"Eco-tourism should be on our shoulders because we're on some of the most beautiful land in the world," explains Selengut.

St. Thomas is the most bustling of the Virgins. This is the destination for any shoppers in your family. St. Thomas' Charlotte Amalie (pronounced a-mal-yah) has a busy cosmopolitan atmosphere with a Caribbean charm all its own.

But beyond Charlotte Amalie's boundaries, the island enjoys a slower pace. Here, on overlooks high above the city's lights, families can share some of the Caribbean's most glorious sunsets. On the island's fringe of powdered sugar beaches, you can catch up on your limin' — just lazing the days away beneath towering palms.

Are We There Yet?

By Air

Both St. Thomas and St. Croix are home to airports with extensive service. St. Croix's Henry E. Rohlsen International Airport is served by

American, American Eagle, Continental Connections, LIAT, US Airways, and several small carriers.

St. Thomas's Cyril E. King International Airport is served by American, American Eagle, Continental and Continental Connections, LIAT, United, US Airways, and others.

From both the St. Croix and the St. Thomas airports, you'll need to take a taxi to your hotels. Hotels and resorts are not allowed to send a hotel van to pick up guests.

Take a day trip between St. Thomas and St. Croix with a quick hop between islands on the **seaplane**, which departs from downtown Christiansted and arrives in downtown Charlotte Amalie. Seaborne Seaplane, Tel. 340/777-6442, provides shuttle service between the two islands; rates are about $79 each way.

By Ferry

St. John does not have an airport, so you'll arrive by boat. Most visitors arrive via ferry service from St. Thomas, Tel. 340/776-6282. From Red Hook, it's a 20-minute, $3 one way cruise ($1 for kids under 12). Ferry service runs from 6:30am to midnight every hour on the hour. A private water taxi from Red Hook is a wonderful luxury; call Per Dohm's Water Taxi, Tel. 340/775-6501.

Getting Around the Island

Taxis are easy to obtain. In Christiansted, stop by the taxi stand on King Street, in Frederiksted the taxi stand is at Fort Frederik. Licensed taxi services bear a license plate that begins with "TP." In St. Thomas, taxis are parked at the Vendors' Market. All taxi fares are fixed and, by law, taxis must carry a list of the fixed fares.

Rental cars are readily available; all you'll need is a valid U.S. driver's license. Remember, though, that driving is on the left side of the road.

Traveling among the USVI is as easy as moving from city to city. You can hop a ferry or seaplane (between St. Croix and St. Thomas), and there's no need to show documents on arrival.

Where Are We Staying?

St. Croix

THE BUCCANEER, Shoys, Tel. 340/712-2100, Fax 340/712-2104. Toll-free US phone number 800/255-3881; www.thebuccaneer.com. Summer rates start $215-$410. Credit cards accepted.

No other hotel in St. Croix , and few in the Caribbean, boasts the impressive history of The Buccaneer, located east of Christiansted. Once owned by Charles Martel, one of the Knights of Malta, the estate had walls three feet thick and was tucked just behind a hill to hide it from view of pirates. Later, the stately manor was the residence of the young Alexander Hamilton.

Today, the original estate is supplemented with modern rooms to complete the 138-room resort but the rich historic atmosphere remains. Every week, guests and staff come together at the manager's cocktail party, hosted in a stone sugar mill that stands as a reminder of the island's early plantation past.

History at the Buccaneer doesn't just end with the facilities — it extends to the resort owners as well. Today the ninth generation of the Armstrong family to reside on St. Croix operates the expansive resort.

The Buccaneer is also well-known for its sports facilities, especially tennis and golf. Eight tennis courts are located halfway down the hill from the main house. Golfers can take their best swing at an 18-hole course with views of the sea. Packages with unlimited golf are available.

One of the top Christmas activities planned by a resort is also found at The Buccaneer. The "Twelve Days of Christmas" kids camp keeps children in the holiday spirit of fun with supervised activities from 10am to 6pm . Children enjoy beach fun, tropical arts and crafts, and outdoor games.

And, of course, the spirit of Christmas rings true here as well. Santa arrives by, what else, a dingy pulled by eight tiny seahorses! For New Years, the celebrations include a tropical luau and fireworks.

CHENAY BAY BEACH RESORT, Green Cay, Tel. 340/773-2918, Fax 340/773-6665. Toll-free reservations Tel. 800/548-4457; www.chenaybay.com. Winter rates $215-$540, Summer rates $158-$360. Credit cards accepted.

Cheney Bay offers a Cruzan Kidz program for children 3-12. The complimentary program runs from 9am to 1pm weekdays and includes tennis lessons, snorkel trips, beach hikes, shell hunts, treasure hunts, and other activities.

The whole family can enjoy Chenay's activities as well. Complimentary snorkeling, tennis, kayaks, and floating mats are provided to guests. And, with its bay location, the calm waters are perfect for young swimmers.

Guests stay in one of 50 West Indian-style cottages, each with kitchenette, mini-bar, cable TV, and private deck with either a garden or ocean view. Family units are two connecting cottages and offer plenty of room for busy children.

DIVI CARINA BAY BEACH RESORT & CASINO, Carina Bay, Tel. 340/773-9700, Fax 340/773-9479. Toll-free US phone number 877/773-9700; www. www.divicarina.com. Winter rates from $174, Summer rates from $151. Credit cards accepted.

Located on a quiet stretch on the south side of the island (you'll probably want to rent a car if you stay here), this resort boasts a 1,000-foot white sand beach. You can also opt for a dip in one of the two pools. Beachside rooms are our favorite (larger villas are located across the road up on the hillside). Rooms are decorated in island style and all include coffee maker, refrigerator and microwave. Kids 15 and under stay free when staying with an adult. Childcare is available for a fee.

HOTEL ON THE CAY, Christiansted, Tel. 340/773-2035, Fax 340/773-7046. Toll-free US phone number 800/524-2035; www.hotelonthecay.com. Winter rates start at $132, Summer rates at $90. Credit cards accepted.

Known to its fans as "Hot C," this charming property is located on a tiny cay with an unbeatable view of Christiansted. Protestant Cay rises from the turquoise waters of the harbor just a one minute ferry ride (free for guests) from downtown.

Along with 55 guest rooms (each with a kitchenette), Hotel on the Cay also offers the only beach in downtown Christiansted. It's enjoyed by guests from many nearby hotels who pay the toll of what must be, considering its length, the priciest ferry ride in the Caribbean: $3 per person for the round trip haul.

HIBISCUS BEACH HOTEL, 4131 LaGrande Princesse, Tel. 340/773-4042, Fax 340/773-4668. Toll-free US phone number 800/442-0121; www.hibiscusbeachresort.com. Summer rates $130-$140 Credit cards accepted.

The 37 guest rooms, each with an ocean view, here are pretty no frills but perfect for the traveling family on a budget. The hotel has a pretty stretch of beach, and this property is very convenient, just 15 minutes from the airport and about 10 minutes from Christiansted.

The best feature, however, is its Friday night (during high season) dance show, a wonderful introduction to the island's heritage for every member of the family. Every Friday, the hotel offers an unbeatable show that pulses with the fervor of island dancing and music. Authentic local steps are performed by the Caribbean Dance Company. The show is available with dinner or as show only. Reservations are required for this popular presentation. The final dance is the Rainbow, where the performers invite the guests to join them on the dance floor. (Kids love this!)

HOTEL CARAVELLE, 444 Queen Cross Street, Tel. 340/773-0687, Fax 340/778-7004. Toll-free US phone number 800/524-0410; www.hotelcaravelle.com. Winter rates $129-$159, Summer rates $105-$125. Credit cards accepted.

This modest European-style hotel is especially convenient for those who want to immerse themselves in the shopping of Christiansted. Located downtown right on the waterfront, this 43-room inn is within walking distance of just about everything in Christiansted, from art galleries to the historic fort to fine dining. It's an excellent choice for anyone on a budget, and you can splurge with the penthouse suite with a living room, full kitchen, large bedroom, and two baths for less than the cost of a standard room at many other island properties.

TAMARIND REEF HOTEL, 501 Tamarind Reef, Christiansted, Tel. 340/773-4455, Fax 340/773-3989. Toll-free US phone number 800/619-0014. Winter rates start at $160, Summer from $145. Credit cards accepted.

This is one of our favorite budget-priced accommodations in the Caribbean, thanks to sparkling clean rooms, an excellent snorkel trail. The property is located east of Christiansted just off the reef. All of the rooms include a refrigerator, coffee maker, air conditioning, phones, and many also include kitchenettes. The atmosphere here is laid-back and comfortable, perfect for families to enjoy the tranquil east end of St. Croix and the snorkel trail in the inlet just in front of the hotel.

Just a few steps from the hotel, the Green Cay Marina is home to boats that offer daily tours to Buck Island as well as deep-sea fishing excursions and scuba diving trips.

Tamarind guests should also consider a kayak trip around Green Cay, a federally protected island (home to the endangered Ground Lizard) just off Tamarind Reef Hotel's beach. Guests of Tamarind Reef Hotel have free access to non-motorized watersports (snorkeling equipment, kayaks, windsurfers); non guests can rent the equipment. The trip to Green Cay is not far and kids 12 and older get there and back with relative ease. Younger kids should go on a two-person kayak with a parent or older sibling.

St. John

CANEEL BAY, St. John, USVI, Tel. 340/776-6111, Fax 340/693-8280. Toll-free US phone number Tel. 888/ROSEWOOD; www.caneelbay.com. Winter rates: $450-$850. Summer rates $300-$700. Credit cards accepted.

Caneel has the air of old-world Caribbean elegance that tells you, without a word, that this resort was a Laurance Rockefeller development. Tucked within the Virgin Islands National Park, Caneel boasts seven beaches and a natural beauty that is surpassed only by the resort's high quality service. Spread out across the lush property, 171 cottages combine "casual elegance" with "St. John camping" to come up with a property where you can feel like you are camping while enjoying plenty of pampering. Cooled by trade winds and a ceiling fan, each cottage has furnishings from the Philippines, screened walls that are open to a pristine view, and cool terrazzo floors as well as an ice chest for daily ice delivery.

Guests check in when they arrive at the airport in St. Thomas and board private ferry service to the resort. Upon arrival, kids are given a special gift and a personalized letter welcoming them to the resort. Complimentary punch is served to kids on the ferry ride over to their home away from home. After check in, children find milk and cookies waiting in their room with a selection of toys chosen for their age. (The ferry service is available several times daily so guests can hop to St. Thomas for a little shopping.) Private ferry service is also available three times a week to the resort's sister property, Little Dix Bay, on Virgin Gorda. (Bring along your passport or proof of citizenship to take this jaunt to the British Virgin Islands.)

Along with plenty of complimentary diversions (including the Peter Burwash International tennis program), introductory scuba diving clinic, windsurfing, Sunfish and kayaks, and movie presentations, other activities are available at additional charge: half- and full-day sails, beach barbecue, sunset cocktail cruise, guided snorkel trips, fishing charters, massages, and boat charters.

Children find plenty of fun at Caneel as well. Turtle Town, the children's center, offers plenty of fun and education. "In Turtle Town, our young visitors learn to appreciate the beauty of our island by going on treasure hunts and nature walks, making arts and crafts with local natural materials, listening to pirate tales, taking Caribbean dance lessons and much more," explains Joanna Werman, Caneel Bay's Children's Program Director.

Each day's fun in Turtle Town follows a special theme. On Marine Life Day, kids enjoy shore exploration, search for sea turtle nests, enjoy aquatic arts and crafts, watch a Sea Life slide show and more. Other themed days include An Island Home (with nature walks), A World of One/East To Be Me Day (featuring local culture), Mystery Day (with a scavenger hunt and costumed hunt for pirate treasure), Magic Day (complete with magic shows and lessons), and Family Fun Day (highlighted by events for the family such as a ride on the Atlantis Submarine or a look at the island's ancient petroglyphs).

However your family chooses to enjoy Caneel, there's one thing sure to please everyone: the resort's beaches. Here seven pristine stretches of sand are available, so guests can visit a different beach every day. Guests can hop aboard the resort shuttle for quick drop off at any of these beaches; don't forget to request a picnic lunch to take along!

CINNAMON BAY CAMPGROUNDS, Cruz Bay, Tel. 340/776-6330, Fax 340/776-6458, www.cinnamonbay.com. Toll-free reservations Tel. 800/539-9998. Winter rates for bare sites are $27 (bare sites) and $110-$140 for cottages, Summer rates are $27 for bare sites and $70-$90 for cottages. Credit cards accepted.

Campers keep the bare sites, tents, and screened shelters of this popular campground full year around. Managed by Caneel Bay, this campground is located on the grounds of the national park and features accommodations near beautiful Cinnamon Bay Beach, St. John's longest stretch of sand.

Tents (which measure 10' x 14') are outfitted with four cots with bedding, a solid floor, an ice chest, water container, and cooking and eating utensils. Outdoors, a propane stove and lantern, charcoal grill, and picnic table are available.

Cottages (15 x 15 feet) are actually screened shelters with the same features as well as electricity. All accommodations share bathhouses with cool water showers.

The atmosphere is very relaxed, as campers enjoy the Caribbean at their campsite, on the beach, and on daily ranger-led tours of the national park. Don't be surprised to see a family of wild burros roaming the grounds.

The most family-friendly cottages are units 10A through D, a seashell's throw from the water. Tent site 21 is the closest to the water, and bare site 24 is best for beach buffs. We hear that you practically have to inherit a reservation to secure these most-popular sites, but give it a try anyway.

ESTATE CONCORDIA STUDIOS, Cruz Bay, Tel. 340/693-5855, Fax 340/693-5960 . Toll-free US reservations Tel. 800/392-9004. Winter rates for cottages from $135, summer from $95 (Eco-tents $110 in winter, $85 in summer). Credit cards accepted.

Like Harmony, Estate Concordia also takes the eco-tourism-with-style approach. Located on the more remote south shore, these units and the neighboring eco-tents are more widely spaced across the landscape than the units at Harmony and Maho. These canvas tent cottages are specifically designed to be light on the land, to rely on high-tech advancements such as ultra light reflective materials, and to provide facilities such as compost toilets, while at the same time being ecologically friendly.

HARMONY STUDIO, Cruz Bay, Tel. 340/776-6240, Fax 340/776-6504. Toll-free reservations Tel. 800/392-9004. Winter rates from $185 summer from $110. Credit cards accepted.

As its name suggests, this was designed to be a resort in tune with nature. Solar power, recycled materials, low flush toilets, and a complete awareness of the environment makes this an eco-sensitive resort, but with a higher number of creature comforts than are found at its sister property, Maho. These units include energy-efficient refrigerators, a computer to track energy use, comfortable furnishings (either two twin beds in the bedroom studio units or two queen beds in the living room studios), private baths, a deck with furniture, and kitchen.

MAHO BAY CAMPS, Cruz Bay, Tel. 340/776-6226, Fax 340/776-6504. Toll-free reservations Tel. 800/392-9004, www.maho.org. Winter rates from $120, Summer rates from $75. Credit cards accepted.

From the minute you arrive at Maho, you'll know that this is no ordinary campground. From the help-yourself center where guests leave unused food, toiletries, books, and other items for other guests' use to the network of raised boardwalks that connect the tent cabins and protect hillside vegetation, this resort's focus is on environmental camping.

Every 16' x 16' unit has screened sides with roll down privacy shades, a sleeping area with mattress-covered beds and bedding, a futon sofa that pulls down into a sleeper, a cooking and dining area with cooler, propane stove, and fan, and an outdoor balcony. Barbecue grills and bathhouses are scattered throughout the property.

WESTIN RESORT ST. JOHN, Tel. 340/693-8000, Fax 340/693-8888. Toll-free US phone number 800/WESTIN-1; www.westin.com or www.westinresortstjohn.com. Rates run from $225-$945. Credit cards accepted.

This resort has long been one of the Caribbean's nicest, a place where guests feel like they're being swept into paradise. Guests are transported to the resort like visiting royalty aboard a private yacht. You'll arrive on St. John at the hotel dock, and soon be off to your room, one of 285 guest accommodations on a hillside over Great Cruz Bay.

Villas

St. John boasts a number of exquisite private villas for the ultimate in privacy. For brochures of these homes, many with private pools, contact a villa broker such as Caribbean Villas, Tel. 340/776-6152, or Villas Caribe, Tel. 340/693-9100

St. Thomas

BOLONGO BAY BEACH CLUB AND VILLAS, four miles from Charlotte Amalie, Tel. 340/775-1800, Fax 340/775-3208. Toll-free reservations Tel. 800/524-4746; www.bolongobay.com. Winter rates from $250, Summer rates begin at $175. Credit cards accepted.

A favorite with family travelers, Bolongo Bay offers 80 guest rooms in standards and superior (beachfront) rooms. All rooms include air-conditioning, ceiling fan, color cable television, private balcony, safe, and telephone. Some rooms include an efficiency kitchen.

Many guests opt for the "all-inclusive" plan with all meals, unlimited beverages, non-motorized watersports, tennis, basketball, beach volleyball, use of spa and fitness center, all-day sailing excursion to St. John, snorkel cruise, introductory scuba lesson, hotel taxes and gratuity in a one price package. If you think you'll be spending much of your time off property, a Continental plan is available with Continental breakfast, watersports, introductory scuba lesson, beach volleyball, tennis basketball, and use of fitness center (and, if you stay for seven nights, the all-day sailing cruise).

Active kids will enjoy Bolongo's many sports offerings: two lighted volleyball courts, two lighted half courts at the basketball club, two tennis courts, a five-star PADI training facility for teens interested in scuba, and an array of watersports that includes water cycles, kayaks, canoes, paddle boats, windsurfers, sunfish, sailboats, snorkel gear, and swim mats.

Children under 12 stay free in the same room with parents (when parents book Continental plan). Cribs are complimentary and baby-sitting services with a licensed day-care provider are available.

MARRIOTT FRENCHMAN'S REEF BEACH RESORT & MARRIOTT MORNING STAR, Estate Bakkeroke, Tel. 340/776-8500, Fax 340/715-6191. Toll-free reservations Tel. 800/228-9290; www.marriott.com. Winter rates from $125, Summer rates from $125. Credit cards accepted.

The hotel-style Frenchman's Reef is popular with conventions and meetings but it also makes a fine place to bring along the family, whether you're on island for business or pure fun.

Families can enjoy plenty of activity together: tennis, golf, snorkeling, sailing, or even a water ferry ride into Charlotte Amalie for a day of duty-free shopping.

Morning Star lies just down the road from Frenchman's Reef but is better designed for families with young children. Like Frenchman's Reef, the resort offers just about any activity you could select: sports, watersports (enjoyed right off the beach at this property), water taxi service into town, and more. However, here families can stroll right from their rooms to the beach, always a favorite with young children anxious to hit the water right away rather than wait for a shuttle.

RITZ-CARLTON, ST. THOMAS, 6900 Great Bay, Tel. 340/775-3333, Fax 340/775-4444. Toll-free US phone number 800/241-3333; www.ritzcarlton.com. Winter rates run $445-1250, Summer rates run $449-549. Credit cards accepted.

Just as you would expect from a member of the Ritz-Carlton family, this resort is really grand. This is one of the most elegant hotels in the Caribbean, an ultra-luxurious resort designed to make its visitors feel like royalty. From the moment you enter the marble entry of this resort styled to replicate a Venetian palace, you'll know that this is a step above even the luxurious resorts for which the island is known. Maintaining a one-to-one guest to staff ratio, the resort is for those vacationers who are ready for privacy and pampering.

The hotel's hibiscus-colored roofs dot the shoreline of Great Bay. Here, amid stark white buildings punctuated with bougainvillea and other tropical splendors, await some of the island's most luxurious guest rooms. Marble baths, seersucker robes, and French doors leading out to private balconies greet guests. Away from their rooms, visitors continue to enjoy the finest in amenities, including sailing, snorkeling, and a private yacht. Nanny service is available for families. Kids ages 4-12 can take part in the Ritz Kids program, offering full- and half-day programs on Mondays, Tuesdays, Wednesdays, Fridays, and Saturdays (a day when evening programs are also available.) Activities at the club range from seashell hunting to feeding the many iguanas that live on property.

SAPPHIRE BEACH RESORT AND MARINA, Smith Bay Route 6, Tel. 340/775-6100, Fax 340/775-2403. Toll-free reservations Tel. 800/524-2090; www.sapphirebeachresort.com. Winter rates $395, Summer rates $225. Credit cards accepted.

Sapphire Beach Resort and Marina is perched on one of the island's most beautiful stretches of sand and offers excellent snorkeling in calm, shallow waters just offshore. Located about half an hour from the airport, this resort includes beachfront and yacht harbor view suites and villas, each with fully equipped kitchens, television, and daily maid service.

If you're traveling with children, try the KidsKlub, a day-long, complimentary program for children ages 4 to 12. Children enjoy swimming, sandcastle building, arts and crafts, story telling, sing-alongs, and more. Presently, the KidsKlub runs from 9 am-4 pm Monday through Friday, and also from 5:30 pm to 10 pm Thursday through Saturday. The 9-4 session includes activities such as swimming, sandcastle building, games, arts and crafts, water bingo, story telling, and more.

Families also have free use of snorkel gear as well as windsurfers and sunfish sailboats. Other watersports are available for a fee: parasailing, deep sea fishing, sea kayaking, scuba diving, and half and full-day sails.

SAPPHIRE VILLAGE, Smith Bay Route 6, Tel. 340/555-1212, Fax 340/775-6220. Toll-free reservations Tel. 800/524-2025; www.antillesresorts.com. Studio $145 in summer, $190 in winter. 1-bedroom $230-270 for 4 people. Credit cards accepted.

Adjacent to the Sapphire Beach Resort, these condominiums offer full housekeeping units for busy families. Studio and one-bedroom suites all include a small kitchen, air-conditioning, TV, phone, in-room safe, private balcony, and maid service.

Guests can use the watersports facilities at the Doubletree, enjoying glass bottom boat rides, snorkeling, paddle boats, or even arranging a sail to the nearby British Virgin Islands.

The beach at Sapphire has long been cited as one of the best on St. Thomas and it's not a claim without justification. A white swath of sand meets the turquoise sea and the waters remain shallow for many yards. A shallow reef comes within feet of the beach, perfect for young snorkelers.

Cribs are available for $10 per night, and kids under 12 stay free.

SECRET HARBOUR BEACH RESORT & VILLAS, 6280 Estate Nazareth, Tel. 340/775-6550, Fax 340/775-1501. Toll-free reservations Tel. 800/524-2250; www.secretharbourvi.com. Winter rates start at $275, Summer rates begin at $149. Credit cards accepted.

Perched on a beautiful swath of sand, this resort offers beach-front studios or one and two bedroom suites, each with fully equipped kitchens, cable TV, air-conditioning, ceiling fans, and beachfront balconies or patios, all looking right out to sea and, in the evenings, to the setting sun.

WYNDHAM SUGAR BAY BEACH CLUB & RESORT, 6500 Estate Smith Bay, St. Thomas, US Virgin Islands. Tel. 340/777-7100, Fax 340/777-7200. Toll-free US reservations number 800/WYNDHAM; www.wyndham.com. Winter from $259, summer from $279. Credit cards accepted.

See Chapter 3, "Best Places to Stay," for a detailed write-up.

Chartered Yachts & Cruises

One of the most exciting ways to explore the Virgin Islands is aboard a chartered yacht. It may sound like the getaway reserved exclusively for the rich and famous, but many families find that these are as reasonable as a floating condominium. These luxurious vessels boast the niceties of a fine hotel room, including private bath, gourmet meals, and television and VCR, and come crewed with a captain and cook. Call **Regency Yacht Vacations**, Tel. 800/524-7676, for information on these unique excursions, where the itinerary is selected based on your needs. A few vessels are small enough for two person charters, but most accommodate between four and 12 persons. Prices are all-inclusive.

Another good option for families are villa homes. For brochures of these homes, many with private pools, contact a villa broker such as Catered To...Ltd., Tel. 800/424-6641, Vacation Vistas, Tel. 340/776-6462, Ocean Property Management, Tel. 800/874-7897, Windspree Tel. 340/693-5423, McLaughlin Anderson Vacations, Ltd., Tel. 800/537-6246 or 800/

666-6246, Caribbean Villas, Tel. 800/338-0987, and Villa Portfolio, Tel. 800/858-7989.

What Can We Do Now?

St. Croix

The best way to see what St. Croix has to offer you and your mate is to get an overview aboard a guided island tour. **St. Croix Safari Tours**, Tel. 340/773-6700 or 800/524-2026, offer excellent tours in open air safari vehicles with bench seats. Tours last about five and a half hours and include visits to both island cities, as well as all the major attractions.

The lavish lifestyle enjoyed by plantation owners during the 19th century is preserved at the **Whim Greathouse**. Here you can visit an elegant home that combined English gentility with Caribbean practicality, filled with fine imported furniture as well as floor-to-ceiling shuttered windows and cool plank floors. If you're lucky, you'll be able to sample some freshly-made johnny cakes, baked in the plantation's detached cookhouse. (And don't miss the gift shop filled with Caribbean cookbooks, perfumes, and crafts.)

St. Croix's southern city, **Frederiksted**, lies just a few miles from the former plantation house. A stop for many cruise ships (a new dock was constructed here in 1994 to replace damage done by Hurricane Hugo), the town is a smaller version of Christiansted with a red, rather than yellow, fortress guarding the waterfront. Shopping includes duty-free boutiques featuring china and crystal to a vendor's market for inexpensive T-shirts and jewelry.

St. Croix's best treasures, however, are not the man-made ones but the natural areas found at opposite ends of the island. From Frederiksted, take Rt. 76 or the Mahogany Road north for a trip to the **rainforest**. The small rainforest has thick vegetation where the sunlight is filtered through mahogany, yellow cedar, and Tibet trees. This forest is also home of **LEAP**, the Life and Environmental Arts Project, where skilled artisans craft everything from sculptures to spoons from the hardwoods found in the rain forest.

St. John

The biggest attraction of St. John is the national park. Start with a visit to the **Virgin Islands National Park Visitors Center**, located on the waterfront in Cruz Bay. Here you'll find information on hiking, camping, snorkeling, and guided programs.

After you have your bearings, head out to the park by taxi or rental jeep. Hike on one of the many marked trails, snorkel the **guided underwater trail** at Trunk Bay, stroll along the self-guided Cinnamon Bay Nature Trail, or visit ruins of Annaberg Sugar Plantation. (A note of caution: at certain times of the year, Annaberg is infested with tiny bugs called no-see-ums. No, you won't see them, but you will definitely feel them when they start to nibble on you. Be sure to apply insect repellent before visiting this site. After three different stops here—and three sets of bites, we've learned the hard way that even a brief visit deserves an application of bug repellent.)

St. Thomas

Our favorite family stop on St. Thomas (and the top tourist attraction on the island) is **Coral World** (Tel. 888/695-2073, www.coralworldvi.com). The park is well worth several hours thanks to its numerous exhibits. The most noticable feature is its Undersea Observatory, located 100 feet offshore and accessible by walkway. You'll descend stairs and have the chance to peek at life 15 feet beneath the surface (including a look at SeaTrek participants wearing helmets and walking on the sea floor.) Twice a day, the obervatory has fish feedings which draw diners in from the surrounding sea.

Fish feeding is also a draw at the Caribbean Reef Encounter exhibit, an 80,000-gallon tank filled with tropical fish and corals. This exhibit is wheelchair accessible and easy for families with strollers. Also easily accessible is the Marine Gardens, a series of smaller aquariums featuring sea inhabitants (including our favorite, the tiny seahorses.) There's also a Deep Reef tank, filled with the predators of the deep including shark and barracuda.

But only a portion of Coral World is behind glass; many of the exhibits are outdoors in the open air (so don't save this for a rainy day option; the outdoor activities are equally as fun as the indoor ones here.) Kids enjoy the Shark Shallows Pool, located next door to the snack bar; you can view the toothy inhabitants both from above and from an underwater window.

Coral World also has plenty of hands-on fun for kids. The Stingray Pool showcases the graceful sea inhabitants;you can feed them at feeding time. The Touch Pool invites young visitors to touch conch, sea cucumbers, and starfish. Other exhibits at the park include a Turtle Pool, nature trail, and Iguana Alley, filled with wild iguanas.

Coral World is located on Coki Beach; your admission ticket means you can visit a while, hit the beach, then return to check out more exhibits or to catch a feeding time. Coki Beach is shallow and calm and good for young children. Also at the park, you can choose to take part in sea kayaking, snorkeling, Sea Trek or Snuba (see the introductory chapter for more on both those activities) or hop a ride on the Nautilus, a semi-submersible. You'll sit beneath the water's surface in front of an underwater window.

Another top family adventure on St. Thomas (albeith an expensive one) is a ride aboard the **Atlantis submarine**, Havensight Mall, Tel. 340/776-5650; www.goatlantis.com. The 30-passenger vessel gives travelers an unbeatable view of the coral reefs and marine life. The entire experience takes two hours including a narrated boat ride out to the dive site and a one-hour dive.

Island tours are an excellent way to get an overview of St. Thomas. Most are conducted in open-air, safari-type buses and include pickup from your hotel and scenic stops at Drake's Seat and Mountain Top, a panoramic stop where you'll have a great view of the British Virgin Islands. Mountain Top claims to be the inventor of the banana daiquiri a complimentary drink is included in most tour prices. Check with your hotel for pick-up times. (A note for parents of young—or wiggly—children: slide all the way to the right (passenger) side of the trams. The left side is completely open to the street below and a little bit scary with young travelers.)

Another way to enjoy a panoramic view is with a ride up the **Paradise Point Tramway** (Tel. 340/777-4540, http://paradisepointtramway.com), just across the street from Havensight Mall and the cruise dock. At the top, you'll find a great view and a small cafe (which does offer a kids' menu with PB&J, grilled cheese sandwiches, and more favorites.) The small trams are enclosed.

Sports & Recreation: St. Croix

Horse lovers can enjoy St. Croix's rainforest on horseback. **Paul and Jill's Equestrian Stables**, Tel. 340/772-2880 or 772-2627, offers rides through this lush area.

Just off the coast of the far northeast side of the island lies St. Croix's other natural treasure: Buck Island. Several outfitters take snorkelers on half and full day trips to this island to swim along the **Buck Island Reef National Monument**. Here, in about 12 feet of water, snorkelers follow a marked trail for a self-guided tour of this undersea world. Several companies offer tours to this site, including Big Beard's Adventure Tours, Tel. 340/773-4482, and Mile Mark Watersports Tel. 340/773-2628, a very friendly group of operators who have a store in downtown Christiansted near the Old Scalehouse.

If the family is ready to head below the water's surface, there are plenty of **dive operators** to take you to coral formations and offshore wrecks in the St. Croix vicinity. In Christiansted, call Mile Mark Charters, Tel. 340/773-2628, or Cane Bay Dive Shop, Tel. 800/338-3843 or 340/773-9913; in Frederiksted, try Cruzan Divers, Tel. 340/772-1852.

Or how would you like your family to be the first Americans to see the day's sunrise? On Point Udall, the easternmost spot in the territorial United States, the US first greets the sunrise. As dawn's rays bathe the Point in light, red Senapol cattle begin another day of grazing on nearby scrub-covered hills. Along a rocky shoreline, where even on the busiest days the sea-grape trees far outnumber the sunbathers, visitors find themselves virtually alone to enjoy daybreak an hour before it reaches the mainland.

Be advised, the road to Point Udall is rugged and requires a four-wheel-drive vehicle and that the last downhill stretch is best traveled on foot.

St. John

St. John is one of a few islands that offer snuba, a unique blend of scuba and snorkeling that allows would-be divers to descend to 20 feet below the surface. Snuba St. John, Tel. 340/693-8063, hooks guests up to a floating air tank so "C" cards are not required. The cost includes equipment, a 1/2 hour orientation, and a one hour dive.

St. Thomas

Deep sea fishing is a favorite activity for many visitors, albeit a pricey one. Charters run about $400 for a boat (holding up to six passengers) for a half-day excursion.

Snorkeling is an excellent way to view the marine life in St. Thomas' waters. Coki Beach is a top spot for many snorkelers; another excellent reef is found at the Doubletree Sapphire Beach Resort, where marine life can be found in waters just two or three feet deep. At Coral World, you can participate in Snuba and Sea Trek (see the introductory chapter for information on both activities.)

What Can We Buy?

St. Croix

In Frederiksted, at a small crafts market located just west of the cruise pier the two of you can shop for homemade hot sauces, T-shirts, and inexpensive jewelry, usually entertained by a live band. There's a fair amount of additional shopping down the street in pricey waterfront shops. For local art, stop by the Frederiksted Gallery, which offers paintings, sculpture, and pottery with an island touch.

Shopping in St. Croix means a trip to Christiansted or Frederiksted. Until recently, most shopping took place in Christiansted, the larger of the two communities, but as the cruise ship business has grown, Frederiksted is offering more duty-free shops aimed at those who have only a few hours to shop.

One of our favorite Christiansted shops is the American West India Company (Strand Street), which also has branches in Key West and on Sint Maarten. This shop offers items from throughout the Caribbean: amber jewelry from the Dominican Republic, art from Haiti, sauces from Jamaica. Caribophiles should save time for a look around this interesting shop.

Larimar, the light blue semi-precious stone known as "the gemstone of the Caribbean," is also sold at many shops on St. Croix. The largest collection is at Larimar Mines in both Frederiksted (on the waterfront) and Christiansted (on the Boardwalk behind King's Alley).

A unique memento of your St. Croix visit is a mocko (rhymes with cocoa) jumbie, seen at Carnival and other special celebrations. The mocko jumbie sways high above the crowd on tall stilts covered with bright pants and wears elaborate headgear. A remembrance of an African tradition, the mocko jumbie is now a Virgin Islands cultural icon. You can buy brightly colored statues of the mocko jumbie at Silver and Tings (Pan Am Pavilion on Strand St.), Many Hands (Pan Am Pavilion), and Folk Art Traders, or gold and silver pendant interpretations at Sonya's.

St. John

St. John offers a very different shopping experience than nearby St. Thomas. Duty-free shopping is available, but by far the emphasis here is on hand-made items: clothing, pottery, jewelry, and artwork.

The most concentrated shopping is found at Mongoose Junction in Cruz Bay across from the National Park dock. Here, look for batik fabrics at the Fabric Mill, beautiful ceramics at the Donald Schneel Studio, where kids can buy "worry stones" made of sand and glass for just a few dollars.

St. Thomas

This is where serious duty-free shoppers come to seek out bargains from around the globe on jewelry, perfumes, leather goods, and gemstones.

The Waterfront Highway (Kyst Vejen), Main Street (Dronningens Gade) and Back Street (Vimmelskaft Gade) run parallel to the waterfront of Charlotte Amalie. These streets, and the alleys that connect Waterfront Highway and Main Street, are filled with non-stop shops. Start near the Vendor's Plaza (good for crafts purchases and inexpensive T-shirts), then begin your walk down crowded Main Street, where the sidewalks are always packed with shoppers and the street is continually lined with taxis and jitneys.

Our favorite shops are tucked in the alleys, refuges from the crowds where you can shop, dine or drink in a little peace. Here the walls are brick, recalling the area's history. In the 19th century, this was the Danish warehouse district.

What Else Do We Need to Know?

Currency. The US dollar is the official currency.

Driving. Driving is on the left side of the road on each of the Virgin Islands.

Information. For brochures on St. Croix and the other United States Virgin Islands, Tel. 800/372-USVI. Information on Island: Information booths are found in both the St. Croix and St. Thomas airports. On St. Croix, stop by the tourist office in Christiansted, located downtown in the Old Scalehouse.

Website. Check out www.usvitourism.vi for additional information.

Island Report Card	
Transportation to island	A+
Transportation around island	A-
Family Resorts	A
Family Restaurants	A-
Friendly atmosphere	A
Activities for kids	B+
Weather	A
New cultures to experience	B+
Safety	B+

Part 2

PLANNING YOUR TRIP

When to Go

Weather is usually a minor factor in planning a Caribbean vacation. It's almost a boring topic, with day after day of spring-like conditions, sometimes punctuated by brief afternoon showers.

One weather topic that concerns most potential Caribbean travelers is hurricane season. These deadly storms are a threat officially from June through November, although the greatest danger is during the later months, basically August through October. (September is the worst.)

But don't forget that the Caribbean is a huge region. Just as a blizzard in Connecticut wouldn't influence travelers to Miami or Denver, a tropical storm doesn't necessarily mean a risk to the whole region. We've been in the Western Caribbean when storms were picking up force in the eastern reaches and never felt a gust of wind or saw a wave over ankle high.

To minimize the chances of a hurricane ruining or postponing your trip, plan a vacation outside the hurricane season or outside the hurricane zone. In the far southern reaches, the islands of Aruba, Bonaire, and Curaçao (also known as the ABC islands) and Trinidad and Tobago are below the hurricane zone and should be safer bets during the summer and fall months.

Overall, the weather in the Caribbean is predictably wonderful. In the summer, days peak at about 95, with lows in the 70s. In the winter, temperatures run about 5 to 10 degrees cooler. The sea remains warm enough for comfortable swimming year around. (Don't forget: The Bahamas are technically not part of the Caribbean, and the temperatures there are slightly cooler.)

However, when to visit the Caribbean may be based more on budget than weather. Prices can vary as much as 40 percent between high and low season.

High season generally extends from December 15 through April 15. During this time, prices are at peak and rooms can even be difficult to reserve (especially during the holiday season). Prices soar during Christmas week. After the holidays, package prices (although sometimes not room rates) drop during January. They rise again by February and remain high until mid-April.

Low season covers the summer and early fall months, for two reasons. First, these are the warmest months in the Northeast, the area of the country that often flees to the sunny Caribbean during the chilly winter months so demand is down. Second, this is hurricane season.

What to Pack

When it comes to packing, there's no doubt that less is more. This axiom is especially true for a Caribbean vacation, where the order of the day is casual and cool. Most guests are comfortable in shorts and T-shirts in the day, switching to something "elegantly casual" in the evening hours: smart shorts sets or simple sundresses for women, khakis and polos for men, and "school clothes" for kids.

We keep a permanent packing list for our Caribbean trips. For a four-night trip, we suggest:

Kids
• 3 pair shorts
• 1 pair jeans or casual pants if you'll be horseback riding
• 3 T-shirts
• 1 old T-shirt to wear while swimming
• 2 dinner outfits, similar to school clothes
• 2 swimsuits (one to wear and one to dry)
• 1 pair beach shoes
• 1 pair sandals
• 1 pair sneakers
• 1 pair swim shoes
• beach toys
• swim diaper (for infants)
• water safety devices

His
- 1 pair casual slacks
- 2 T-shirts
- 1 pair jeans or very casual pants if you'll be horseback riding
- 2 polo or short sleeve shirts
- 2 pair of shorts
- 2 swimsuits
- 1 pair walking shoes
- 1 pair walking sandals
- 1 pair swim shoes

Hers
- 1 pair casual slacks (for the plane)
- 1 pair nice slacks or khakis
- 1 casual skirt
- 1 pair jeans or casual pants if you'll be horseback riding
- 1 dress
- 1 T-shirt
- 2 short sleeve/sleeveless blouses
- 2 pair of shorts
- 2 swimsuits
- 1 pair sandals or tennis shoes
- 1 pair evening sandals
- 1 swimsuit cover-up
- 1 pair swim shoes

We also carry all the necessary accessories (which, on some islands, can be expensive or difficult to buy):
- film and camera, extra camera battery
- sunscreen (usually two bottles of different strengths)
- snorkel gear (and certified divers must bring a "C" card)
- aqua shoes
- insect repellent
- all prescriptions (in prescription bottles)
- 2 pairs of sunglasses each
- paperback book or two
- antiseptic for bug bites
- aloe vera lotion for sunburn
- first aid kit with aspirin, stomach medicine, bandages, children's aspirin, etc.
- passports
- airline tickets
- mini-address book for postcard writing

Parents with infants will find baby needs readily available on most islands. In a few cases, disposable diapers are difficult to locate (on small islands like Little Cayman). If you have favorite brands, bring them from home. Prices are likely to be steeper on the islands, and the selection can be limited.

Passports

In the past, passports were an optional item for Americans headed to Caribbean. No more! Beginning in 2006, you'll need a valid passport to RETURN to the US from any Caribbean trip (that means for both sea and air travel, regardless of your age.)

NOTE: *Remember, this new passport requirement doesn't include Puerto Rico and US Virgin Islands, since both are part of the US.*

Getting into the Caribbean, the entry requirements vary from country to country but none require anything more than a valid passport. American citizens don't need to worry about visas for any Caribbean island.

Obtaining a Passport

To obtain a passport, you may apply in person at the nearest passport office (see chart) or at one of the several thousand federal or state courts or U.S. post offices authorized to accept passport applications. Not every post office will accept passport applications; it's usually one of the largest offices in the city. For your first passport application, you must apply in person.

We can't stress enough the importance of applying for a passport early. The heaviest demand period is January through August (because of summer travel), with September through December being the speediest period. Even during the latter, however, you should allow at least eight weeks for your passport application to be processed. With today's increasing security, it is more important than ever to apply for a passport months before your travel date.

Note: As part of the US, both the USVI and Puerto Rico are exempt from the new passport requirements; however, parents traveling with children will need proof of identification for their children such as an official birth certificate. If children are traveling without both birth parents, it's suggested that you follow the procedures for traveling without both parents including a certified letter of permission from the absent parent.

How to Get Your First Passport

If this will be your first passport, you'll have to apply in person. You can search the Department of State's website which includes 6000 passport acceptance offices to find the one closest to you. Search here http://iafdb.travel.state.gov/

When you make your application, you'll need to bring with you a certified birth certificate issued by the city, county or state. What's a certified birth certificate? One with *a* registrar's raised, embossed, impressed or multicolored seal, registrar's signature, and the date the certificate was filed with the registrar's office, which must be within 1 year of your birth. If you were board abroad, you'll need a Consular Report of Birth Abroad or Certification of Birth.

Also, you can provide citizenship with a Naturalization Certificate or Certificate of Citizenship if you became a US citizen later in life. If you don't have the above information, it's a little more complicated; check out the State Department site for other documents you can substitute http://www.travel.state.gov/passport/get/first/first_830.html .

You'll also have to bring proof of identity which can be:
•Current, valid Driver's license
•A previous U.S. passport (mutilated, altered, or damaged passports are not acceptable as proof of identity)
•Naturalization Certificate
•Certificate of Citizenship
•Government ID: city, state or federal
•Military ID: military and dependents

NOTE: *Your Social Security Card does NOT prove your identity* .

You'll also need two passport pictures. Don't just grab any old snapshots, though; there are certain specifications for these photos. (The easiest thing to do is visit your local print shop or chain drug store; most make passport photos in minutes for just a few dollars.) Passport photos must be:
•2x2 inches in size
•Identical
•Taken within the past 6 months, showing current appearance
•In color
•Show your full face, front view with a plain white or off-white background
•Allow between 1 inch and 1 3/8 inches from the bottom of the chin to the top of the head
•Show you in normal street attire (no uniforms, sunglasses, hats, etc.)

Passports for Children Under Age 14

Special rules cover passports for children under the age of 14. Basically, you'll need to prove the citizenship and identify of both your child and yourselves as parents as well as proof of your relationship to the child.

For proof of citizenship, you need to provide on of these items for your child:

- Certified U.S. birth certificate (one with a raised seal)
- Previous fully valid U.S. Passport
- Report of Birth Abroad (Form FS-240)
- Certification of Birth Abroad (Form DS-1350)
- Certificate of Citizenship or Naturalization

You also need to prove that you are the child's parents. Parents need to supply one of the following:

- Certified U.S. birth certificate (with parents' names
- Certified Foreign Birth Certificate (with parents' names and translation, if necessary
- Report of Birth Abroad (Form FS-240) (with parents' names)
- Certification of Birth Abroad (Form DS-1350) (with parents' names)
- Adoption Decree (with adopting parents' names)
- Court Order Establishing Custody
- Court Order Establishing Guardianship

That establishes your relationship to your child. Next, you need to prove who you are with one of the following:

- Valid Drivers License
- Valid Official U.S. Military ID
- Valid U.S. Gov't ID
- Valid U.S. or Foreign Passport with recognizable photo
- Naturalization/Citizenship Certificate from BCIS with recognizable photo
- Alien Resident Card from BCIS

It's easiest for both parents to appear together to obtain the child's passport. If that's not possible or practical, though, one of you can appear with the proper paperwork and with some additional proof from the second parent that it's OK for the child to obtain a passport. This proof can be:

- **notarized statement of consent** authorizing passport issuance for the child (see Form DS-3053, Statement of Consent: Issuance of a Passport to a Minor Under Age 14, available at http://www.travel.state.gov/passport/forms/ds3053/ds3053_846.html), or a written statement with the same information on a sheet of paper from the non-appearing parent that includes the child's name and date of birth, as well as parent's identification information or a copy of his/her ID may be used for this purpose)
- evidence of your sole authority to apply for the passport. This proof can be a birth certificate listing only one parent, an adoption decree listing only one adopting parent, a court order that gives you the permission to

travel with the child, a court document that declares the non-applying parent incompetent, or the death certificate of the other parent.

Once this is all accomplished, you'll need to provide two passport photos of your child just like those mentioned in the above section on adult passports.

Passports for Teens

Teens between the ages of 14 and 17 have some additional rules to follow. The teen must appear in person to obtain the passport. Parental consent for the passport may be requested.

If your teen has identification (see the above list) of his own, he can provide that but, if he doesn't yet have official identification, you need to accompany your child, present your own identification, and co-sign the passport application.

How Long Does It Take?

The time frame can vary by time of year (expect early spring to be slow as travelers look ahead to European summer trips) but the State Department says to allow six weeks to receive your passport.

In a hurry? They offer an expediting service for $60 which trims the delivery time (if you pay for overnight delivery) to two weeks.

In even a bigger hurry? The fastest way to get a passport is to get it at one of the 13 passport agencies. You have to have an appointment but there is no charge for an appointment. These offices are just for travelers who are traveling with two weeks. Here's a list of the passport agencies:

BOSTON Passport Agency
Thomas P. O'Neill Federal Building
10 Causeway Street,
Suite 247
Boston, MA 02222-1094
 Automated Appointment Number: 877/487-2778

CHICAGO Passport Agency
Kluczynski Federal Building
230 S. Dearborn Street
18th Floor
Chicago, IL 60604-1564
Automated Appointment Number: 312/341-6020

CONNECTICUT Passport Agency
50 Washington Street

Norwalk, CT 06854
Automated Appointment Number: 877/487-2778

HONOLULU Passport Agency
Prince Kuhio Federal Building
300 Ala Moana Blvd.
Suite 1-330
Honolulu, HI 96850
Automated Appointment Number: 877/487-2778

HOUSTON Passport Agency
Mickey Leland Federal Building
1919 Smith Street
Suite 1400
Houston, TX 77002-8049
Automated Appointment Number: 713/751-0294

LOS ANGELES Passport Agency
Federal Building
11000 Wilshire Blvd.
Suite 1000
Los Angeles, CA 90024-3615
Automated Appointment Number: 310/575-5700

MIAMI Passport Agency
Claude Pepper Federal Office Building
51 SW First Avenue
3rd Floor
Miami, FL 33130-1680
Automated Appointment Number: 305/539-3600

NEW ORLEANS Passport Agency
One Canal Place (corner of Canal and North Peters Streets)
365 Canal Street, Suite 1300
New Orleans, LA 70130-6508
Automated Appointment Number: 504/412-2600

NEW YORK Passport Agency
376 Hudson Street
New York, NY 10014
Automated Appointment Number: 877/487-2778

PHILADELPHIA Passport Agency
U.S. Custom House
200 Chestnut Street
Room 103
Philadelphia, PA 19106-2970
Automated Appointment Number: 215/418-5937

SAN FRANCISCO Passport Agency
95 Hawthorne Street
5th Floor
San Francisco, CA 94105-3901
Automated Appointment Number: 415/538-2700

SEATTLE Passport Agency
Henry Jackson Federal Building
915 Second Avenue
Suite 992
Seattle, WA 98174-1091
Automated Appointment Number: 206/808-5700

WASHINGTON Passport Agency
1111 19th Street, N.W.
First Floor, Sidewalk Level
Washington, D.C. 20036
Automated Appointment Number: 877/487-2778

Fees

Passports for teens age 16 and over and for adults cost $97, which includes a whole batch of fees. Passports for children under the age of 16 cost $82, including the fees.

Children Traveling Without Both Birth Parents

Children traveling without both birth parents should have a notarized letter from the non-present parent stating permission for the child to travel with the other parent. Why all the fuss? Parental kidnappings has skyrocketed and foreign countries are trying their best to stop parental abductors from entering their countries. In Mexico, law requires that a child traveling alone or with only one parent carries a written, notarized consent letter from the absent parent. (This includes children traveling with grandparents.) Generally, this is not a problem in the Caribbean but better safe than sorry. This also applies if your child is bringing along a friend on the trip; you'll want to get a notarized letter of consent from the child's parents stating that it's OK for the child to travel.

Also, you'll want to make sure your child (or any child you're traveling with) has permission to receive medical treatment during the trip. If you don't have this letter, you won't be able to obtain medical treatment for the child until parents can be contacted.

Just what should this letter say? Here's a general idea:

Consent for Minor Child to Travel without Both Birth Parents

I (we) YOUR NAMES give my/our authorization for my/our minor child(ren) CHILD'S NAME/S to travel to DESTINATION aboard AIRLINE/FLIGHT NUMBER with NAME OF ADULTS ON TRIP. The scheduled date of return is DATE.

Also, I/we authorize NAME OF ADULTS ON TRIP to obtain any necessary medical treatment for my/our child on this trip.

Signed: PARENT'S NAME
Signed: PARENT'S NAME
Address: YOUR ADDRESS
Telephone: YOUR TELEPHONE

Sworn to and signed before me, a Notary Public,
this _____ day of _____, 20_____

_____
Notary Public Signature and Seal

U.S. Consulates & Embassies

Emergency Situations

When we think of the State Department assisting Americans abroad, we usually picture political tensions or Americans who have run into trouble with the law.

However, the State Department's Bureau of Consular Affairs will also assist travelers during an emergency situations, such as a hurricane.

The State Department sets up a task force to disseminate information on the crisis, including responding to relatives and friends who are inquiring about the safety of those abroad. If you are involved in an emergency situation, go to the nearest US embassy or consular office and register. Bring along your passport and a location where you can be reached. The Embassy can also assist you with these situations:

Lost Passport: If you lose your passport or have it stolen, first report the loss to the local police. Get a police declaration then report to the consul for a replacement passport. If you have extra passport photos, bring these along. It also helps to travel with a copy of the identification page of your passport tucked somewhere in your belongings. In case of a lost passport, this will speed along the reissuance. Know, however, that in these days of heightened security, obtaining a replacement passport will be a lengthy process.

Medical Assistance: Contact the consular office for a list of local doctors, dentists, and medical specialists. If you are injured or become seriously ill, a consul will help you find medical assistance and, at your request, inform your family or friends. The State Department cannot assist you in funding an emergency trip back to the States—that's what travel insurance is all about.

Financial Assistance: Lose your money? The consular office can help you contact your family, bank, or employer to arrange for them to send you funds.

Below is a list of American embassies and consulates in the region:

BAHAMAS
American Embassy
Queen Street
Nassau, Bahamas
Tel. 242/322-1181 or 328-2206

BARBADOS
American Embassy
Canadian Imperial Bank of Commerce Bldg.
Broadstreet
Bridgetown, Barbados
Tel. 246/436-4950

American Consulate
ALICO Building
Cheapside
Bridgetown, Barbados
Tel. 246/431-0225

DOMINICAN REPUBLIC
American Embassy
Calle Cesar Nicolas Penson and Calle Leopoldo Navarro
Santo Domingo, Dominican Republic
Tel. 809/221-2171

JAMAICA
American Embassy
16 Oxford Road
Kingston, Jamaica
Tel. (876)935-6044

American Consular Agent
St. James Place, 2nd Floor, Gloucester Avenue
Montego Bay, Jamaica
Tel. (876)952-0160
Assists Americans in Jamaica.

NETHERLANDS ANTILLES
American Consulate General
J.B. Gorsiraweg No. 1
Willemstad, Curaçao
Tel. 599-9/461-3066

TRINIDAD AND TOBAGO
American Embassy
15 Queen's Park West
Port of Spain, Trinidad
Tel. 868/622-6371

Several islands also have available resident consular agents:

CAYMAN ISLANDS
American Consular Agent
George Town, Grand Cayman
Tel. 246/949-7955

ANTIGUA AND BARBUDA
American Consular Agent
Hospital Hill, Nelson's Dockyard P.O.
English Harbour, Antigua
Tel. 268/460-1569
Note: Assists Americans in Antigua & Barbuda, St. Kitts & Nevis, and the British West Indies.

DOMINICAN REPUBLIC
American Consular Agent
Calle Beller 51, Second Floor, Office 6

Puerto Plata, Dominican Republic
Tel. (809) 731-4294

Foreign Embassies in the US
For diplomatic relations with the US and to assist their citizens while in the US, other nations have embassies located within the US. These offices can help with specific questions on the country's entry requirements, political situations, etc.

EMBASSY OF ANTIGUA AND BARBUDA
3216 New Mexico Avenue, N.W.
Washington, DC 20016
Tel. 202/362-5211
Fax 202/362-5225

EMBASSY OF THE BAHAMAS
2220 Massachusetts Avenue, N.W.
Washington, DC 20008
Tel. 202/319-2660
Fax 202/319-2668

EMBASSY OF BARBADOS
2144 Wyoming Avenue, NW
Washington, DC 20008
Tel. 202/939-9200
Fax 202/332-7467

CONSULATE OF THE COMMONWEALTH OF DOMINICA
800 2nd Avenue, Suite 400 H
New York, NY 10017
Tel. 212/599-8478
Fax 212/661-0979

EMBASSY OF THE DOMINICAN REPUBLIC
1715 22nd Street., NW
Washington, DC 20008
Tel. 202/332-6280
Fax 202/265-8057
www.domrep.org

EMBASSY OF FRANCE
4101 Reservoir Road, NW
Washington, DC 20007

Tel. 202/944-6000
Fax 202/944-6166
www.info-france-usa.org

EMBASSY OF JAMAICA
1520 New Hampshire Avenue, NW
Washington, DC 20036
Tel. 202/452-0660
Fax 202/452-0081
www.emjamusa.org

EMBASSY OF THE NETHERLANDS
4200 Linnean Avenue, NW
Washington, DC 20008
Tel. 202/244-5300
Fax 202/362-3430
www.netherlands-embassy.org

EMBASSY OF ST. KITTS AND NEVIS
3216 New Mexico Avenue, NW
Washington, DC 20016
Tel. 202/686-2636
Fax. 202/686-5740
www.stkittsnevis.org

EMBASSY OF ST. LUCIA
3216 New Mexico Avenue, NW
Washington, DC 20016
Tel. 202/364-6792
Fax 202/364-6723

EMBASSY OF TRINIDAD AND TOBAGO
1708 Massachusetts Avenue, NW
Washington, DC 20036
Tel. 202/467-6490
Fax 202/785-3130
http://ttembassy.cjb.net/

BRITISH EMBASSY
3100 Massachusetts Avenue, NW
Washington, DC 20008
Tel. 202/588-7800

Fax (Consulate department) 202/588-7850
www.britainusa.com

Customs & Entry Requirements

US Customs

Arriving home means a trip first through immigration and then through US Customs. (A few islands have Customs Pre-Clearance so you can go through the declaration before returning home, usually a faster process.)

You can return with $800 worth of items duty-free (as long as they're brought back with you in carry-on or checked luggage). Up to two liters of alcohol per adult can be included in your exemption.

If you are returning from the USVI, you can bring back $1600 under your duty-free exemption!

You'll complete a customs declaration form, one per household, identifying the total amount of your expenditures while out of the country. Each person has the exemption of and families can pool their exemptions so a family of four can bring back $3200 worth of merchandise from most islands.

Some items cannot be brought back to the US. These include:
• books or cassettes made without authorized copyright ("pirated" copies)
• any type of drug paraphernalia
• firearms
• fruits and vegetables
• meats and their by-products (such as paté)
• plants, cuttings
• tortoise shell jewelry or other turtle products (which you will see sold in the Cayman Islands, among others)

Here are some tips to make your passage through Customs a little easier:
• keep your sales slips
• pack so your purchases can be reached easily
• get a copy of the "Know Before You Go" brochure (Publication 512) from the US Customs Service at your airport – or write the US Customs Service, PO Box 7407, Washington, DC 20044 or see *www.customs.ustreas.gov.*

Canadian Customs:

If you are a Canadian citizen, you can claim up to CAN$200 worth of goods without paying duty if you've been away 48 hours or longer (make that CAN$750 if you've been traveling seven days or more). This is your personal exemption. These goods need to be with you and you can't include alcohol or tobacco in this exemption amount. You must have the goods with you when you arrive, and you cannot include tobacco products or alcoholic beverages in this exemption.For more info: http://www.cbsa-asfc.gc.ca/

Immunizations

Immunizations are not required for any islands in the Caribbean. Travelers should have their immunizations current however and anyone traveling should make sure their tetanus inoculation was within the past five years.

Check with your pediatrician several months before departure to make sure your children's shots are up-to-date.

Using Travel Specialists

Travel agents offer a (usually) free service, making hotel and air reservations and issuing airline tickets. They can shop around for the lowest rate for you and often know about sales that aren't known to the general public.

Stop by a travel agency and talk to an agent during an off-peak time, usually early morning or mid-day. Tell him or her your likes and dislikes and your budget range. The agent can help you start to narrow your choices to a few islands and perhaps a few resorts. Pick up some brochures, head home, and talk over the choices with your family.

Now the fun part: doing some research. Rent some travel videos. Look at some guidebooks and travel magazines. Get on the Internet and check out some travel forums for other people's views. Talk about your options.

When you have your minds made up—or at least narrowed down—return to the travel agent for some help. If it's a large office, ask for the agent who specializes in the Caribbean.

Now the agent can assist you with the nitty-gritty of the travel task: making your reservations. Often you'll need to put down a deposit on reservations or packages. This deposit may be non-refundable so make sure that you have made your final selection both in terms of resort and travel dates.

Flying to the Caribbean

Getting to the Caribbean is an easier job that it once was. Daily flights serve most islands. Most connections from major mainland US cities are made through Miami or San Juan's Luis Muñoz Marin Airport, the

American Airlines hub for many Caribbean flights to smaller islands. From San Juan, American Eagle serves many neighboring islands.

Those air arrivals are met with expanded and improved airports on many islands. Terminals in Aruba, Jamaica (Montego Bay), Bermuda, St. Kitts, San Juan, Puerto Rico and the Cayman Islands offer new and improved facilities.

The following carriers offer flights to at least one Caribbean destination. You'll find that the flight schedule varies by season (the most flights, and for some airlines the *only* flights, are offered during peak season from mid-December to mid-April). The airlines include:

- **Air Canada**   Tel. 888/247-2262
                          www.aircanada.com
- **Air Jamaica**   Tel. 800/523-5585
                          www.airjamaica.com
- **ALM**   Tel. 800/327-7230
                          www.airalm.com
- **American Airlines**   Tel. 800/433-7300
                          www.aa.com
- **Bahamasair**   Tel. 800/222-4262
                          www.bahamasair.com
- **BWIA**   Tel. 800/538-2942
                          www.bwee.com
- **Cayman Airways**   Tel. 800/422-9626
                          www.caymanairways.com
- **Continental**   Tel. 800/231-0856
                          www.continental.com
- **Delta**   Tel. 800/221-1212
                          www.delta.com
- **Northwest**   Tel. 800/447-4747
                          www.nwa.com
- **United**   Tel. 800/538-2929
                          www.united.com
- **USAirways**   Tel. 800/428-4322
                          www.usairways.com

Helping Your Kids Enjoy Flying

Faced with nightly newscasts and heightened security, flying with children, never an easy task, can be an even tenser undertaking. You can make the journey easier on both yourself and your children, however, by preparing everyone before the trip. Talk to your children about the flight, especially if they're first-time fliers; help older children to pack so that it will easy your trip through airport security. Here are some tips for making your journey as smooth as possible:

•Talk to your kids about flying, from the sounds they'll hear to the layout of the plane and the behavior that will be expected of them. Talk with them about the security measures and what they can expect when going through security.

•Pack with an eye for security to minimize your time passing through security. This means no scissors, razors, or other prohibited items in your carry on bag. Dress your children with a minimum of metal (belt buckles, jewelry, etc.) to make setting off the metal detectors less likely.

•Book seat assignments early so the family sits together. (If you're flying on a charter carrier that doesn't pre-assign seats, get to the airport extra early to ensure that your group will stay together.)

•Bring snacks. With recent cutbacks, fewer airlines now serve meals on flights to the Caribbean. Call yours and check. Be sure to pack snacks for the flight.

•Minimize your luggage. You'll travel lighter (remember the "lug" in luggage!) and check-in will be faster.

•Arrive at the airport early. Security lines can be lengthy at some airports to arrive no less than two hours (and arriving even earlier doesn't hurt).

•Consider preboarding if you want to get seated before the mad dash onto the plane begins. However, if your child is restless, this will only add to total time on the ground before takeoff.

•Bring bottles and pacifiers for young children to ease the pressure on the inner ear during take off and landings. For older children, bring chewing gum.

•Pack some special activities in a secret "goody bag" to keep your child's hands busy until the trip is underway.

Several airlines offer package deals that provide a complete vacation: room, transfers, air, and, for all-inclusives, meals, drinks, and tips. Is this cheaper than putting a package together on your own? Usually. Check it out for yourself by calling the hotel reservation numbers, asking for their room rate and adding it to the cost of an airline ticket. You'll usually see a substantial savings, since, after all, the airlines are buying rooms in bulk and therefore have much more purchasing power than an ordinary consumer.

Packages are also offered by charter airlines, carriers that offer service at lower cost, usually with few frills. (Often only one class of service is available, seat assignments are given only at check-in, and carry on allowances may be only one bag per passenger due to an increased number of seats onboard.) Some companies offering Caribbean service include Adventure Tours, FunJet, Apple Vacations, GoGo, and others. See your travel agent for information on charters available from your area.

If you're concerned about the credibility of a charter company or a tour package, check it out before signing on that dotted line. Call the **American Society of Travel Agents**, Tel. 703/739-2782, w*ww.astanet.com*, or write 1101 King Street, Alexandria, VA 22314, to see if complaints have been lodged against the company. Another good source of information is your local Better Business Bureau.

If you don't want the package vacation, some of these charters also sell "air-only," just the airline tickets themselves.

Child Restraint Devices

Parents flying with infants or small children may also want to pack another important piece of equipment: a child restraint device or CRD. The Federal Aviation Administration strongly recommends that children under 40 pounds be secured in a CRD.

A CRD should have hard sides and back. It attaches to the seat through channels; you just thread the seatbelt through the channels to secure the device. Many carriers will say they are approved for motor vehicles and on aircraft; another tip is to look for the "FMVSS.213" insignia. Some car carriers recently issued work both in planes and automobiles but don't assume that every carrier will perform both functions. Carriers shouldn't be wider than 16 inches or they won't fit the airline seat properly. Also, make sure the carrier correctly fits your child; the shoulder straps should come out of the seat back just above the child's shoulders.

Children under 20 pounds should face the rear of the seat; kids 20-40 pounds face out. Once you're on the flight, the CRD can be used in seats that face forward and are not in an exit row. The window seat is best.

If you have questions and would like more information on air safety for children, call the **FAA consumer information hotline**, Tel. 800/322-7873.

Getting Around the Caribbean

By Air

Want to island-hop? It's fun and, if you're visiting small islands, a necessary part of a Caribbean vacation.

Two carriers offer special passes designed for island hopping. **LIAT**, *Tel.* 888/844-5428, www.liatairline.com, and **BWIA**, Tel. 800/538-2942, www.bwee.com, each offers a special pass that permits you to hop from island to island—with certain restrictions. The catch is that you must make all your travel in one direction, except for the return flight back to the island from which you started. Passes must be purchased and ticketed (a very important detail) outside the Caribbean. They cannot be purchased in the islands.

Several other carriers offer frequent flights around the Caribbean. Check with these carriers for their coverage:

- **Caribbean Star, www.flycaribbeanstar.com,** Tel. 268/GO1-STAR
- **Air Jamaica Express, www.airjamaica.com,** Tel. 800/523-5585

By Ferry

Ferry travel is available between some islands: Trinidad and Tobago, St. Martin and both St. Barts and Anguilla, St. Kitts and Nevis, the British Virgin Islands and St. John and St. Thomas, and others.

Ferry travel between islands can be a fun way to extend your knowledge of the region and to travel like a local. Prices are generally very economical but expect timetables to be taken less seriously than you might expect. Arrive plenty early and bring along your passport for voyages between countries such as Anguilla and St. Martin.

By Bus

Public transportation can be a fun and inexpensive way to travel around the island and feel like a local. However, you'll find that it's not the fast way. Be prepared for plenty of stops and starts (on many islands buses stop anywhere they're flagged). Smaller islands such as Anguilla do not have bus service. To flag down a bus or taxi in the islands, hold out your hand and pat down, like you're bouncing a ball.

By Car

Modes of transportation vary from island to island, but for the most part taxis are the best means of travel. Even the smallest islands like tiny Salt Cay in the Turks and Caicos have taxi service, and you'll find that they're generally operated by professionals who are happy to talk about their island. We've had some of our most interesting conversations about island life with taxi drivers, who are well informed about history and tourist attractions. Often drivers will present their business card at the end of the journey in case you have further need for transportation.

Car rentals can be expensive in the islands but on some islands, such as Anguilla, present a more economical option than taxis. If you'll be doing some exploring, a rental car is often the easiest and most economical way to get around.

Prices vary by island, type of vehicle, and even time of year. Most car rentals begin at about US $30-40 per day; expect to pay about $10 more per day for a 4X4 vehicle. Prices are higher on some islands such as St. Barts where rental cars average about $60 a day in the winter months, falling to about $35 a day during the summer. In this sellers' market, major credit cards are accepted but most request a two- or three-day minimum rental. Know that gasoline can be very expensive throughout the region (although driving distances aren't that far on most islands.)

On many islands, a temporary driver's license is required; you can usually obtain this from the rental agency by presenting a valid driver's license. Prices vary from about $5-10. You must also show a major credit card.

Remember that driving is on the LEFT side of the road on Caribbean islands with a British heritage including Anguilla, Cayman Islands, Jamaica, St. Kitts and Nevis, the US and British Virgin Islands, and others. Even though driving is on the left side, many vehicles are right hand drive; however, most 4X4s have a left-hand stick shift.

Even if you won't be driving during your stay, remember that driving is on the left and stress this to your family members. Crossing a road becomes a challenge under these circumstances: remind everyone to look RIGHT then left. Take special care when getting out of tour vans, taxis, and buses.

Throughout most islands, speed limits are far lower than those in the US and Canada. Speed limits are maximum 30 mph on many islands (20 mph in some areas). Look for tall traffic bumps called "sleeping policemen" to slow down speeders.

Family-friendly Accommodations

Whatever you're looking for in the way of accommodations— high-rise hotel, seaside bungalow, contemporary condominium, small traditional hotel, or private villa — you'll find it in the Caribbean.

Just as varied as the type of accommodations is the range of prices of these properties. Everything from budget motels with Spartan furnishings to private islands that attract royalty and Hollywood types is available.

This guidebook covers things in between, places where the everyday vacationing family can enjoy safety and comfort in surroundings where fun can flourish. The resorts, hotels, and villas featured on these pages cover all levels of activity. Some offer around-the-clock fun and evening theme parties for their guests; others point the way for families to find their own entertainment. Some are located on the beach; others up in the mountains with grandiose views. Some are full-service properties with everything from beauty salons to jewelry shops; others are simple accommodations where the guests enjoy dinner in former greathouses built over 200 years ago.

Choosing a Caribbean accommodation is even more important than selecting a hotel at other destinations. You'll find that a Caribbean hotel, unlike a property in a downtown US city, for example, becomes your home away from home. This is not just where you spend your nights, but also a good portion of your days, languishing on the beach, lying beneath towering palms, and luxuriating in a warm sea.

What form will your paradise take? White sandy beaches? Rugged limestone cliffs that fall into baby blue water? Mountainside vistas? A resort with daily activities and a complete children's program? Or a quiet getaway where the only footprints are your own? The choice is yours.

Resorts

What is a resort? A resort is a hotel, but a hotel is not necessarily a resort. Confused?

Actually the distinction is fairly simple. A resort is a place where you could, if you chose, stay your entire vacation. You'll find restaurants, watersports, shops, you name it, all within the hotel grounds. It's a place that caters to the leisure traveler, although you may also see a mix of business travelers at some properties.

Resorts offer many different packages. These include:

EP, European Plan. This is a room-only plan. You've paid for a place to sleep but all meals, drinks, and recreation are extra.

MAP, Modified American Plan. Breakfast and dinner are included. This is a good option for those who plan to be out exploring the island during the day.

AP, American Plan. All meals are included. This is not an all-inclusive plan however, since drinks may or not be included and usually watersports, tips, and any other kind of recreation are not part of the package.

All-inclusive Resorts

As the name suggests, all-inclusive means that all activities, meals, drinks, transfers, and tips are included in the price.

This all-inclusive policy means that you're free to try anything you like without getting out the credit cards. You've already paid for it in the package price.

Some folks don't like all-inclusive because of the concern (not unfounded) that once you've paid for the whole package you'll be unlikely to leave the property to sample local restaurants and explore the island.

If your family wants to try it all: scuba diving, sailing, windsurfing, golf, or tennis, an all-inclusive is just the ticket for you as well. The one-price-pays-all policy will be a better deal than paying for individual lessons.

Our family loves all-inclusive resorts, but we are careful to balance a stay there with island tours or visits to off-property restaurants. Even with these extra expenditures, we've found most of these resorts to be economical choices. Our family has enjoyed several all-inclusive stays which have relieved strain (both on parent-child relations and on the budget) as the kids to be able to order whatever they want without an eye on the pocketbook.

It makes it even easier to get picky eaters just to "try" a bite of a new dish like fungi or callaloo when you know that you've already paid for it.

The all-inclusive concept was born in Jamaica over a decade and a half ago with SuperClubs. "Here all our guests are equally rich because you can't spend money while you're here," says founder John Issa. With an all-inclusive vacation, you're enjoying a stay without tips, bar tabs, transfers, or bills of any kind.

Today Jamaica is still the king of the all-inclusive market, and properties offer fun for travelers of all ages. Some popular all-inclusive chains in the Caribbean especially popular with families are Beaches (part of the Sandals family), SuperClubs, and some members of the Club Med family.

Condominiums

Like your own island apartment, condominiums give you the freedom of housekeeping, whether that means doing a quick load of laundry or making bowls of cereal in the morning. Condominiums are not found on every island but are an especially popular option on Grand Cayman.

Condominiums can be a favorite money-saver for many families because of the option to make meals in-house. Here are some additional money-saving tips whether you're staying in a condominium or a resort:

Beaches & Sesame Street

Beaches Resorts has signed a multi-year agreement that launches a Sesame Street sponsorship called The Beaches Resorts Caribbean Adventure with Sesame Street. The program will include appearances by Bert, Ernie, Elmo, Cookie Monster, Grover and Zoe at all Beaches resorts. Twice a week, your family will be able to enjoy live stage shows created just for Beaches by the producers of Sesame Street Live.

At the resorts, you'll find the characters walking around the property, ready to pose for pictures with young (and, we found, many not-so-young) guests. Other activities include story time with Elmo, baking with Cookie Monster, learning to dance with Zoe, going global with Grover, making music with Bert and Ernie, character breakfasts (surcharge), themed birthday parties (surcharge), character parades, and more.

•Consider bringing some food with you or making a stop at a supermarket.

•Pick up coupon booklets. These can offer 10%-off coupons and other bargains at eateries. This type of booklet is often distributed at the visitors' booth at the airport arrival area.

•Look for two-for-one specials (popular on Sunday nights).

•Buy rum on island and make your own cocktails. Buy soft drinks and juices for the kids.

•Double check the gratuity. Some restaurants add a 15% gratuity to the bill, so make sure you don't inadvertently tip twice.

•Check for laundry facilities if you rent a condominium.

•Look for early bird specials at some restaurants. Dining before 6pm can save money and it's smart with children.•Make sure you understand whether the menu prices you are reading are marked in US or local currency.

•Look for free attractions. Remember, a stop doesn't necessarily have to be labeled "tourist attraction" to be fun and educational. We always make a stop at the local grocery store to compare brands and have a look at local specialties. Outdoor food markets are also terrific fun. Buy a banana or pineapple from a local vendor for an impromptu picnic.

Small Hotels

If you're looking for peace and quiet, small inns offer good getaways and a chance to immerse yourself in more of the local atmosphere. Often the owners of the inn reside right on property, so you'll receive personal attention.

Our favorite inns make us feel like we're guests of the family returning for another stay. We enjoy chatting with other guests, usually experienced travelers, and with the owners, who give us an insight into island life. Over the years, we've shared dinner conversations with hoteliers about hurricanes, gardening, local specialties, local sports, and island life in general. It has given us a perspective on these destinations that we would never have received at a larger property.

How do small properties feel about kids? This book includes only small properties that welcome families but for other properties you'll have to ask. Some do not allow children, period. That includes anyone under age 18. Others welcome children during non-peak months. And still others welcome kids with open arms any time of year.

Villas

For some families, the idea of a real getaway is a private villa, without other guests. Your family gets the treat of feeling like you're living on the island in your own home, except for the occasional visit by a cook or maid who is there to meet your special requests, to introduce you to island cuisine, and to make you feel pampered in what really is your home away from home. There's no better solution for families who want to enjoy a vacation together with plenty of room, facilities to satisfy even picky eaters, and a genuine island atmosphere.

The top islands for villa getaways are St. John and St. Thomas in the US Virgin Islands, Jamaica, and Barbados.

Like resorts, villas come in different budget categories, but generally are more pricey than a hotel or resort stay. Also, you should not assume that every villa comes with the range of facilities you might expect from a resort.

Before you select a villa, check on some details. Is maid service offered? Many villas offer maid service before your arrival and after your departure; additional cleaning can be arranged for a surcharge. At other properties, you may have daily maid service. Check with your villa management company.

Can you send a deposit for groceries and have a cook stock up before your arrival? Finding a refrigerator and cabinets ready with your favorites can be a big boost after a long flight. Is cook service available? Many villas can arrange for cook service as you choose: three meals a day, dinner only, or just one special meal. In Jamaica, villas typically include cook service. Check your options. Is the villa air-conditioned? Don't assume your villa is air conditioned; ever-present trade winds make this an optional feature. If it's more of a necessity than an option to you, inquire.

Do you need to rent a car? Many villas are located away from the resort areas. See if you should rent a car to avoid pricey taxi rides for long hauls. Is there a minimum stay? Unlike hotel minimums of three nights, villas often require a minimum seven night rental.

Travel with Teens

The recipe for a successful Caribbean with kids is simple: sand, sun, and, for some, supervised kids' programs. Many children enjoy independent time away from parents and the chance to meet other kids at the resort.

But don't expect the same response from pre-teens and teenagers. Kids' clubs are just a little too close to babysitting to suit most teens, even though some kids' programs welcome teen participants.

So what's the key to a successful Caribbean with teens trip? Know your teen. (OK, we understand. Let's revise that to say "know your teen as best as you can know any teen.") Ask yourself:

•Does my teen want to hang out with other teens while on vacation, even though they are strangers at first?

•Would my teen be happy hanging out with us on vacation?

•Would my teen enjoy the vacation more if there were a way he/she could bring along a friend from home?

If you answered "yes" to question one, look closely at the growing number of programs (no, whatever you do, don't call them kids' clubs) aimed specifically at teens. Check out Club Med Punta Cana (see the Dominican Republic chapter in this book) and the Westin Rio Mar Beach Resort (see the Puerto Rico chapter) for examples of good teen-oriented programs.

If you think your teen would be happy hanging out with you on vacation, consider a getaway that gets you all out and about, whether that means renting ATVs and exploring the countryside of Aruba or ziplining over the lush countryside of Jamaica. You might want to select a destination like the USVI or the Cayman Islands where it's easy to rent a car and explore like local citizens.

If your teen would like to bring along a friend (and has one that you can vacation with pleasantly), be sure to ask yourself if you feel comfortable turning the pair loose, even within the confines of a resort. Some destinations are much more comfortable than others in terms of safety and drug availability. Teens are prime targets for drug salesmen in the islands (see our section on Crime in Chapter Four.) Also, remember that teens traveling without parents will need a notarized permission letter stating that it is OK to leave the country without parents. (Check the "Traveling without Both Birth Parents" section earlier in this chapter for more information on traveling without parents.)

Basic Information

The Caribbean is the land of "no problem" and, for the most part, it's just that. Here's a look at some basic details to make your family's visit carefree.

Business Hours
Business hours vary from island to island but plan for most shops to be open 8am to noon, often closing from noon to 2pm. When cruise ships are in port, however, look for shops to keep their doors open throughout the day.

Cost of Travel
This item really varies by island. Some islands are pricey and proud of it. Destinations like Anguilla and St. Barts are aimed at travelers who won't flinch at high price tags. Other destinations, such as Puerto Rico, Jamaica, the US Virgin Islands, and St. Martin, offer plenty of elegant properties but also a mix of modest accommodations.

Crime
There's no escape from crime, period. However, in general, crime is

an infrequent problem in this region and often the result of travelers taking a vacation from their everyday precautions. On vacation, use the same common sense you would exhibit at home, especially at night. Don't bring expensive jewelry. Use safes and safety deposit boxes provided by hotels. Also, don't leave valuables on the beach while you are in the water—one of the most common scenarios for theft.

Also, make sure your children know some basic information in case you are separated. Children should know the name of the hotel where you are staying. Also, make sure that very young children know your name, first and last, rather than just Mommy or Daddy.

Depending on the island you visit (Jamaica is the most notable example), you may be offered illegal drugs from a smooth-talking local salesman. These ingenious entrepreneurs offer their goods both on and off land. We've had more than one swim interrupted by salesmen in canoes, boats, and, once, even on horseback in the shallow water. A polite "no, thank you" usually ends the transaction without further problems.

Marijuana, or *ganja* as it's known locally, is illegal throughout the Caribbean. Drug penalties are becoming stiffer, and drug prevention measures more stringent in many countries. Customs carefully screens bags (using dogs in most cases) both when leaving the island and when returning to the mainland.

Have a good talk with teenagers before a trip to the islands. They're prime targets for ganja salesmen, especially in Jamaica. Explain to teenagers that they may be approached and offered drugs for sale, and also explain to them how to politely refuse and move on without further discussion.

We also caution vacationers not to carry any packages that they have not personally packed. We have been approached by locals asking us to mail packages for them once we arrived in the US. The requests may have been legitimate, but the risk is too great.

Etiquette

The citizens of the West Indies are modest, conservative people who generally frown upon displays of skin. Although nudity or topless bathing is permitted on some beaches, it is typically not practiced by locals. Most islanders follow a more conservative style of dress than seen in US beach communities, perhaps echoing back to the European influences felt on many isles.

Bathing suits are appropriate only for swimming; when off the beach grab a cover up. Bare chests are also frowned upon outside the beach. However, leisure wear — T-shirts, shorts, sundresses and sandals—will be readily accepted in any Caribbean community.

Throughout the West Indies, it is customary to greet folks before blurting out a question or request. A polite "good morning" or "good afternoon" will help you fit in and get your interaction off to a good start.

Electricity

Fortunately you don't need to worry about bringing many electrical appliances on a family Caribbean vacation. For those who insist on carrying a hair dryer (which many resorts will supply), electric shaver, or curling iron, however, know that the electric current may not be the same as that you have at home. And on those islands where it is, you may find yourself faced with electric outlets that don't at all resemble those you use every day.

Most Caribbean islands do offer 110 power, 60 cycles with American plugs (after all, American travelers make up the biggest portion of their business). However, on the French islands, St. Kitts and Nevis, and many others, you'll find 220 volts. The French islands use 220 AC, 60 cycles, and all appliances made in the US and Canada will require French plug converters and transformers. Most hotels offer both voltages and different plug configurations but bring converters to be safe.

Festivals

The Caribbean is undoubtedly one place that knows how to party. Besides a whole slew of national holidays (more than found in the US and Canada), you'll also find that the islands celebrate with many special festivals. The biggest blowout on every island is Carnival, scheduled at different times on different islands. Like Mardi Gras, this party lasts for many days (and nights) and may or may not be the best time for your family's visit.

Many smaller festivals are also planned throughout the year on every island. Some can be a wonderful glimpse into another culture, from music that echoes back to the island's early days to flavorful foods that give a taste of the island's bounty.

Be forewarned, however: islands just about shut down during any festival or holiday. Don't expect shops and stand-alone restaurants outside the hotels and resorts to be open for business.

Here's a sampling of some of the festivals planned annually in this region:

January
Bahamas: Junkanoo parades
Jamaica: Maroon Festival
St. Kitts and Nevis: Carnival parade
USVI: Crucian Christmas Children's Parade

February
Curaçao: Carnival
Jamaica: Bob Marley Birthday Bash
Trinidad and Tobago: Carnival

March
Anguilla: Moonsplash
Bahamas: Winter Sailing Championships
St. Maarten: Heineken Regatta
Trinidad and Tobago: Leatherback turtle nesting period

April
Barbados: Congaline Festival
Cayman Islands: Schooner race
Jamaica: Carnival
St. Maarten: Carnival
Tobago: Goat and Crab Race
USVI: Rolex Cup Regatta, St. Thomas Carnival

May
BVI: Spring Caribbean Arts Festival
Cayman Islands: Annual National Children's Festival of the Arts
Curaçao: KLM Jazz Festival
Trinidad: Steelpan Competition
Turks and Caicos: Annual Regatta

June
Cayman Islands: Annual Million Dollar Month International Fishing
Tournament
Puerto Rico: Casals Festival
St. John, USVI: Carnival

July
Cayman Islands: Summer Bash Weekend
Puerto Rico: Barranquitas Artisans Fair
Tobago: Tobago Heritage Festival
Turks and Caicos: Rake and Scrape Festival

August
Jamaica: Jamaica Independence Day Parade
Turks and Caicos: Cactusfest

September
BVI: Foxy's Wooden Boat Regatta
Puerto Rico: Inter-American Festival of the Arts
Turks and Caicos: National Youth Day

October
Cayman Islands: Pirates Week
USVI: St. Croix Jazz and Caribbean Music and Art Festival

December
Anguilla: Christmas Fair
Nassau, Bahamas: Night of Christmas Music
Jamaica: Devon House's Christmas Fair
Puerto Rico: Criollisimo Show, Dec.; Lighting of the Giant Christmas Tree; Nutcracker Suite Ballet
St. Lucia: Christmas Folk Festival
Turks and Caicos: Christmas Tree Lighting Ceremony
St. Croix, USVI: Christmas Spoken Here

Handicapped Access

If a member of your family uses a wheelchair, you'll find the same ADA rules in effect in Puerto Rico and the US Virgin Islands as you'd find on the mainland of the US. You'll find ramps (also great for strollers), handicapped accessible guest rooms and restrooms, etc. On other islands, handicapped access varies, although many resorts offer special handicapped accessible rooms.

Health Concerns

Stomach problems from food and water are at a minimum in the Caribbean. Most stomach distress is caused by, not the food itself, but by larger-than-usual amounts of food (a problem visitors to the all-inclusive resorts will easily understand due to massive buffets).

Nothing will ruin a vacation any faster than a sunburn, your biggest danger in the Caribbean. You'll be surprised, even if you don't burn easily or if you already have a good base tan, how easily the sun will sneak up on you. At this southern latitude, good sunscreen, applied liberally and often, is a must.

Bring along children's sunblock for tender young skin. Reapply often and make sure that it goes everywhere, even into thin hair. Many parents bring along a T-shirt for children to wear in the water. Young snorkelers can fry like fish in these waters and while snorkeling it's especially easy to forget that your back is exposed.

Also bring along mosquito and bug repellent. The worst insect in the Caribbean are sand fleas. Popularly known as no-see-'ums, these pesky critters raise itchy welts where they bite, usually along the ankles. Use an insect repellent if you'll be on the beach near sunset, the worst time of the day for these unwelcome beach bums.

Here are a few other dangers to share with your family:

•**Fire coral:** There are many varieties but all edged in white and will burn you if you brush against it. The safest thing is to teach children not to touch any kind of coral because coral will die if touched.

•**Jellyfish:** These cause painful stings with their tentacles.

•**Manchineel trees:** These present an unusual danger. These plants have highly acidic leaves and fruit. During a rain, water dropping off the leaves can leave painful burns on your skin and the tree's tiny apples will also burn when stepped on. In most resorts, manchineel trees have been removed or are clearly marked, often with signs and with trunks painted red. Don't let kids touch the trees or play beneath them.

•**No-See-Ums:** Tucked into that oh-so-wonderful sand lie tiny sand fleas, waiting to bite when the sand cools. You won't feel their bites, but just wait a day or two: welts like jumbo mosquito bites will make themselves apparent and they'll itch for days. To avoid the no-see-ums, stay off the sand at sunset. The fleas are most active when the sand cools.

•**Scorpionfish:** This mottled pinkish fish hangs out on coral and is so ugly it actually looks dangerous.

•**Sea urchins:** These are painful if you step on their brittle spines. We recommend bringing old sneakers or swim shoes for every member of the family.

•**Stingrays:** These are dangerous only if stepped on and can be avoided by dragging your feet when wading.

Language

English is the primary language of most Caribbean islands, but you'll quickly find that you may not understand everything, especially if locals are talking to one another. English is spoken with a distinct Caribbean lilt, a delightful sing-song rhythm. Each island has its own patois as well; local words are often a mixture of African languages dating back to the island's slave days. Jamaica's patois is perhaps the most distinctive and also most difficult to understand.

Money & Banking

You'll find that US currency is accepted on many Caribbean islands, although you'll often receive change back in the local currency. You'll find that US currency is accepted on many Caribbean islands, although you'll often receive change back in the local currency.

We recommend using a credit card for everything but tips and street purchases. Besides avoiding the hassle of currency conversion (and back again when you leave). you'll usually receive the best possible exchange rate on a credit card. The credit card company shops for the best exchange rate for you—saving you some extra pennies and time.

Currency exchange rates shift as suddenly as sand on a beach, but here are some US dollar conversion rates at press time:
- **Barbados dollars (BBD)**: $1US=1.95 BBD
- **Dominican pesos (DOP)**: $1US=28 DOP
- **Cayman dollars (KYD)**: $1US=83 cents KYD
- **Jamaican dollars (JMD)**: $1US=50 JMD
- **Trinidad dollars (TTD)**: $1US=6.21 TTD

Nudity

Depending on the island you visit (the French islands are the most notable example, although it is practiced on other islands as well), your family may very well encounter topless bathers. A routine part of sunbathing for European women, top-less vacationers are often seen on many beaches. We've explained to our children that topless sunbathing, like different foods and different languages, is just another example of the cultural differences that make travel interesting and necessary.

> ### Keeping Current with Currencies
>
> You'll find that the French islands now use the **Euro**, although dollars are seen more frequently. Other islands, such as Jamaica, Trinidad and Tobago, Dominican Republic, Cayman Islands, and Bahamas, have their own currency used only by that island. Several islands use Eastern Caribbean or **EC** currency (not to be confused with EU); this money can be used in locations including St. Kitts, Nevis, St. Lucia, Antigua, and Anguilla.

Post Office

Don't forget to bring along your friends' addresses for those obligatory postcards. Most resorts sell postcard stamps and generally the front desk will handle mailing. It's also fun to make a stop in the local post office to buy a selection of local stamps, which might begin a lifelong philatelic interest for your youngster. Stamps are also a good way to learn more about island life, from the national bird to the past leaders.

Telephone

Telephone service from the Caribbean is generally very good, although it is expensive. Generally the highest rates are found on islands that are not part of the US dialing system such as the French and the Dutch isles. A brief phone call from these islands can be as much as US $40.

However, even on islands near the US and part of the US dialing system such as the Turks and Caicos, rates are pricey, often as much as US $2.50 per minute. Make the call directly from your hotel room and you'll also be slapped with hotel telephone surcharges, sometimes as much as 100-

200% of the call itself. The answer? Make a quick call and ask the receiver to call you back. Calls from the mainland to the islands are much less pricey.

Fax service is available at just about all the resorts and is another good way to keep in touch. Many charge nothing to receive a fax and only a few dollars to transmit.

Television

Most Caribbean resorts offer far more television than you'll probably want. Satellite transmissions mean that you're only steps away from all the network channels.

Some resorts recognize that not all guests want a television and do not offer sets in the rooms.

Time

The Caribbean straddles two time zones. The western islands— Jamaica and Cayman—fall in the Eastern time zone, the same as the east coast of the US.

The eastern islands fall in the Atlantic time zone, one hour ahead of Eastern time.

Also, most islands do not observe Daylight Savings Time. During the summer months, the western islands are the same as the Central time zone; the eastern islands the same as the Eastern time zone. A few islands, such as the Turks and Caicos, do observe Daylight Savings Time, however.

Tipping

Between 10 and 15% is traditional for tips for waitstaff and taxi drivers. Some islands typically add tips to restaurant bills so check before paying.

Water

The water is safe to drink on almost every island in the Caribbean with the exception of Hispaniola (Haiti and the Dominican Republic) and the Mexican Caribbean. If you are in a location with a questionable water supply, consider buying bottled water (and some resorts, like Breezes in the Dominican Republic, will give it you in your rooms.) Also, avoid fruits and vegetables that have been washed in water; the safest bet is to get fruit that can be peeled.

Tips for Staying Healthy in the Caribbean

Here are some tips from SunVacations.org for traveling with kids to destinations with so-so water supplies or if you're a little concerned about the food:

• Bring a travel kettle to boil tap water to wash your kids sippy cups, plastic cutlery etc. Put a small amount of dish soap in a Tupperware dish and use that for soap.

• Even if your hotel room tap water says it is drinkable don't drink it. Sometimes just a change in water even safe water can send toddlers and some adult's stomachs/bowels for a turn. Therefore brush and rinse your teeth and tooth brushes with bottled water too. Just keep getting extra bottles in your mini fridge.

• Bring lots of their favorite dry snacks from home for munching in the hotel room and by the pool or beach.

• Eat fruit that has to be peeled e.g. bananas, pineapple, mangoes, oranges etc.

• If your toddler is a fussy eater, do not worry; they will manage fine on fruit, crackers, toast, pancakes, yogurt, ice cream, French fries, muffins, hot dogs and pizza; not ideal but it is only for seven days.

• Bring along a large pack of juice drink boxes, the single serving applesauce and mini Oreos and mini cereal bars.

• Bring along lots of extra baby face cloths as you go through them very fast. You only get a couple of face cloths in your room.

• If you are worried about high chairs or other eating surfaces bring along a pack of bacterial wipes.

• Bring the rubber bath mat from your tub to stop slipping in the shower/tub at the hotel.

• Bring a large mesh laundry bag as you will have a fair amount of damp laundry and it can get smelly or moldy. If you have a balcony, keep the bag outside.

• If you don't have walky-talkies consider getting a set. It will make your life much easier when you need to locate each other if one of you is in the room and the other at the pool etc.

• Bring many more diapers then you think you would need them as changes in food bring changes in bowel movements and frequency of them.

• A small medical kit is very helpful should children become ill when traveling. The kit should contain medications for illnesses that children experience at home and for potential travel-related illnesses, and it should contain the telephone numbers of all the children's health-care providers.

Getting the Kids Ready

Learning Through Books

One of the best ways to build excitement about an upcoming trip is to start the vacation before you ever leave home. Look for Caribbean restaurants in your area or select a Caribbean recipe for your family to make together and try. Read about the region. Rent movies that feature island locales. Surf the Internet and look for island news, notices, and even photos of your destination and resort.

We've compiled here a list of books for different ages, from preschool through teens. Introducing your children to the islands through books can be a way to enrich your experience and to minimize culture shock, helping young travelers learn to appreciate and enjoy the differences between countries.

Picture Books

Bloom, Valerie and David Axtell (Illustrator). *Fruits : A Caribbean Counting Poem*. Henry Holt, 1997.

This preschool book follows a young Jamaican girl and her sister as they count tropical fruits, including guava, sweet-sop, and guinep. The book is written in Jamaican patois.

Lessac, Frane. *My Little Island*. Harpercrest, 1985.

Aimed at babies to preschoolers, this colorful book follows a young boy and his friend back to the island of his birth.

Elementary Readers

Agard, John, Grace Nichols, Cynthia Jabar (Illustrator). *No Hickory No Dickory No Dock: Caribbean Nursery Rhymes*. Candlewick Press, 1995.

Ages 4-8 will enjoy these lilting nursery rhymes.

Agard, John. *Under the Moon & Over the Sea : A Collection of Caribbean Poems*. Candlewick Press, 2003.

School Library Journal described this book as "A collection of more than 50 poems guaranteed to chase away any winter blahs."

Burgie, Irving, and Frane Lessac (Illustrator). *Caribbean Carnival: Songs of the West Indies*. William Morrow, 1992.

For ages 4-8, this collection includes easy piano and guitar arrangements for many calypso and folk songs. Irving Burgie is the composer of "Day-O," "Jamaica Farewell," and other calypso classics, and includes those tunes as well as "Michael Row the Boat Ashore" and "Yellow Bird."

Caribbean Canvas. Boyds Mills Press, 1994.

This collection of poems and proverbs of West Indian writers is accompanied by folk paintings with all the beauty and color of the region.

Conolly, Yvonne, Gloria Cameron, and Sonia Singham. *Mango Spice: 44 Caribbean Songs.* A&C Black, 1994.

Ages 9-12 will enjoy this book of spirited songs.

Elder, J.D., Bess Lomax Hawes, and Alan Lomax (Compiler). *Brown Girl in the Ring: An Anthology of Song Games from the Eastern Caribbean.* Pantheon Books, 1997.

This collection of 68 children's songs includes not only the music and the lyrics but also the stories behind them.

Faustin, Charles. *A Caribbean Counting Book.* Houghton Mifflin, 1996.

It's easy to catch the Caribbean spirit with this fun counting book for ages 5-7. Publisher's Weekly said about this book, "The sights and sounds of the Caribbean burst into life in this vibrant collection of traditional counting rhymes."

Gunning, Monica and Frane Lessac (Illustrator). *Not a Copper Penny in Me House: Poems for the Caribbean.* Mills Press, 1993.

For all age levels, this collection of poems talks about growing up in the Caribbean.

Hallworth, Grace (Editor) and Caroline Binch (Illustrator). *Down by the River: Afro-Caribbean Rhymes, Games, and Songs for Children.* Cartwheel Books, 1996.

For ages 4-8, this collection includes rhymes, chants, and games of Afro-Caribbean origins. Girls will love the jump rope rhymes and hand-clapping games.

Isadora, Rachel. *Caribbean Dream.* Putnam Publishing Group, 2002.

Vivid watercolors capture the spirit of the Caribbean in this story of island life.

Joseph, Lynn and Sandra Speidel (Illustrator). *Coconut Kind of Day: Island Poems.* William Morrow, 1990

For ages 4-8, this book of poems follows a Trinidad girl through her day.

Rau, Dana Meachen and Katie Lee (Illustrator). *Undersea City: A Story of a Caribbean Coral Reef.* Soundprints Corp. Audio, 1997.

This story follows a land hermit crab in the Dominican Republic in his search for a new shell.

Sherlock, Philip and Petrina Wright (illustrator). *The Illustrated Anansi: Four Caribbean Folk Tales.* MacMillan Publishers Ltd., 1995.

Ages 4-8 enjoy the tales of the Caribbean's most popular folk character: spider named Anansi.

Staub, Frank. *Children of Cuba.* Carolrhoda, 1996.

For ages 4-8, this book portrays the daily life of Cuban children against the backdrop of their history and customs.

Young Adult Books

Abodaher, David J. *Puerto Rico: America's 51st State* (An Impact Book). Franklin Watts, 1993.

This book looks at the history of the Caribbean's fourth largest island and includes discussion on the debate for statehood.

Black, Clinton V. *Pirates of the West Indies.* Cambridge University Press, 1989.

Teens can learn more about the real pirates of the Caribbean with this volume.

Broberg, Merle. *Barbados (Let's Visit Places and Peoples of the World).* Chelsea House Publishers, 1989.

This guide covers all of Barbados in a language for young readers: history, people, culture, and topography.

Dolan, Sean. *Juan Ponce De Leon* (Hispanics of Achievement). Chelsea House Publishers, 1995.

Ferris, Jean. *Song of the Sea (American Dreams).* Flare, 1996.

This novel follows Rose as she escapes from a British sea captain and meets up with Jean LaFitte.

Stevenson, Robert Louis. *Treasure Island.*

This classic tale (which was inspired by an island in the British Virgin Islands) is a fun way to set the mood for a Caribbean vacation for young readers.

Taylor, Theodore. *Timothy of the Cay*. Flare, 1994.
This sequel to the immensely popular The Cay follows Philip and Timothy after their rescue.

Bring Home Vacation Memories

Every vacationer wants to return home with memories of the experience that will help him relive the trip time after time. Adults rely on cameras to capture these memories, but children all too often fall prey to overpriced souvenirs as a poor substitute.

There is a way to help your child bring back vacation memories — without breaking your trip budget. No matter where you travel, free (or low cost) souvenirs are yours for the asking. Your children can collect everything ranging from postcards to matchbooks and placemats. They are available in restaurants, campgrounds, motels, tourist attractions, and service stations, potentially every place your family might stop. By showing your child the fun of searching for (not just buying) souvenirs, you can involve him in the excitement of seeking out free souvenirs and keep him away from the trinket stands which plague so many tourist attractions.

Your first step begins before the vacation at your neighborhood five-and-dime. Buy each child an inexpensive photo album ($1-2) with adhesive pages. These pages allow small fingers to stick memorabilia in the book, and they will survive several rearrangements before you have to resort to glue.

Keep an eye out for these souvenirs:

Restaurants: You'll find special children's placemats in many family restaurants, often with pictures or a map of local attractions. Free children's menus, containing a game or a puzzle, are available in many restaurants. And don't overlook tiny sugar packets with the restaurant's name or picture on it. These can act as miniature postcards, ready to assume a place in your child's scrapbook.

Postcards: For about a quarter each, you can carry home a professional photo of almost any attraction in the world. These are a great bargain, and a much better buy than the slides sold at many places, which have often faded under fluorescent lights. And if you've heard your child complain "I never get any mail," encourage them to send a postcard to themselves! They'll act as miniature vacation diaries when they return home, and give returning vacationers a little something to look forward to as well.

Matchbooks: Many restaurants and hotels give away free matchbooks. Minus the matches, of course, these make good additions to the scrapbook. Also, your young travelers may want to start a matchbook collection in a jar once they return home.

Foreign Money: A sample of foreign currency can be a good souvenir and a great way to learn about a country. Foreign coins can be fun to collect and could even interest your child in an entirely new hobby.

Stamps: Foreign stamps are also an excellent and inexpensive way to bring home souvenirs. Your child will learn about the government, national heroes, and often the national bird and flower through stamps.

Sports & Recreation

The Caribbean presents a variety of sporting opportunities, whether it's for the toddler or teen, the non-swimmer or the certified scuba diver. Here's an overview of some of the top activities in the Caribbean.

Some of these sporting activities such as scuba diving require previous knowledge and skills; others can be learned with a quick lesson on site. Whatever activities you and your family select, know your limitations and the limitations of your children before signing up for any of these sports. For watersports, make sure that life vests are available. The scruples of the sports operator should not mandate your safety level and don't forsake safety for fun. Know what you can and cannot do.

Scuba Diving

The Caribbean is universally recognized as one of the world's top dive destinations. Thousands of sites lure divers of all abilities, from beginners looking for shore excursions and shallow reef dives to advanced divers seeking wreck and cave explorations.

You'll find professional assistance from dive operators on every island, including resort courses where you'll have the opportunity to sample diving after a one-day course. Full certification courses will award you a "C" card, and advanced courses to teach you the use of scuba computers, the skills of drift diving, and even underwater photography.

Resort courses can be a good way to introduce your teens to the world of scuba diving without sacrificing much of your vacation. Only children age 10 and over are allowed to participate in PADI Discover Scuba courses. The day begins with a lesson on scuba diving, followed by practice at up to a 20 feet depth. It's a thrilling introduction to a new sport and is available at most larger resorts (complimentary at many all-inclusives).

Other novice divers decide to go for full certification and take courses at home before the big vacation. You can opt to do everything but your certification dive at home and then finish up in the Caribbean if you'd like.

Incredible visibility, measured at 100 to 150 feet, helps make these islands such spectacular dive destinations. With year-around water temperatures of 77 to 83 degrees, visitors can dive comfortably and enjoy an underwater playground that's filled with marine life.

Although good scuba spots are found off most islands, top scuba destinations are Grand Cayman, the Bahamas, Turks and Caicos, Anguilla (wreck diving for advanced only).

Sea Trek

Wonder what it would be like to walk on the moon? You might never get closer than a walk on the ocean floor in an old-fashioned dive helmet, an adventure you can do through Sea Trek on several islands. The minimum age is eight, and there is a minimum weight of 80 pounds. Kids with asthma can't participate either due to the pressurized air that's used.

We've done Sea Trek in Aruba with our youngest daughter and it was great fun, an experience we all continue to talk about. How does it work? You'll take a short "course" on the helmet, what to expect, signaling underwater, etc.; plan on about 20 minutes for the briefing.

Next, you'll put on an optional wet suit (since you'll be underwater for nearly half an hour, it can get a little cool, even in the Caribbean) and line up at the ladder to enter the water. One at a time, you'll go down the ladder until the water's chin deep. When just your head is out of water, a high-tech dive bell that weighs 70 pounds will be lowered onto your shoulders; don't worry about supporting the weight because you'll lower yourself on down the ladder as the helmet goes onto your head. From that point on, the helmet's just about weightless due to the water's bouyancy.

Slowly, you'll step down the ladder with the help of scuba divers who will remain with you throughout your time underwater. At the foot of the ladder, you'll find a rope outlining the walkway you'll follow. Single file, behind the other "divers," you'll walk along this walkway as if in slow motion. The only sound is your own breathing, echoed inside your helmet. The surface is never more than a signal away (one gesture and the certified divers who are accompanying you will whisk you to the top.)

What's neat about the experience? You don't have to have any dive experience to do it; you don't even have to know how to swim. Anyone in your family who wears glasses can wear their glasses as usual because everything (including your hair) remains dry under the helmet. Best of all, the experience gives you the feeling of being just another fish in the Caribbean Sea. Fish will come right up to you and you'll have a look at the sea in a way no one but a scuba diver has the opportunity to do.

At present time, you'll find Sea Trek operations in Montego Bay, Jamaica (at Doctor's Cave Beach), at St. Thomas' Coral World, Aruba's DePalm Island, and in the Turks and Caicos. For more on Sea Trek, visit www.sea-trek.com/.

Tethered Scuba

For those curious about the undersea world but not ready to take the plunge for a full certification course, several outfits in the islands offer a **tethered scuba** experience to depths of 20 feet. In Grand Cayman and St. John, tethered scuba operators give you the option of shallow scuba diving. You'll start with a simple class on use of the gear then wade out for a shallow water dive. At all times, you are connected to the air tank floating on the surface by a 20-foot tube. With this tube, you'll breathe just like any other scuba diver.

SASY

If you would like to introduce your children to the joys of scuba diving, Cayman is the place. Thanks to a program operated by Red Sail Sports, children as young as four can now have a taste of scuba diving. **SASY**, or **Supplied Air Snorkeling for Youths**, is a scuba unit customized for young bodies. Developed in the Cayman Islands by Capt. Wayne Hasson, a father of two young children, the unit combines a regulator so young divers can breath from a continuous air supply and a buoyancy compensator to keep children floating safely near the surface. Units are available for use at Red Sail Sports (www.redsail.com) locations at the Hyatt Regency Grand Cayman, Westin Casuarina Resort and Marriott Grand Cayman.

Submarines

For more underwater fun, several islands are home to submarines that give you the chance to see beneath the waves without ever getting wet. Atlantis submarines, found on Grand Cayman, St. Thomas, Barbados, and Aruba, plunge to a depth of 100 feet below the surface.

On other islands, semi-submersible subs are another option. On these vessels, the boat never submerges but visitors walk down into a glass hull for a look at the undersea world. These are a good choice for the budget conscious and for those whose children might not do well in the enclosed environment of a true sub.

Underwater Photography

A great way to get your children interested in the world beneath the sea is with an inexpensive underwater camera. Disposable models are available for about $15 and are good to a depth of 10-15 feet. They're perfect for capturing the memories of a snorkel trip or even for wading out in the clear waters and taking a picture of the beautiful corals.

Snorkeling

Snorkeling is an excellent introduction to the underwater beauty and rich marine life found in the Caribbean waters. Many scenic reefs can be enjoyed with equipment as limited as a mask and a snorkel.

Just yards from shore, you can enjoy a look at colorful corals, graceful fans, and fish like friendly sergeant majors, butterfly fish, and shy damselfish.

Most resorts offer snorkel equipment for little or no charge. To prevent your mask from fogging, rub saliva on the inside of your lenses. Dishwashing liquid and special alcohol-based non-fogging formulas may also be used.

Even non-swimmers can enjoy a look below the waves with snorkel gear. Don a mask, stand in the shallows, and just stick your head in the warm water for a look at another world just inches away.

How much will all this underwater fun cost? Here's a rundown of the average prices for underwater activities, in US dollars:

- Snorkel Equipment Rental: free-$8
- Half Day Snorkel Trip: $20-$35
- Full Day Snorkel Trip: $38-$45
- One Tank Scuba Dive: $35-$45
- Two Tank Scuba Dive: $55-$65
- Night Scuba Dive: $25-$50
- Resort scuba course: $75-$90
- Scuba Certification Course: $250-$400

Above-Water Fun

Sailing excursions are another popular way to enjoy the islands. Charters, sunset cruises, booze cruises, rollicking "pirate" cruises, and more are offered to entertain vacationers. Do it yourselfers will find plenty of smaller watercrafts: ocean kayaks, Sunfish, Hobie cats, waverunners, and more.

Rental prices vary by location, but expect to pay anywhere from $25 to $100 an hour, depending on type of vessel. Catamaran rentals run about $35-$40 per hour.

Yachting is another favorite sport. While it may sound like the stuff of a vacation for only the rich and famous, many families enjoy yacht excursions in the Caribbean. Yacht companies in the US Virgin Islands, British Virgin Islands, Sint Maarten, and others offer both bareboat (where you captain the vessel) and crewed yachts. A crewed yacht is similar to a floating hotel. Your meals will be cooked for you and you can help set the course for the day. The size of the vessels vary, so you can choose to have a yacht just for your family or share with others.

Water Toys

You'll find plenty of less serious water fun in the islands as well, especially at the major resort centers. Waverunners, aqua trikes, viewboards, Sunsearcher floats, banana boat rides, paddle cats, paddleboats, and toys for kids of all ages are available for rent. Look along the busier beaches throughout the region: Orient Beach on St. Martin, Seven Mile Beach in Negril, Jamaica, and Seven Mile Beach on Grand Cayman. Top resorts also offer a good array of water toys, often available for guests to use free of charge.

It's also fun to take along some of your child's water toys. Small pails, shovels, and even spoons can keep youngsters busy for hours.

Parasailing

If you or your older children are ready to enjoy a bird's eye view, sign up for a parasail ride. Cost averages about $45 for the ride, which lasts about than 10 minutes. Here are some other average prices for watersports activities, in US dollars:

- •Windsurfing rentals per hour: $20-$30
- •Wave Runner rentals per half hour: $35-$60
- •Sailboat rentals per hour: $20-$30
- •Ocean kayak rentals per hour: $15-$22
- •Catamaran rentals per hour: $35
- •Glass bottom boat ride per trip: $22-$33
- •Dinner cruises: $45-$68
- •Day sail cruise: $35-$100

Fishing

Fishing is a popular activity on many Caribbean islands. Several different types of fishing are available throughout the region:

Shore Fishing: From the beach and the shallow waters just beyond, anglers find plenty of challenge. One advantage of shore fishing is that you can enjoy it with just a minimum of scheduling and cost. Bonefish, tarpon, permit, common pompano, and barracuda are some species commonly caught from the shore.

Reef Fishing: The many miles of reefs in the Caribbean provide a playground for fishermen looking for light tackle action. After chumming to attract the fish, a variety of species can be sought, usually with live bait such as squid and conch. At the reef, grouper, jack crevalle, mutton snapper, yellowtail snapper, and others are common catches.

Deep Sea Fishing: Charters seek gamefish including blue marlin, yellowfin tuna, wahoo, dolphin (dorado) and barracuda, all caught year-around. Strikes can occur as close as a quarter mile from land at the point where the turquoise shallows drop into inky darkness. Chartering a boat is not an inexpensive proposition, but for many visitors it's the highlight of their trip. A half day charter begins at about US $400 and may range as high as $1000 for a full day trip aboard a large charter with state-of-the art equipment and tackle. Blue marlin, dolphin (not the mammal but a popular gamefish), yellowfin tuna, blackfin tuna, skipjack tuna, and wahoo are favorites with deep sea anglers.

Costs for fishing activities vary by operator, by island, and by time of year, but here's a cost estimate in US dollars (tipping, which is traditional, is extra):

- •Deep sea charters, full-day $450-$1,000
- •Offshore charters, half-day $325-$650
- •Bone, tarpon and reef fishing $300-$600
  full day (up to four anglers, $50 for each additional fisherman)
- •Bone, tarpon, and reef fishing $200-$400
  half day (up to four anglers, $50 for each additional fisherman)
- •Bonefishing guide, half day $250
  (maximum two anglers)

Hiking & Walking

Hikers will find marked trails on many islands. Some are self-guided walks and can be enjoyed by any family member, others are recommended only for serious hikers.

Note that mid-day heat can be intense, especially once you enter the interior of the island away from the cooling breezes on the beach. Always carry water with you and be aware of signs of heat exhaustion and sunstroke.

Horseback Riding

Horseback riding is an excellent opportunity to tour some of the island's quieter sections and to romp along the beach. Some operators also offer pony rides for children.

Use your best judgment with horseback operators. Ask your hotel concierge for recommendations and check out the operation. Does the equipment look well tended? Do the horses look healthy? While there are several top-notch riding facilities in the Caribbean, a few have very old equipment. If your children have not had experience with horses, make sure you select a reputable operator.

Food & Drink

For most travelers, dining is an important part of their trip. After all, not everyone will snorkel, scuba dive, or fish, but everyone eats three times a day. It's also a chance to further delve into a national culture, to learn more about the bounty of the land and the sea.

A richly diverse region, the Caribbean presents a full menu of offerings that reflect the many cultures that settled this area. From East Indian rotis served throughout Trinidad and Tobago to Dutch keshi yena served on

Aruba, Curaçao, and St. Maarten, the islands are a cornucopia of cultures and cuisines.

One thing island cuisines have in common is attention to flavor. Dishes are rich with flavor and are often spicy. Some dishes trace their origin back to the earliest days of the island when the Arawak Indians first barbecued meats. Later, distinctive seasonings were developed by Africans who came to the islands as slaves. A century later, Chinese and East Indian influences made their way to the islands, when indentured laborers who replaced slaves after emancipation also brought their own culinary talents. Today curried dishes grace nearly every menu, using local meats such as goat, chicken, and seafood.

You will find, however, that at most resorts local dishes are "toned down" to more American tastes. Also, many resort restaurants also offer plenty of American dishes for even the pickiest eater in the family. Beyond the resorts, you'll find fast food outlets on many islands. Don't laugh, even a trip to a fast food eatery can be a cultural experience. In Aruba, we enjoyed an inexpensive lunch under the golden arches, surrounded by locals speaking in Papiamento.

Here's a sampling of island dishes found on many Caribbean menus:

Breakfast:
•ackee and saltfish, the national dish of Jamaica. Ackee is a small fruit that is harvested only when it bursts and reveals its black seeds; before that time the fruit is poisonous. Ackee is cooked and resembles (and tastes) much like scrambled eggs.
•johnny cakes and boiled fish for breakfast in the Bahamas

Soups:
•pepperpot, a spicy stew
•*asopao*, a chicken and rice soup in Puerto Rico.
•*stoba di cabrito* (goat stew) in Curaçao

Restless Restaurant Dining
OK, this is a warning: service in Caribbean restaurants is not speedy. Whether you are going to a resort restaurant for a nice night out or a side of the road jerk stand, recognize that these are not American fast food joints. Service will not be speedy. You will wait. Your kids will wait.

And they may not wait gracefully. Evening meals can stretch out for several hours at some Caribbean restaurants, and even the most patient diners can become restless. Here are a few tips for dealing with young (and not so young) restless diners:
•consider buffets. Many resorts offer buffet lunches, and buffet serving is often offered at least once a week (most do a "beach night" and serve barbecue).

•move around. Consider placing the order, then taking the kids out for a walk.

•bring activities. The wait for food is a perfect time to catch up on postcard writing, travel diaries, and other "desk" activities for schoolage children.

•use the time to discuss your day and plan the next day's activities. Go around the table and ask everyone what their favorite activity that day was. Their favorite food? Their favorite song on the island?

Entrees:
•fried fish
•stewed lamb with *pan bati* (pancake) on Dutch islands
•*keshi yena* (a hollowed wheel of Edam cheese filled with meat and baked to combine flavors) on Dutch islands
•conch (pronounced konk), a shellfish served chopped, battered and fried in conch fritters
•grouper, a large fish caught in the waters just offshore, also appears on every menu
•flying fish
•fried plantains
•pattie, a turnover filled with spicy meat that's a favorite lunch snack with locals in Jamaica
•jerk, pork, chicken, or fish is marinated with a fiery mixture of spices including fiery Scotch bonnet peppers, pimento or allspice, nutmeg, escallion, and thyme. This is a favorite dish in Jamaica.
•*empanadillas*, little meat turnovers in Puerto Rico.
•roti, a burrito-like fast food that traces its roots to India; served in Trinidad and Tobago. Look for "buss up shot" at most diners; this is a roti that's torn up like a "busted up shirt" and is eaten with a fork rather than by hand.

Side Dishes:
•peas (usually red beans or pigeon peas) and rice: the number one side dish in the Caribbean
•cou-cou (a cornmeal and okra dish) in Barbados
•jug-jug (a dish made of Guinea corn and green peas) in Barbados
•christophine, a type of squash
•dasheen (a root vegetable similar to a potato)
•*mofongo*, fried plantains mixed with fried pork rinds and seasoned with garlic, in Puerto Rico
•afungi, a pudding of cornmeal and okra
•fungi (pronounced foon-gee), a tasty accompaniment that's somewhat like cornbread dressing; in the Virgin Islands.

Dessert:

•ducana, a pudding made from grated sweet potato and coconut, sugar, and spices, and boiled in a banana leaf

•*flan*, a wonderful custard

•*tembleque*, a custard made with coconut milk and sprinkled with cinnamon in Puerto Rico.

Caribbean Tourist Offices

Anguilla Tourist Information Office
Old Factory Plaza
The Valley, Anguilla, BWI
Tel. 800/553-4939, 264/497-2759
Fax 264/497-2710
www.anguilla-vacation.com

Antigua and Barbuda Tourist Office
Government Complex
Queen Elizabeth Highway
St John's, Antigua W.I.
Tel. 268/462-0480
Fax 268/462-2483Fax 268/462-24836
www.antigua-barbuda.org

Aruba Tourism Authority
1000 Harbor Boulevard
Weehawken, NJ 07087
Tel. 800/TO-ARUBA or 201/330-0800
Fax 201/330-8757
www.aruba.com

Bahamas Tourism Centre
150 East 52nd Street
28th Floor North
New York, NY 10022
Tel. 800/4-BAHAMAS or 212/758-2777
www.bahamas.com

Barbados Tourism Authority
800 2nd Avenue
2nd Floor
New York, NY 10017

Tel. 800/221-9831
Fax 212/573-9850
www.barbados.org

Bermuda Department of Tourism
205 East 42nd Street
16th Floor
New York, NY 10017
Tel. 800/BERMUDA, 212/818-9800
Fax 212/983-5289
www.bermudatourism.com

British Virgin Islands Tourist Board
1270 Broadway, Suite 705
New York, NY 10001
Tel. 800/835-8530 or 212/696-0400
Fax 212/ 563-2263
www.bvitouristboard.com

Cayman Islands Department of Tourism
3 Park Avenue, 39th floor
New York, NY 10016
Tel. 800/346-3313 or 212/889-9009
Fax 212/889-9125
www.caymanislands.ky

Curaçao Tourist Board
19 Pietermaai
PO Box 3266 Willemstad, Curaçao
800/328-7222 or 599/9-434-8200
Fax 599/9-461-2305
www.curacao-tourism.com

Jamaica Tourist Board
1320 South Dixie Highway
Suite 1101
Coral Gables, FL 33146
Tel. 800/233-4JTB or 305/665-0557
Fax 305/666-7239
www.jamaicatravel.com

Puerto Rico Tourism Company
666 Fifth Ave.

15th Floor
New York, NY 10103
Tel. 866/2GOTOPR
Fax 212/586-1212
www.gotopuertorico.com

St. Kitts and Nevis Tourism Offices

St. Kitts:
414 East 75th Street
New York, NY 10021
Tel. 800/582-6208, 212/535-1234
Fax 212/734-6511
www.stkitts-tourism.com

Nevis:
Nevis Tourism Authority
Main St.
Charlestown, Nevis
Tel. 866/55 NEVIS or 869/469-7550
Fax 869/469-7551
www.nevisisland.com

St. Lucia Tourist Board

800 Second Avenue
9th Floor
New York, NY 10017
Tel. 800/4-ST LUCIA or 212/867-2950
Fax 212/867-2795
www.stlucia.org

St. Martin Tourist Board/French Govt. Tourist Office

444 Madison Ave.
New York, NY 10022
Tel. 877/956-1234 or 212/475-8970
Fax: 212/260-8481
www.st-martin.org

St. Maarten Tourist Office

675 Third Avenue
Suite 1807
New York, NY 10017
Tel. 800/STMAARTEN or 212/475-8970

Fax 212/786-2278
www.st-maarten.com

Trinidad and Tobago
10-14 Philipps Street,
Port-of-Spain,
Trinidad, West Indies
Tel. 888/535-5617 or 868/675-7034/5/6/7
Fax 868/638-3560
www.visittnt.com

Turks and Caicos Tourist Board
128 Front Street,
Grand Turk, Turks & Caicos Islands, B.W.I.
Tel. 800/241-0824 or 649/946-2321
Fax 649/946-2737
www.turksandcaicostourism.com

US Virgin Islands Division of Tourism
1270 Avenue of the Americas
Suite 2108
New York, NY 10020
Tel. 800/372-USVI or 212/332-2222
Fax 212/332-2223
www.usvitourism.vi

Index

Things Change!

Phone numbers, prices, addresses, quality of food, etc, all change. If you come across any new information, we'd appreciate hearing from you. No item is too small! Drop us an email note at: Jopenroad@aol.com, or write us at:

Caribbean With Kids
Open Road Publishing
P.O. Box 284
Cold Spring Harbor, NY 11724

About the Authors

John Bigley and Paris Permenter fell in love with the Caribbean on their honeymoon and have turned their extensive knowledge of the region into an occupation. As professional travel writers and photographers, Paris and John travel once a month to explore new destinations.

Along with *Caribbean with Kids*, the husband-wife team has also authored *National Parks with Kids* and *Las Vegas with Kids* for Open Road Publishing. The writers have also produced *Lovetripper.com's Guide to Caribbean Destination Weddings, Adventure Guide to Jamaica, Adventure Guide to the Cayman Islands, Adventure Guide to the Leeward Islands, Cayman Islands Alive!, Jamaica: A Taste of the Island, Jamaica Alive!, Nassau and the Best of the Bahamas Alive!* and others.

Paris and John are also frequent television and radio talk show guests on the subject of travel, featured in two one-hour programs on the Fine Living Network. Both are members of the prestigious Society of American Travel Writers (SATW).

Readers can follow the couple's travels on their websites: Caribbean Travels with Paris and John (www.parisandjohn.com) and Lovetripper.com Romantic Travel Magazine (www.lovetripper.com), an extensive site featuring over 5,000 pages on romantic getaways, honeymoons, and destination weddings worldwide.

Great Family Guidebooks for Great Family Destinations!

Hawaii with Kids, $14.95

Italy With Kids, $16.95

L.A. with Kids, $14.95

Las Vegas With Kids, $14.95

London with Kids, $14.95

National Parks With Kids, $14.95

New York City with Kids, $14.95

Paris with Kids, $14.95

Washington DC with Kids, $14.95